Introduction to PL/I Programming
for Library and Information Science

LIBRARY AND INFORMATION SCIENCE

CONSULTING EDITOR: *Harold Borko*

GRADUATE SCHOOL OF LIBRARY SCIENCE

UNIVERSITY OF CALIFORNIA, LOS ANGELES

Introduction to PL/I Programming for Library and Information Science

THOMAS H. MOTT, Jr.

SUSAN ARTANDI

LENY STRUMINGER

Rutgers University

A C A D E M I C P R E S S   *New York and London*

ACADEMIC PRESS, INC.
111 Fifth Avenue, New York, New York 10003

United Kingdom Edition published by
ACADEMIC PRESS, INC. (LONDON) LTD.
24/28 Oval Road, London NW1

LIBRARY OF CONGRESS CATALOG CARD NUMBER: 78-182675

PRINTED IN THE UNITED STATES OF AMERICA

TO

Judi, Cathi, Janin, and Ronald

Contents

Chapter 4. **Character Data**

Chapter 5. **Character Manipulation**

Chapter 6. **Statement Label Data**

Chapter 7. **The DO Statement**

Chapter 8. **Arrays and Structures**

Chapter 9. **Basic Concepts of Boolean Algebra**

Chapter 10. **A Logical Analysis of Document Retrieval**

Chapter 11. **Binary Vectors, Bit String Manipulation, and Document Retrieval**

Chapter 12. **Program Organization**

Chapter 13. **File Data Management**

Chapter 14. **Based Variables for List Processing**

Solutions to Exercises

Selected Bibliography

Preface

The purpose of this text is to provide the student of library and information science with an introduction to certain fundamentals of a widely used computer programming language, so that he may understand and appreciate some of its applications in those areas of librarianship and information science that deal with the organization, storage, and retrieval of information—in short, information handling. To accomplish this purpose, a simple introduction to the concepts of Boolean algebra is also provided in the text. By this means, the student is furnished with the basic knowledge needed to acquire an understanding of the role of the programmer in the development of computer-based information handling activities.

The programming language chosen for study in the text—albeit at an elementary level—is the PL/I language. This is a recently developed, general purpose computer language that enjoys wide usage and acceptance in scientific and engineering circles and within the business and commercial fields. Several programming texts are available that offer a complete catalog and description of the features and characteristics of PL/I. Some texts deal with its capabilities as a language for scientific programming, while others treat its advantages for business and commercial applications. The major objective of the present text is to describe the extensive capabilities that render PL/I useful as a symbol manipulating language for handling nonnumeric data as contrasted with its features as a language for scientific computing and business data processing. Various facilities are available in PL/I that enable the computer to function as a logic machine for processing data structures comprised of characters, words, and symbols. These facilities permit the manipulation and logical processing of data structures having information content in their own right, but which also function as parts of a larger network or hierarchy of information-bearing structures. With this goal in mind, numerous sample PL/I programs are presented in the text to illustrate how PL/I is applicable to a variety of information handling tasks that occur in circulation control, serial control, acquisition procedures, document retrieval, and similar library and information management activities.

The text also offers an elementary introduction to the basic concepts of Boolean algebra and shows how this useful theoretical tool can be applied to areas of information handling in order to gain a better understanding of the logical framework underlying these important applications in library and information science. No special mathematical background is assumed. Anyone who has had high school mathematics and science and has also a modest degree of mathematical or analytical maturity should be able to assimilate the material with profit.

The authors believe that presenting many examples to illustrate the salient points of the discussion is the key to a good theory and programming text. All of the programming examples presented have been run on a computer to ensure their correctness. Exercises included in the chapters are designed to give the reader the opportunity to show his understanding of the material presented in the chapter. Programming solutions to all the exercises are included.

Acknowledgments

All this material has been presented several times over in a graduate seminar on programming theory for information handling. The authors are grateful to the students for the benefit of their advice, counsel, and criticism. Grateful acknowledgment is also made to Professor Oliver H. Buchanan of Pratt Institute of Technology, Mrs. Susan Martin of Harvard University, and Dr. Harold Borko of the University of California at Los Angeles for their many valuable comments and excellent suggestions. We are also indebted to Mrs. Phyllis Pohl for her careful typing of the several stages of a difficult manuscript.

Symbology of Flowcharts

A program is a series of instructions describing the sequence of steps to be performed by the computer for the completion of a job. The instructions must be explicit and given in great detail so that the computer knows what to do with the data that is fed into it under every conceivable combination of circumstances.

The technique which facilitates the development of the logic that is to be incorporated in a computer program so that it can satisfy the requirements given above is called "flowcharting."

A flowchart shows, in graphic form, the steps and decisions involved in the performance of a job or the achievement of a stated objective. Each decision on a flowchart is formulated in terms of a set of conditions that is tested and the outcome of each test can only be yes or no. The condition is either present or not and the chart must indicate the steps to be taken in either case. This approach is compatible with the way in which computers make decisions and while flowcharting is a useful tool for the analysis and design of any routine operation, manual or machine, the technique is particularly suited to the development and description of algorithms that form the basis of computer programs.

A series of standard symbols are used in flowcharting. These symbols, indicating decisions or actions, are connected by arrows indicating the direction of actions. The text in the area enclosed by the symbols describes the action or decision that must be made at that point. The standard symbols used in this text book are defined as follows.

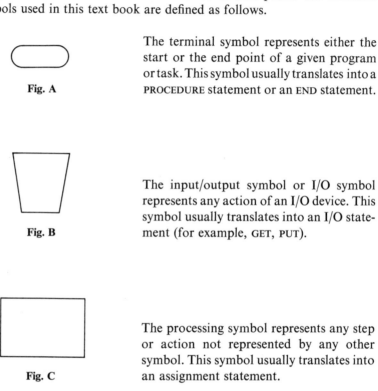

The terminal symbol represents either the start or the end point of a given program or task. This symbol usually translates into a PROCEDURE statement or an END statement.

Fig. A

The input/output symbol or I/O symbol represents any action of an I/O device. This symbol usually translates into an I/O statement (for example, GET, PUT).

Fig. B

The processing symbol represents any step or action not represented by any other symbol. This symbol usually translates into an assignment statement.

Fig. C

The decision symbol represents the point at which some decision as to further steps is made. This decision is made as a result of an analysis of the current value of the data (for example, Is A equal to 1? or Is B equal to C?). All possible results of the analysis must be accounted for by branches exiting from the decision symbol. This symbol usually translates into an IF statement where the alternative branches are indicated by the THEN clause or the ELSE clause.

Fig. D

List of Sample Programs

CHAPTER 1

Computers in Libraries

Because of the well known increase in the amount of published and un-published literature in practically all fields of human endeavor and because of the sophisticated information needs of the individual in today's complex society, problems of information handling have been receiving considerable attention. Research and development activities relating to these problems have centered around the broad objective of developing methods by which it is possible to recover information stored as symbols from their storage places in response to requests from prospective users. The exploration of the relevance of computers to this major objective has become an important aspect of current activities in information science.

In a number of areas in information science computers have been used relatively successfully and large-scale operational systems are in existence. In other areas computers have been used mainly in experimental projects. All of these applications, however, have the significant common character-istic that they demand the capability of processing textual information as contrasted with business and scientific applications in which the emphasis is on numerical computation. Consequently, information science applications require the exploration of the computer's capabilities as symbol manipulation devices for the processing of data that is to a very large extent composed of characters, words, and other symbols.

Document retrieval systems represent a significant area of computer applications in information science. These systems are designed to retrieve documents which should, with some degree of certainty, contain the information sought by the user. In this case the user is at least one step removed from the actual information (unless what he seeks is only a list of document references or some data contained in the document record itself) and the computer is used to search a file of document representations. Document representations most frequently consist of index tags indicating the subject matter and possibly some other characteristics of the document which are considered potentially useful to the user. In the majority of existing systems index tags are assigned by human indexers prior to input to the computer. In addition to mechanical searching, the retrieval file created in this manner is also frequently used to produce printed indexes, catalogs, or cards for manual searching. A file of similar content can serve as a basis for on-line document retrieval systems which are accessed by the user through remote terminals as well as for Selective Dissemination of Information (SDI) systems operating in a batch-processing mode. In applications that are exclusively concerned with the production of printed indexes or catalogs, the computer is frequently used only as a sorting and printing device to order and format entries and no mechanical search capability is required.

Areas of applications involving text processing that are still largely experimental today are automatic indexing and automatic translation. In automatic indexing the computer is used to generate index terms from the natural language text of the document. The only commercially successful product in this category of computer application is the KWIC type index, which in its basic form is a machine-generated concordance of document titles. Each word in the title that is *not* included in an exclusion list is selected by the computer to be printed as an index term in its proper alphabetical place—either surrounded or followed by the full title. The problems of automatic translation are largely unresolved because of insufficient linguistic knowledge and a lack of understanding of the extra-linguistic knowledge used by the human translator in the translation process.

An important area of computer applications in libraries relates to what may be referred to as "housekeeping functions," such as circulation control, serial control, acquisition procedures, and other similar routines, all of which require some capability for processing nonnumeric information.

Since the data base of all of these systems is predominantly textual, a major processing requirement in these computer applications is to be able to manipulate characters as individual symbols or as strings of symbols of variable lengths.

PL/I was selected as the programming language for this introductory text on information handling because the ease with which it can handle nonnumeric data makes it extremely suitable for the applications just described. While most of the high-level, widely used programming languages were originally designed for numerical processing and are difficult to adapt to nonnumeric types of symbolic processing, PL/I was designed to accommodate a variety of applications with extensive capabilities for handling nonnumeric problems. A variety of commands are available in the language for the manipulation of strings of characters constituting words or phrases. Some of these operations are direct counterparts of those performed upon numeric data, others are unique to character data.

The text takes advantage of perhaps the most useful feature of the PL/I language: its modularity. While the full language is extremely complete, without losing its integrity as a language PL/I can also be applied by using only parts of it to suit the requirements and backgrounds of the users. Thus, it is possible to write fairly complex programs with the subset of the language presented in this text.

CHAPTER **2**

Programming Fundamentals

2.1 Program Execution

A computer is designed to execute a set of specified operations. The sequence of steps to be performed by the computer must be stated in the form of explicit and detailed instructions. This series of instructions constitutes a *program* and the notation in which it is written is called a *programming language*. When a program is written in a high-level machine-independent language such as PL/I, its instructions cannot be executed by the computer in the form in which they are written. A computer can respond only to machine language that is specific for a given type of machine and is represented in a binary code consisting of strings of zeros and ones. Because of this, the program written in a high-level language, called the *source program*, needs to be translated into a machine language program, called the *object program*, before the computer can execute it. This translation from the source program into the object program is performed by

4

the *compiler*, a program designed for this purpose. The compiler examines each high-level instruction, determines what sequence of machine language instructions will be required to produce the same actions, and then produces these instructions in machine language. In a sense the compiler acts as an automatic machine language programmer. This explains why it is often referred to as a *language processor*.

One instruction written in a high-level language usually corresponds to several instructions in the corresponding machine language program. This greatly reduces the number of instructions to be written by the programmer. Also, writing a program in machine language requires that it be written in the machine coding of the particular computer and places the full burden of the organization of the program and responsibility for assignment of storage directly on the programmer (see the programming illustration in Section 2.2). For these reasons, although programming was actually done in machine language in the early days of computers, simplifications were introduced fairly soon. Symbolic addresses and mnemonics for the operations were introduced in what is called *symbolic* or *assembly language* programming. The program that translates from symbolic or assembly language into machine language is called an *assembler*. The assembler program produces one machine language instruction for each mnemonic instruction with the exception of *macro-instructions*. A macro-instruction causes the assembler to generate a sequence of machine language instructions instead of a single one. While symbolic programming and macro-instructions will free the programmer from some machine detail, he still must consider the particular computer to be programmed; that is, his program is still machine dependent.

Programming in a high-level language makes the programmer, to a very large extent, independent of the machine. In contrast with machine language or assembly language, which must take into consideration the structure and organization of particular computers, high-level languages reflect the structure and organization of the language of the problem area. For this reason they are frequently referred to as *problem-oriented* languages.

PL/I is a high-level problem-oriented language that was developed to meet the need for a broad base language that is able to accommodate a variety of types of problems. Some of the problems that the language was developed to handle represent new types of computer applications that require the processing of data represented by characters, words, and symbols rather than exclusively numerical values. The type of logical processing required of these types of nonnumeric applications is often difficult to program in languages that were primarily designed for numerical applications.

The ability of PL/I to handle characters as individual symbols and as strings makes it particularly useful for the processing of data that is primarily composed of text.

Another advantage of PL/I from the point of view of text processing is that it can handle a large set of unique characters. Two hundred and fifty-six different characters are recognized by the processor, and for inclusion in the statements within programs themselves, the language makes use of 60 unique alphanumeric characters (see Section 2.3).

PL/I provides many options for statements and for ways of describing data. Whenever there is an alternative available, and if the choice is not stated explicitly by the programmer, the compiler chooses by default the standard alternative that would be required in the majority of cases. This *default concept* contributes a great deal to the simplicity of the language.

The language is also designed to handle conveniently interrupt features present in many of today's computer systems and can be used without regard to the type of terminal through which the user is communicating with the system. Because of its modularity, PL/I allows the use of parts of the full language to suit the requirements of particular users while still maintaining the effectiveness and integrity of the full language.

2.2   The PL/I Program

Writing a program in a high-level language such as PL/I greatly simplifies the process of instructing the computer to execute specified commands.

Suppose we are given two values, X and Y, and we want to calculate a value Z representing their sum. In ordinary mathematical notation, we would write

$$Z = X + Y$$

In order to calculate this sum, a computer must be provided with a series of machine language instructions in which addition itself plays a rather small role.

In narrative form, the series of machine language instructions required to instruct the computer to perform the simple addition $Z = X + Y$ might appear as follows:

1. Start program.
2. Reserve space in computer memory to store value of X. (We will refer to the location of this memory space as the *address* of X.)

3. Reserve a second memory location to store value of Y.

4. Reserve a third memory location to store value of Z after it has been computed.

5. Take note of the particular peripheral device that will transmit the values of X and Y for internal storing.

6. Bring in the current values of X and Y from the device specified in step 5.

7. Store the two values just received in addresses X and Y, respectively.

8. Take the value currently stored at address X (that is, the *content* of the memory location whose address is X) and make a copy of it at the memory location whose address is Z.

9. Take the value currently stored at address Y (that is, the content of Y) and add it to current value stored at Z.

10. Note the particular peripheral device on which the results are to be displayed.

11. Send to the device specified in step 10 the current values (that is, contents) of memory locations X, Y, and Z.

12. End program; there are no further instructions to be executed.

In contrast with the above, the corresponding PL/I program shown on the left below illustrates the simplicity of the PL/I statements that are required in order for the computer to perform the same addition. The PL/I statements are automatically translated by the compiler into the series of 12 machine language instructions discussed above.

PL/I program (source)	Machine language (object) program created by action of processor
PROCEDURE OPTIONS (MAIN);	Step 1
DECLARE X, Y, Z;	Steps 2–4. By *default* (that is, in absence of further specifications), PL/I compiler assumes X, Y, Z will take numbers as values rather than letters or other symbols.
GET LIST (X, Y);	Steps 5–7. The assignment of particular I/O devices are made. By default, PL/I refers to the card reader.
Z = X + Y;	Steps 8–9
PUT LIST (X, Y, Z);	Steps 10–11. Again by default a standard I/O device is assumed, in this case the high speed printer.
END;	Step 12

As part of the process of compilation, the PL/I source program receives an extensive diagnostic analysis in the course of which a number is assigned to each statement. The source program is then printed out with diagnostic messages referring to specific numbered statements in the source program. This allows the programmer to refer directly to the statement in question and make the necessary corrections. Once the source program is debugged in this manner and successfully compiled, the resulting object program (sometimes referred to as the "processing program") is the one actually used during the stage of program execution and processing of the data.

The execution of the object program is under the control of a master supervisory or control program, known as the *operating system*, that resides permanently in the computer. The operating system is responsible for the execution of the instructions of the object program, allocation of storage locations, and assignment of the necessary input/output devices.

Processing generally requires the following configuration of input data:

1. Instructions to the control program identifying user, job, and type of operation.
2. Object program.
3. Instructions indicating that the data to be processed follows.
4. Data.
5. Indication of the end of the job.

2.3   PL/I Character Set

PL/I characters may be grouped in three broad categories:

1. *The extended alphabet*, consisting of 29 characters (the alphabet A–Z) and three special characters $, #, @.
2. *Numeric characters*, consisting of the digits 0–9.
3. *Special characters*, consisting of 21 characters.

One group of special characters indicate separation between terms, statements, or parts of a PL/I program. These are the following:

Blank   Used as a separator between terms in a PL/I statement or between items of data.

Comma   ,   Used as a separator between elements in a list or separating items of data.
Semicolon   ;   Used to separate one PL/I statement from the next.
Colon   :   Used to separate any label from the body of a statement.
Parenthesis   ( )   Used to separate one part of a PL/I statement from others.

A second group of eight special characters in PL/I are called *comparison operators*. Each operator causes a comparison to be made between two arithmetic variables or expressions. The result of the comparison will be either true or false, depending upon the comparison being made and the numerical values of the variables at the time of the comparison.

Comparison (relational) operator	Meaning
<	Less than
¬<	Not less than
<=	Less than or equal to
=	Equal to
¬=	Not equal to
>=	Greater than or equal to
>	Greater than
¬>	Not greater than

EXAMPLES

$$A < B$$
$$K \neg = L$$

The first of the expressions above will be true provided that the numerical value of A is less than the numerical value of B, and the second will be true if the numerical value of K is not equal to the numerical value of L; otherwise the expressions will be false.

Observe that no blank can occur between compound comparison operators such as ¬= or >=. On the other hand, where blanks are permissible, it does not make any difference how many blanks occur. For example, PUT   LIST or PUT   LIST would be interpreted as the same.

A third group of special characters are called *logical operators*. A major function of these operations is to allow simple expressions, such as those in the example above, to be combined into more complex logical expressions. To accommodate this, three logical operators are available in PL/I, corresponding to the basic Boolean operations of logical negation, logical sum, and logical product.

Logical operator	Meaning
¬	Not
&	And
|	Or

The meanings attached to the logical operators are the same as the conventional meanings for the Boolean AND, OR, and NOT operators. A more detailed discussion of these basic Boolean operations and their relationship to other important Boolean functions is found in Section 9.2.

As we mentioned above, comparison operators and logical operators are used in forming expressions that take as their value the logical constants "true" and "false." For this reason they are known as logical expressions, as contrasted with arithmetic expressions that take as their value numerical constants (see Section 3.3 for a discussion of arithmetic expressions). In addition, such logical expressions are called *conditional expressions* because they express a condition which can be tested to determine the truth or falsity of the expression. If what is stated in the condition is found to be the case, the expression is said to be true; otherwise it is false. Simple conditional expressions are formed by combining two arithmetic expressions with one of the eight comparison operators. The logical operators are used to combine simple conditional expressions into compound conditional expressions. Thus it is possible in a PL/I program to represent the outcome of several comparisons by means of a single compound conditional expression, as shown in the following examples:

$$(A < B) \,\&\, (K \,\neg\, = L)$$
$$(C > = D) \,|\, (X = Y)$$
$$\neg(A < = D)$$

Conditional expressions find a major use in PL/I programming in connection with the IF statement. In Section 3.5 we shall explain the basic forms of the IF statement, and in Section 4.6 we shall illustrate the use of character strings in the IF statement. It should be kept in mind that not only simple conditional expressions can be used in IF statements, but also more complex IF statements can be constructed by combining the outcome of several comparisons into a compound conditional expression. In either case, the conditional expression as part of the IF statement is an important tool to effect branching within a PL/I program.

The PL/I language character set is shown in Table 2.1.

TABLE 2.1

PL/I *Language Character Set*

Character	Description
A–Z	Alphabetic
$, @, #	Alphabetic
0–9	Numeric
	Blank[a]
=	Equal
+	Plus
−	Minus
*	Asterisk
/	Slash
(	Left parenthesis
)	Right parenthesis
,	Comma
.	Period
'	Single quote
%	Percent
;	Semicolon
:	Colon
¬	Not
&	And
|	Or
<	Less than
—	Break
?	Question mark
>	Greater than
||	Concatenate[b]

[a] Whenever it is appropriate, the symbol ƀ may be used in the text to denote a blank.

[b] Technically, \|\| is a compound character and should not be included in the basic character set. Similar remarks apply to the compound characters **, /*, */, ¬<, ¬>, ¬=, <=, etc.

2.4 Format Rules

Each command in PL/I is represented by a *statement*. While the length of a statement is not limited, the most widely used specification is that columns 2–72 on a punched card are available for statements. There are no restrictions on the starting column for a statement, the number of statements on a card, or the length of a statement. However, each statement must end with a semicolon indicating to the compiler the end of the statement. It is possible to have multiple statements per card or to start a statement on one card and to continue on another, but the interruption should occur in column 72 and the statement should continue in column 2 of the next card.

EXAMPLE

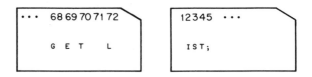

Statements can be identified by assigning them unique names; such a name-tag is called a *statement label*. A statement label can be any combination of PL/I characters with the following restrictions:

1. The name must begin with one of the 29 characters of the extended alphabet (A–Z, $, #, @); subsequent characters can be alphabetic characters or digits.
2. The length cannot exceed 31 characters.
3. No blank may appear anywhere in the statement label.
4. If a group of words are used as a label, they have to be connected by the break character.

EXAMPLES

    ASSESS1: PROCEDURE OPTIONS (MAIN);
     START: DECLARE TEXT;
    GET_WORD: GET LIST (WORD);

In the various types of PL/I statements there are certain words called *keywords* which have a special status in that their presence in the statement is always necessary since they convey certain information to the compiler. In the sample PL/I statements shown above, the keywords are PROCEDURE OPTIONS (MAIN), DECLARE, and GET LIST. Some keywords have abbreviations which are recognized by the compiler as completely synonymous and interchangeable with the keyword they represent. For example, the abbreviation of the keyword DECLARE is DCL, and the abbreviation of PROCEDURE is PROC. We shall discuss many of the PL/I keywords later in the text as we consider the various types of PL/I statements. For those keywords that can be abbreviated, we shall follow the practice of including the abbreviation in parentheses when first introducing the keyword in the text.

In addition to keywords, PL/I statements contain words that are called *identifiers*. Besides the statement labels ASSESS1, START, and GET_WORD, which are identifiers, the sample PL/I statements shown above also contain two other identifiers, TEXT and WORD. As used in PL/I, then, the term "identifier" refers to the name of any variable associated with the three basic types of data recognized by the language. That is, an identifier is the name of any variable of the following types:

> arithmetic data variables
> string data (character or bit) variables
> program control or label data variables.

The above four restrictions on use of PL/I characters for forming statement labels apply generally to any identifier. Other examples of identifiers are

  USER,   RATE,   DEC,   X,   NEW_LIST,   A1,   F5,   ALPHA,   BIN

It should be noted that keywords and their abbreviations are available for use by the programmer as identifiers, if one so chooses, and no confusion will result so long as the 60-character set is used. Thus, while DEC and BIN are abbreviations for the keyword attributes DECIMAL and BINARY (see Section 3.2), they may also be used by the programmer as names of data variables. It should also be observed that uppercase letter type will be used throughout the text to express identifiers. The same type of upper case letter format will apply to PL/I keywords and their abbreviations.

It is possible to include *comments* of any length as part of a PL/I program to serve as documentation. Comments are printed as part of the program listing but are not taken into consideration in the compilation and execution of the program. Comments may be of any length and may appear almost anywhere but must appear as follows:

/*comment*/

The beginning symbol /* and the ending symbol */ must be written as shown, without a blank separating the slash and asterisk. Sample Program 6: ASSESS6 illustrates the use of comments in a PL/I program.

EXERCISE

1. Which of the following is a valid PL/I identifier?
    (a) STEP 1
    (b) STEP-1
    (c) STEP_1
    (d) STEP/1
    (e) STEP1
    (f) STEP(1)
    (g) 1STEP
    (h) #1STEP

CHAPTER 3

Basic Instruction Types in PL/I

3.1 Defining the Boundaries of a Program

A PL/I program consists of one or more blocks of programming statements called *procedures*. Although a program may consist of several procedures, for the present we shall consider a program as consisting of a single procedure, deferring the discussion of programs having several procedures until Chapter 12.

It is necessary to provide the processor with information defining the beginning and end of a procedure. The start of a PL/I program is indicated by the statement

        label: PROCEDURE OPTIONS (MAIN);

where "label" is an identifier for naming the program, PROCEDURE has as its abbreviation PROC, and OPTIONS (MAIN) tells the processor this is the first procedure in the program. Each statement must terminate with a semicolon (;), which signals to the compiler the end of a statement. The use of label can be extended to any statement in the program so that any program statement can have a unique name associated with it. For any statement so named, the statement label must precede the statement to which it applies and must be separated from it by a colon (:).

All procedures must end with the statement

END label;

where "label" may be omitted.

3.2   Storage Allocation

The general form of the programming statement for reserving storage is

DECLARE name;

where "name" is an identifier assigned by the programmer, and the keyword DECLARE has DCL as its abbreviation.

By including the names of several identifiers in a single DECLARE statement, storage location can be reserved for multiple quantities of data. Thus the statement

DECLARE X, X1, X2, X3;

will reserve four storage locations that are identified for the duration of the program by the names x, x1, x2, and x3.

The type of data that a variable may assume is determined explicitly by the attributes specified in the DECLARE statement or by the default ones assigned by the compiler. PL/I deals with arithmetic data, string data (character or bit), and program control data such as statement labels, subroutine names, and other program entry points. Arithmetic data can be fixed or floating point, binary or decimal, real or complex. The corresponding keyword attributes for arithmetic data are FIXED, FLOAT, BINARY (abbreviated: BIN), DECIMAL (abbreviated: DEC), REAL, and COMPLEX (abbreviated: CPLX), respectively.

An example of a DECLARE statement with explicitly specified data attributes is

DECLARE X FIXED DECIMAL, WORD CHARACTER (8), BEGIN LABEL;

where x, WORD, and BEGIN are names of arithmetic, string, and program control variables, respectively, standing for designated storage locations in the computer. Thus stored in location x is fixed decimal data (for example, 23.589), stored in location WORD is a string of eight characters (for example, RETRIEVE), and in location BEGIN is any identifier which is a label in the program (for example, START).

If the names begin with letters I–N, arithmetic data is *by default* assumed to be in integer form (for example, 33, 1, 5748, 2, 301, 906); if the names start with the letters A–H or O–Z, $, #, @,† the data has the form

$$\pm n.d\textsc{e} \pm pp$$

where n is a single digit, d is a number *d* digits long and pp is a two-digit number representing the power of 10 by which the number n.d is to be multiplied. This representation is called *floating point*. By default, *d* is automatically set by the PL/I compiler at some fixed value, usually 5.

Floating point form	Number
2.00000E + 00	2.0
3.12000E + 01	31.2
3.12000E + 04	31200.0
3.12000E − 06	0.00000312
−2.10400E − 01	−.2104

Without attributes, the previous DECLARE statement would appear as follows.

DECLARE X, WORD, BEGIN;

and, by default, all three locations X, WORD, and BEGIN will store floating point arithmetic data instead of arithmetic, character, and program control data. It is important for the programmer to define the attributes, especially when the default ones are not the ones required by the problem, since failure to do so is a very common error condition when executing a program. Moreover, the DECLARE statement defines only the *type* of data to be stored in the location named by an identifier; it does not specify the *value* of the data. For example, in the illustration above, the identifier X is declared to be only the *name* of arithmetic data that must be specified in floating point form; the *value* of X is not specified. Thus X may take as its

---

†In PL/I, the dollar mark ($), the number sign (#), and the at sign (@) are considered alphabetic characters (see Section 2.3).

initial value any of the floating point numbers shown above, or for that matter any others, and indeed its value need not remain fixed but may change during the course of program execution.

3.3   Assignment Statements

The assignment statement allows the programmer to:

1.   generate new data internally (as opposed to introducing it from an external source);
2.   perform mathematical and logical operations on data; and
3.   shift and exchange information in memory.

The general form of the assignment statement is

$$\text{name} = \text{expression};$$

where " name " is a variable (that is, identifier) assigned by the programmer and " expression " is one or more variables and/or constants connected by operators. An example of an assignment statement is

$$X = A + B + 3;$$

Interpretation of Symbol " = " in PL/I

Because actual values are represented by the contents of locations in memory, we must interpret " = " as an abbreviation for " *is replaced by.*" For example, in a program for the calculation of fines for overdue books, the assignment statement

$$FINE = DAYS * RATE;$$

would be interpreted by the processor as " multiply the current content of memory location designated by DAYS by the contents of storage location called RATE, and replace the content of location named FINE by the resulting product."

By the rules of ordinary algebra, the statement

$$X = X + 3;$$

is meaningless, since no number can be both itself and three more than itself. In PL/I, however, $x = x + 3$ is said to mean "take the current content of location x, increase it by 3, and store the result back in location x, destroying its previous content."

Generation of Numeric Values

The assignment statement in PL/I can be used as a declaration to allocate storage under a name and assign a numeric content to the location without use of a separate DECLARE statement. For example, execution of the assignment statement

$$\text{RATE} = 25;$$

would result in the storage of the constant 25 in a location named RATE.

The general form of the assignment statement when used for this purpose is

$$\text{name, name, name, etc.} = \text{constant};$$

Hence, the three assignment statements

$$x = 14;$$
$$y = 14;$$
$$z = 14;$$

are equivalent to and can be replaced by the single assignment statement

$$x, y, z = 14;$$

Arithmetic Operations

Five basic arithmetic operations are available in PL/I to connect constants and variables to form arithmetic expressions in assignment statements.

Symbol	Operation	Level of priority
+	Addition	1 (lowest)
−	Subtraction	1
*	Multiplication	2
/	Division	2
**	Exponentiation	3 (highest)

Correct and incorrect ways of expressing in PL/I the algebraic equation

$$Y = \frac{2X + 7}{3X - 4}$$

are

> *Correct*:   Y = (2 * X + 7)/(3 * X − 4);
> *Incorrect*:   Y = 2 * X + 7/3 * X − 4;

By inserting parentheses, it is always possible to specify unambiguously the order in which operations are performed in an arithmetic expression. In the absence of parentheses, or within parentheses, the order of evaluation is based on the following priority scheme: level 3 operators are performed first, level 2 operators next, and level 1 operators last. If more than one level 3 operator appears in the same expression, the order of priority of these operators is from right to left. However, if two or more level 2 operators appear in the same expression, they are evaluated from left to right, and similarly for the order of evaluation of two or more level 1 operators. Applying these rules to the two PL/I expressions shown above, the reader may verify that the one on the top is indeed a correct version of the given algebraic equation, and that the one on the bottom has as its evaluation the algebraic equation

$$Y = (2X + \tfrac{7}{3}X) - 4 = \frac{13X - 12}{3}$$

Priority of Operators

With the exception of the concatenation operator ($\|$), to be discussed in Section 5.1, all the operators that can be used to form expressions in a PL/I assignment statement have now been introduced. These include the arithmetic operators

$$+, -, *, /, **$$

the comparison operators

$$<, \neg<, <=, =, \neg=, >=, >, \neg>$$

and the logical operators

$$\neg, \&, \,|$$

As in arithmetic expressions, the order in which operators are evaluated in logical expressions also has an effect on the meaning or result of the evaluation. In the absence of parentheses, or within parentheses, the precise evaluation of a logical expression is obtained by the rule of priority shown in the table below, which establishes a ranking of arithmetic and logical operators for compound expressions.

Operator	Level of priority
$\|$	1 (lowest)
&	2
$<, \neg <, <=, =, \neg =, >=, >, \neg >$	3
$\|\|$	4
$+, -$	5
$*, /$	6
$**, \neg$	7 (highest)

Operators of higher priority in an expression are evaluated before operators of lower priority. If more than one level 7 operator appears in the same expression, the order of priority of these operators is from right to left; otherwise, for two or more operators of the same level other than level 7 appearing in an expression, the order of priority is from left to right.

EXAMPLES

Expression	Result of evaluation
A & B $\neg = $ C $*$ D $\|$ F	((A & (B $\neg = $ (C $*$ D))) $\|$ F)
A $**$ B $<$ C $*$ D & $\neg$ F	(((A $**$ B) $<$ (C $*$ D)) & ($\neg$ F))

Shifting and Exchanging Data in Memory

To transfer the content of one location to another location, it suffices to use the single assignment statement

$$Y = Z;$$

This results in the content of location Z being copied into location Y, destroying the previous content of Y. After this operation is completed the contents of both locations will be identical.

To exchange the contents of Y and Z, a set of PL/I statements is required as follows.

DECLARE Y, Z;
HOLD = Y;
Y = Z;
Z = HOLD;

Note that the identifier HOLD does not have to be declared explicitly.

3.4   Input–Output Statements

Input–output (I/O) statements are used for sending information to and from computer memory. PL/I has a number of options available that enable the user to select the type of I/O instructions which will be most suited to his problem. In PL/I there are two basic modes of data transmission, known as (1) *stream* I/O and (2) *record* I/O.

In Chapter 13 we shall describe briefly several features of "record I/O" that are useful in file data management; otherwise the discussion in the text will be limited to "stream I/O." In this basic mode of data transmission, both input and output is treated as a continuous stream of data separated by blanks or commas, in which the flow of the stream is turned on and off by the action of the program. This mode of transmission is not dependent on format or the amount of data involved and it allows the user to input or output data as a stream of numeric and alphanumeric characters.

List-Directed I/O

A basic form of input command for "stream I/O" is

GET LIST (name 1, name 2, etc.);

and the corresponding form of output command is

PUT LIST (name 1, name 2, etc.);

where name 1, name 2, etc. are identifiers that provide names for the data and specify their storage locations.

The order in which these names appear in the input statement is important because each data item in the input stream is matched with the corresponding identifier in the GET statement.

For example, if the input data consisted of a stream of document numbers 1, 5, 7, 6, 9, 11 as shown below

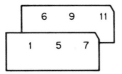

the input statement

GET LIST (A,B,C,D,E,F);

would result in A = 1, B = 5, C = 7, D = 6, E = 9, F = 11. In other words, document number 1 would be placed in storage location A, document number 5 in location B, document number 7 in location C, and so forth. However, if the data cards became reversed and the order of the input data were

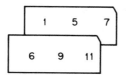

then A = 6, B = 9, C = 11, D = 1, E = 5, and F = 7. In this case, document number 6 would be placed in location A and document number 1 in location D.

If one wanted to store at locations A,B,C,D, respectively, only the first two data items appearing on the above pair of data cards, then an input statement like the following would be required.

GET LIST (A,B,DUMMY,C,D);

This results in A = 6, B = 9, C = 1, and D = 5. In other words, the third data item is read and stored in the computer (at a location called DUMMY), but it need not be further accessed by the program.

The PUT LIST statement causes the computer to obtain the data contained in the specified storage locations and list them as output in the order in which they appear in the PUT LIST statement. Based on the example of the first GET LIST statement above,

PUT LIST (A,B,C,D,E,F);

will produce as output document numbers 1,5,7,6,9,11 in this order; on the other hand,

PUT LIST (D,E,F,B,C,A);

will produce a list of the document numbers 6,9,11,5,7,1 in this order.

When the PUT LIST statement is used in this form, the physical positioning of the output will be left to the compiler.

The output statement

PUT SKIP LIST (name 1, name 2, etc.);

allows the programmer to specify a new line. Thus

PUT LIST (A,B,C);
PUT SKIP LIST (E,D,F);

will produce two separate lines of output. If we assume the values specified in the previous example, the two lines of output would be

1 5 7
6 9 11

It should be noted that input statements in PL/I cause the processor to allocate storage as part of the input process. Thus the two statements

DECLARE A,B,C;
GET LIST (A,B,C);

represent a redundancy. If certain default options are accepted, the GET LIST statement alone would be sufficient.

Data-Directed I/O

A second form of input/output for stream-oriented transmission of data is *data-directed* I/O.

The basic form of the GET statement for data-directed input is

GET DATA (name 1, name 2, etc.);

where "name 1," "name 2," and so on are identifiers that represent internal storage locations to which data items in the input stream are assigned. The identifiers are the same as those described for a GET LIST statement, with certain differences that we shall explain below. The data in the input stream is also like the data processed by a GET LIST statement except that it is in the form of a set of assignment statements, separated by either a comma or a blank, and terminated by a semicolon:

identifier = constant, identifier = constant, etc.;

The input stream for data-directed transmission, therefore, might appear as

DATE = 12, BOOK = 'QC36.A5', RATE = 10, USER = 'SMITH';

The semicolon determines how many data items in the input stream are to be processed by a single GET DATA statement and stored in the computer. Unlike the GET LIST statement, the order in which identifiers appear in a GET DATA statement does not have to match the order in which data items appear in the input stream. Thus, the following two GET DATA statements are equally valid for reading in the data in the input stream above.

GET DATA (DATE, BOOK, RATE, USER);
GET DATA (USER, BOOK, DATE, RATE);

Moreover, identifiers appearing in the input stream need not appear explicitly in the GET DATA statement (although they must be declared). Conversely, identifiers appearing in the GET DATA statement need not appear in an assignment statement in the input stream, in which case no data transmission occurs for such identifiers and their values are left unchanged. Thus, the following two GET DATA statements are also valid for reading in the data in the foregoing input stream.

GET DATA (DATE, RATE);
GET DATA (USER, BOOK, DUEDATE, FINE);

The values for DUEDATE and FINE are left unchanged, because no assignment statements for them appear in the input stream.

The basic form of the PUT statement for data-directed output is

PUT DATA (name 1, name 2, etc.);

where the data items in the output stream are separated by blanks and terminated by a semicolon:

name 1 = constant   name 2 = constant   etc.;

Since the output from PUT DATA statements is automatically labeled, use of data-directed output is convenient for purposes of debugging and program testing. For example, if the input stream is

'SMITH', 25

the input statement for reading in and storing these values in the computer could be

GET LIST (USER, DUEDATE);

This statement could then be immediately followed by the statement

PUT DATA (USER, DUEDATE);

which produces as labeled output

USER = 'SMITH'   DUEDATE = 25;

Edit-Directed I/O

A third form of input/output for stream-oriented transmission of data is *edit-directed* I/O. Edit-directed transmission allows the programmer to specify the variables to which data is to be assigned as well as to specify the format of the data on the external storage medium.

Unlike list-directed and data-directed I/O statements, edit-directed I/O statements require the use of two lists: a data list containing identifiers for the data, and a format list containing specifications, in column-by-column detail, of the form of the data.

The basic form of the GET statement for edit-directed input is

GET EDIT (name 1, name 2, etc.) (format 1, format 2, etc.);

and the output statement is

PUT EDIT (name 1, name 2, etc.) (format 1, format 2, etc.);

where "name 1," "name 2," and so on are identifiers that represent internal storage areas to which data items are assigned, and "format 1," "format 2," and so on are format specifications for the data associated with the identifiers.

The following are examples of edit-directed I/O statements.

GET EDIT (CALLNO) (F(3));
GET EDIT (USER, ADDRESS, ID) (A(10), A(40), F(3,2));
PUT EDIT (FINE, SUM, TOTAL) (F(5,2), E(6,1), E(8,2));

In an input statement, format specifications relate only to the way in which data is to be transmitted; they do not control the form of the data when it is stored. The form which the data assumes in storage is determined by the attributes assigned to the identifiers in a DECLARE statement, or by default ones.

In an output statement, format specifications indicate the form of the printed output.

For either input or output, the first format specification is associated with the first item in the data list, the second format specification with the second item in the data list, and so on.

If a format list contains fewer format specifications than the number of data items, the format specifications are reused. If the number of format specifications exceeds the number of items in the data list, the extra ones are ignored.

When a given format specification appears successively in a format list, it is possible to cite it only once and precede it by an iteration factor which specifies how many times it is to be used. For example, suppose that we wish to read in data for three identifiers which have been declared to accept eight-character strings as values; then the following edit-directed input statements are equivalent, and any one of them may be used.

GET EDIT (USER, CALLNO, DATE) (A(8), A(8), A(8));
GET EDIT (USER, CALLNO, DATE) (A(8));
GET EDIT (USER, CALLNO, DATE) (3 A(8));

The following three categories of format items can appear in the format list of edit-directed I/O statements:

1. *data-format items*, describing the external format of a single data item;

2. *control-format items*, specifying the layout of data associated with a file; and

3. *the remote-format item*, specifying the label of a FORMAT statement that contains a format list which is to replace the remote-format item.

1. *Data-Format Items.* The F-*format item* describes the external representation of decimal arithmetic data in fixed-point format. It can have one of the following forms

$$F(w), \quad F(w,d), \quad F(w,d,p)$$

where w specifies the length of the field, inclusive of the sign and the decimal point; d specifies the number of digits to the right of the decimal point; and p specifies a scaling factor (an exponent of 10). If the input stream is 234,

GET EDIT (A) (F(3));

assigns the value 234 to the variable A.

GET EDIT (A) (F(3,0));

assigns the value 234 to the variable A.

GET EDIT (A) (F(3,2));

assigns the value 2.34 to the variable A.

GET EDIT (A) (F(3,2,1));

assigns the value 23.4 to the variable A. If no decimal point appears in the input string and p is not specified, then d specifies the number of digits to the right of the assumed decimal point as in the third statement above. If p is specified, then the value of the data item is multiplied by 10^p, which means that when p is positive the decimal point is moved p places to the right of its assumed position and when p is negative the decimal point is moved p places to the left of the assumed position, as in the fourth statement above.

If a decimal point appears in the data stream, it overrides the value of d in the format specification. For example, if the input data stream is 23.58916321,

GET EDIT (RATE, BOOKNO, USERNO) (F(4,2), F(4), F(3,0,2));

assigns the following values to the variables.

RATE = 23.5
BOOKNO = 8916
USERNO = 32100

The first format specification reads four characters from the input stream. Because p is not specified and because one of the input characters is a decimal point, the value for RATE is set to the value shown. The second

format item reads the next four characters and interprets them as a
decimal value for BOOKNO. The third format specification reads three
characters and because p is specified to be 2, the number represented by
these characters is multiplied by 10^2 and the result stored in location
USERNO.

If only w is specified in the F-format, then only the integer portion of
the number is printed in the output. If the value of a fixed-point number is
less than zero, a minus sign is printed as the first character of the field;
therefore the field-width specification (w) must include a count of the
minus sign and of the decimal point. For example, if A $= -18$, then

PUT EDIT (A) (F(4,1));

prints

$-$	1	.	8

PUT EDIT (A) (F(6,2));

prints

b	$-$	1	.	8	0

If the number of fractional digits is smaller than d, trailing zeros are
supplied. If, as in the second statement above, w is larger than the number
of digits, then the number is preceded by blanks.

In edit-directed output if TOTAL $= 12000.50$ and BOOKNO $= 123.45$, then

PUT EDIT (TOTAL, BOOKNO) (F(9,2), F(6,2));

would print

$-$	1	2	0	0	0	.	5	0	1	2	3	.	4	5

PUT EDIT (TOTAL, BOOKNO) (F(12,2), F(9,3));

would print

b	b	b	$-$	1	2	0	0	0	.	5	0	b	b	1	2	3	.	4	5	0

The E-*format item* describes the external representation of decimal arithmetic data in floating point format. As shown in Section 3.2, a floating point number has the representation

$$\pm n.dE \pm pp$$

where $\pm n.d$ is called the *mantissa* and $\pm pp$ is called the *exponent*.

The specifications for an E-format item can be of the form

$$E(w), \quad E(w,d), \quad \text{or} \quad E(w,d,s)$$

where w, d are the same as in F-format and s represents the number of digits to be printed in the mantissa and is used only for *output edit-directed data*.

On input if the data is a fixed-point number, the exponent is assumed to be zero and the mantissa must be a decimal fixed-point constant. When no decimal point appears in the input stream, then d specifies the number of digits to the right of the assumed decimal point in the mantissa. A decimal point in the input stream overrides the value of d. The value of w for the E-format item includes the mantissa sign, the exponent sign, the letter E, the decimal point, and the number of digits in the mantissa. The exponent is a decimal integer constant.

If the input is

$$12.13E-03$$
GET EDIT (A) (E(9,4));

assigns the value 12.13×10^{-3} to the variable A.

On output the exponent is automatically adjusted so that the leading digit of the mantissa is other than zero. If the number does not fill the specified field on output, then leading blanks are supplied (as in F-format).

If s is not specified, then the number of digits for the mantissa is taken to be one plus the number of digits specified by d. When s is not given, the mantissa is represented by only one digit to the left of the decimal point. The following statements illustrate the use of s in an E-format specification.

If $A = 1234.67$,

PUT EDIT (A) (E(8,2));

prints

```
1 . 2 3 E + 0 3
```

PUT EDIT (A) (E(9,2,4));

prints

```
1 2 . 3 5 E + 0 2
```

PUT EDIT (A) (E(12,3,6));

prints

```
␢ 1 2 3 . 4 6 7 E + 0 1
```

The A-*format item* describes the external representation of a character string. Its specification is

$$A(w)$$

where w specifies the length of the input or output field.

If the input stream is

BROWN1234

GET EDIT (NAME, ACCT) (A(5), A(4));

assigns to NAME the character string 'BROWN' and to the identifier ACCT the character string '1234'. On input w is always required and if it has a value less than or equal to zero, a null string is assumed.

On output the value of the variable is converted to a character string and is truncated or is extended with blanks on the right to the specified field length (w) before it is placed into the data stream.

If USER1 = 'SMITH' and USER2 = 'JAMES',

PUT EDIT (USER1, USER2) (A(8));

prints

```
S M I T H ␢ ␢ ␢ J A M E S ␢ ␢ ␢
```

On output if w is not specified, it is assumed to be equal to the length of the character string of the identifier specified in the data list. For example, for the same values of the identifiers USER1, USER2 as shown above,

PUT EDIT (USER1, USER2) (A);

would print

SMITHJAMES

Another way of using the A-format item is

PUT EDIT ('THE BOOKS RECEIVED ARE:') (A);

The B-*format item* describes the external representation of a bit string. Its specification has the form

B(w)

where w specifies the number of characters contained in the bit string.

On input the character representation of the bit string may occur anyplace in the field w and blanks are ignored before or after the bit string in the field.

If the input string is

ᵬ 1 0 1 0 1 1 ᵬ ᵬ
GET EDIT (A) (B(6));

assigns the value '101011'B to the variable A.

GET EDIT (A) (B(8));

similarly assigns the value '101011'B to the variable A.

The input string should contain only the characters 0 and 1. Any other character in the input string will stop execution of the input statement, including blanks. If the input string is

ᵬ 1 0 ᵬ 1 1 1 ᵬ
GET EDIT (A) (B(7));

cannot be executed but the statement

GET EDIT (A,B) (B(4), B(3));

could be used. However, if the input string is

ᵬ 1 0 ᵬ 1 ᵬ 0

then an error will occur in the execution of the statement above.

On output the character representation of the bit string is padded with blanks on the right to match the length specified by w. If TERMS = '101110'B

PUT EDIT (TERMS) (B(6));

would print

```
| 1  0  1  1  1  0 |
```

PUT EDIT (TERMS) (B(10));

would print

```
| 1  0  1  1  1  0 ɓ ɓ ɓ ɓ |
```

PUT EDIT (TERMS) (B);

would print

```
| 1  0  1  1  1  0 |
```

Note that the use of B-format does not print the identifying letter B for bit string.

2. *Control-Format Items.*   The x-*format item* controls the spacing of data items in the data stream. Its form is

$$x(w)$$

where w specifies the number of character positions to skip or space. On input the x-format indicates that the next w incoming characters are to be skipped. On output the x-format item indicates the number of columns to be skipped before printing continues.

PAGE-*format* indicates the start of a new page. It has the form

PAGE

COLUMN-*format* indicates a column on the current input card or output page. It has the form

COLUMN(w)

where w specifies the column at which reading or printing is to commence. (COL is an abbreviation for COLUMN.)

LINE-*format* indicates a line on the output and it has the form

LINE(w)

where w specifies the line of the current page at which printing should begin.

SKIP-*format* indicates that the next input card is to be read or printing is to commence on the next line of the output page. It has the form

SKIP   or   SKIP(w)

where w specifies the number of lines to be skipped in printing. When w is not given, its value is assumed to be one.

For example, the edit-directed output statement

PUT EDIT (A,B,C) (PAGE, SKIP, COL(3), F(6,2),
X(2), F(7,3), COL(50), A(10));

causes the printer to advance to the next page, to skip down one line on that page, to skip to the third column of that line; to print the value of A as a fixed decimal number in a field six characters long, to skip two spaces on the line, print the value of B, skip to column 50, and print the contents of C.

3. *Remote-Format Items.*   The following specifies the format list as a separate statement

GET EDIT (data list) (R(label));
label: FORMAT (X(2), A(10), SKIP);

where "data list" is one or more variables to be transmitted and "label" is the name of the statement containing the format specifications. An illustration of the use of this type of format specification is found in Chapter 11 in Sample Program 19: RETRIEVE1.

Sample Program 1:   ASSESS1

The following sample program is intended to illustrate the use of some of the statements discussed so far.

In library operations the fine procedure frequently is part of the circulation control system. The objective of the fine procedure is to compute the amount of money owed by the user on the basis of the number of days his book is overdue and the daily overdue rate charged by the particular library. The amount of the fine is calculated by multiplying the number of days by the daily rate.

Let us call the procedure ASSESS1. The objective is to determine the value of the FINE to be paid by the USER on the basis of DAYS and RATE. Below are a sample flowchart and program to accomplish this. For the reader not familiar with the technique of flowcharting, an introduction to the symbology of flowcharts is included in the front matter.

ASSESS1:

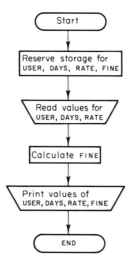

ASSESS1: PROCEDURE OPTIONS (MAIN);
DECLARE USER, DAYS, RATE, FINE;
GET LIST (USER, DAYS, RATE);
FINE = DAYS * RATE;
PUT LIST (USER, DAYS, RATE, FINE);
END ASSESS1;

3.5 Control and Decision Statements

Looping

ASSESS1 as written above will perform the fine procedure only once and no provision is made to repeat the process to calculate the amount of the next user's fine.

The technique which will allow a sequence of instructions to be repeated is called *looping*, and the particular sequence to be repeated is called a *loop*. Repetitive processing can be accomplished by use of the GO TO statement.

The GO TO Statement

The unconditional GO TO (abbreviated: GOTO) statement has the general form

GO TO label;

where "label" represents the name of the identifier assigned to the particular statement in the program where the loop begins.

Sample Program 2: ASSESS2

To remove the limitation in ASSESS1 that the program calculates only the fine of one user, a loop (L) can be introduced into the program by repeating the procedure that begins with the GET LIST statement. In this way new data is obtained for the calculation of the fine for the next user. This may be accomplished by use of the GO TO statement and a statement label is shown in the flowchart and program below.

ASSESS2:

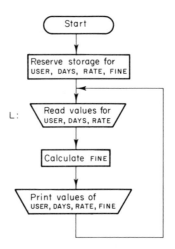

```
ASSESS2:    PROCEDURE OPTIONS (MAIN);
            DECLARE USER, DAYS, RATE, FINE;
     L:     GET LIST (USER, DAYS, RATE);
            FINE = DAYS * RATE;
            PUT LIST (USER, DAYS, RATE, FINE);
            GO TO L;
            END ASSESS2;
```

It is obvious that use of the unconditional GO TO statement in ASSESS2 above creates an infinite loop and does not make provision for ending the loop. A conditional loop can be accomplished by use of the IF statement.

The IF Statement

The IF statement has the general form

IF conditional expression THEN statement 1;
Statement 2;

Since the IF statement is designed to test a condition of truth, use of the IF statement in conjunction with the GO TO statement will result in a *conditional* loop. If the condition specified in the expression is true, the computer will execute statement 1; otherwise the computer will ignore statement 1 and execute statement 2 (immediately following the IF statement).

By placing the word ELSE in front of the statement 2, the programmer can make that statement act as an alternative to the statement introduced by THEN.

IF conditional expression THEN statement 1;
ELSE statement 2;
Statement 3;

In this case, if the conditional expression is true, statement 1 is executed followed by the statement 3 because the compiler recognizes the word ELSE and skips over statement 2. If the expression is false, the computer will proceed in the normal way to execute statement 2, followed by statement 3.

The use of conditional expressions in IF statements offers a convenient method for the comparison of character strings in search procedures. This application of IF statements is illustrated in Section 4.6.

IF statements can be nested as in the following example.

IF X = 0 THEN IF Y = 1 THEN W = Z;
ELSE W = R;
ELSE GO TO L;

In Section 7.3, an illustration of nested IF statements is shown in the Sample Program 14: COUNT.

Sample Program 3:   ASSESS3

If we know in advance how many library fines are to be processed, then a particular storage location can be reserved to be used as a counter. Let us assume that we have 50 fine records to process and a loop is to be set up on that basis.

Below are the flowchart and program to calculate the fines of 50 overdue book borrowers.

ASSESS3:

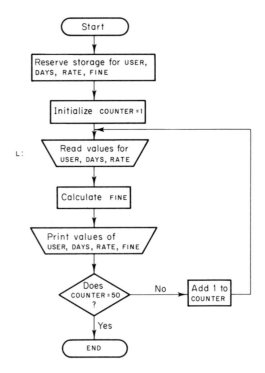

ASSESS3:   PROCEDURE OPTIONS (MAIN);
           DECLARE USER, DAYS, RATE, FINE;
           COUNTER = 1;
    L: GET LIST (USER, DAYS, RATE);
           FINE = DAYS * RATE;
           PUT LIST (USER, DAYS, RATE, FINE);
           IF COUNTER = 50 THEN GO TO STOP;
           COUNTER = COUNTER + 1;
           GO TO L:
    STOP: END ASSESS3;

Observe that COUNTER does not have to be declared explicitly because of its appearance on the left-hand side of an assignment statement.

Sample Program 4:   ASSESS4

Since we seldom know in advance how many library fines will have to be calculated, it is desirable to modify the program in such a way that the number of fines to be computed can vary each time the program is used. This may be done by designating a storage location into which will be read the number of fines to be computed during a given execution of the program. We shall call the location in which is stored the number of fines to be calculated HOWMANY. The flowchart and program follow.

ASSESS4:

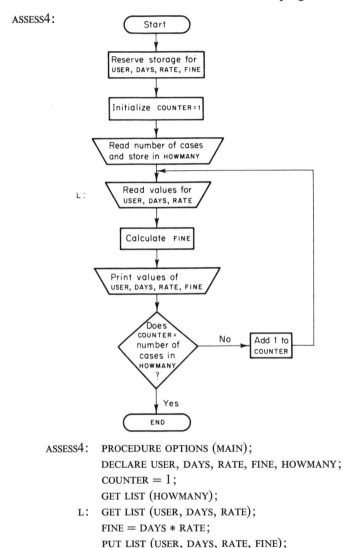

ASSESS4:   PROCEDURE OPTIONS (MAIN);
            DECLARE USER, DAYS, RATE, FINE, HOWMANY;
            COUNTER = 1;
            GET LIST (HOWMANY);
       L: GET LIST (USER, DAYS, RATE);
            FINE = DAYS * RATE;
            PUT LIST (USER, DAYS, RATE, FINE);
            IF COUNTER = HOWMANY THEN GO TO STOP;
            COUNTER = COUNTER + 1;
            GO TO L;
   STOP: END ASSESS4;

Sample Program 5:   ASSESS5

Another way of handling the problem of calculating a varying number of fines is to terminate the loop by setting up a condition that can never be true.

Often it may not be known in advance how many fines are to be calculated during a given execution of the program. Let us assume that the value of the user's identity number can never be zero. Thus it is possible to use a dummy record with zeros for the user's identification to indicate the end of the data for a particular run.

Using this method in our illustration, we obtain the following program.

```
ASSESS5:   PROCEDURE OPTIONS (MAIN);
           DECLARE USER, DAYS, RATE, FINE;
      L:   GET LIST (USER, DAYS, RATE);
           IF USER = 0 THEN GO TO STOP;
           FINE = DAYS * RATE;
           PUT LIST (USER, DAYS, RATE, FINE);
           GO TO L;
   STOP:   END ASSESS5;
```

While the previous examples were intended to illustrate methods of looping, it should be pointed out that in most actual library situations the number of days that the book is overdue is not included as explicit data in each record but is generated from other input data during processing.

Sample Program 6:   ASSESS6

In its simplest form, a circulation record includes book information, borrower information, and date due. However, two additional pieces of information (which remain constant for a particular run) are needed for the processing of overdue fines: (1) current date (stored in DATE) and (2) daily overdue rate (stored in RATE).

The following sample program ASSESS6 assumes that book information is recorded in the form of an accession number and that the borrower information is the borrower's identification number. It assumes that no overdues are carried over from one month to the next, and it identifies the users for which overdue fines are to be calculated by checking whether DATE (the current date) is larger than DUEDATE (the date the book is due to be returned). If larger, the program proceeds to calculate and print the user's name and fine; otherwise it obtains the next set of user data.

```
ASSESS6:   PROCEDURE OPTIONS (MAIN);
           DECLARE (BOOK, USER, DUEDATE, RATE, DATE, FINE) FIXED;
           GET LIST (RATE, DATE);
      L:   GET LIST (BOOK, USER, DUEDATE);
           IF USER = 0 THEN GO TO STOP;
           /* CHECK FOR END OF INPUT DATA */
              IF DATE < = DUEDATE THEN GO TO L;
           /* IF DUEDATE IS LARGER THAN CURRENT DATE,
              BYPASS THIS USER AND READ NEXT ONE */
           FINE = (DATE − DUEDATE) * RATE;
           PUT SKIP LIST (BOOK, USER, FINE);
           GO TO L;
   STOP:   END ASSESS6;
```

The program illustrates the use of *comments* to clarify the action that occurs at a given point for someone unfamiliar with the logic of the program. Comments can be inserted in a PL/I program anywhere that a blank can be inserted. As noted in Section 2.4, they consist of a beginning symbol /*, any string of characters recognized by the computer hardware (including those that are not in the PL/I character set), and an ending symbol */.

The input data for the program would be as follows.

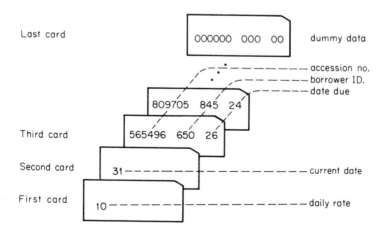

The output of this program is a list of accession numbers with the values of the individuals having the corresponding books on loan and their respective fines in cents, as follows.

565496	650	50
809705	845	70
⋮	⋮	⋮
accession number of book	borrower's ID number	fine in cents

Note that the data is not in floating point representation because in the DECLARE statement the attribute FIXED is specified for all data.

EXERCISES

1. In Section 3.3 the discussion of priority of operators ends with two examples of compound logical expressions containing the variables A, B, C, D, and F. Identify the arithmetic variables in each of the two expressions.

2. In the discussion of IF statements in Section 3.5, the following example of nesting is provided.

$$\text{IF } X = 0 \text{ THEN IF } Y = 1 \text{ THEN } W = Z;$$
$$\text{ELSE } W = R;$$
$$\text{ELSE GO TO L};$$

Determine the statement to be executed next when (1) $X = 0$ is false and $Y = 1$ is true, (2) $X = 0$ is true and $Y = 1$ is false, (3) both $X = 0$ and $Y = 1$ are true, and (4) both are false.

3. A drawback of Sample Program 6: ASSESS6 is that the program does not keep a tally of the total number of fines that are calculated during a given execution of the program, nor is a record kept of the overall sum of the fines calculated for a particular run. Draw a flowchart and rewrite the program to include this additional information in the printout.

CHAPTER **4**

Character Data

4.1 Representation of Character Strings

PL/I provides facilities for handling two types of nonnumeric data: string data and program control or label data. String data is a sequence of arbitrary characters, or binary zeros and ones, treated as a single item of data and, accordingly, is divided into character-string data and bit-string data. Both kinds of string data can be processed in a variety of ways. We shall discuss character strings first, devoting this chapter and the next to their description and function, returning to bit-string manipulation in Chapter 11. Facilities for handling label data in PL/I will be described in Chapter 6.

A character string may contain any alphabetic, numeric, or special characters in any combination. The PL/I processor recognizes a character string by the presence of a single quotation mark ' at the beginning and at the end of the string. When the string already includes quotation marks, it is necessary to include an extra quotation mark for every quotation mark in the string.

Examples of character strings in PL/I are

'THIS IS A STRING OF LENGTH 30.'
'RUTGERS UNIVERSITY'
'525.6'
'z567.5A25'
'SHAKESPEARE''S HAMLET'
''''DON''T KNOW'''' SHE SAID.'

4.2   Declaration of Character Variables

The method of declaring names for strings of characters is the same as that used for arithmetic variables.

Character strings have two attributes: the CHARACTER (abbreviated: CHAR) attribute, which specifies a character string (or more precisely, that the value of the variable declared is a character data item); and a length attribute, which specifies the number of characters in the string.

The general form of declaring a character variable is

DECLARE name CHARACTER (n)

where "name" is the identifier naming the variable assigned by the programmer and "n" is a decimal integer specifying the number of characters that the string will contain.

4.3   The VARYING Attribute

In some applications the length of a character string will always remain fixed, but in other applications it may vary. For example, when processing a book list, the character strings representing authors and titles may be of varying length. To provide for this, a character-string variable may be assigned the VARYING (abbreviated: VAR) attribute in a DECLARE statement. In this case the length specification (n) indicates the *maximum* length of the string rather than a fixed length.

The statement

DECLARE (BOOK, AUTHOR) CHARACTER (20) VARYING;

specifies that the identifiers BOOK and AUTHOR take as values character strings of varying length, each containing a maximum of 20 characters.

4.4   The INITIAL Attribute

All three kinds of PL/I data, arithmetic, string, and label, can be set to initial values by means of the INITIAL (abbreviated: INIT) attribute in a DECLARE statement. The general form of a DECLARE statement with the INITIAL attribute is

DECLARE name attribute(s) INITIAL (value);

where "attribute(s)" may be any appropriate attribute or (valid combination of attributes for arithmetic data), and "value" is a constant of the appropriate data type.

EXAMPLES

DECLARE AUTHOR CHARACTER (20) INITIAL ('WILLIAM WHITE');
DCL SBN CHAR (5) VAR INIT ('001'), LOC CHAR (5) INIT ((5)'*');

Although the declared length of AUTHOR is 20 characters, the actual length of the string assigned by the INITIAL attribute is only 13 characters, requiring the addition of 7 blanks on the right when the string is stored at AUTHOR. On the other hand, because of the VARYING attribute, the character variable SBN is assigned the initial value '001' without the addition of blanks, although the maximum length of SBN is declared to be 5 characters. Finally, the character variable LOC is assigned the value '*****' when storage is allocated to the variables.

The notation

$$(5)'*'$$

used in the example above indicates that the characters in quotation marks following the enclosed integer constant are to be repeated the number of times specified by the integer. The latter is sometimes called a *replication factor*. The following character constants are identical in value

'ABABABAB'
(2)'ABAB'
(4)'AB'

4.5   Character Data as Output

The GET LIST and the PUT LIST statements can be used for character data in the same way as for arithmetic data.

An additional optional capability for character output is that character strings can be generated as part of the PUT LIST statement itself.

For example,

PUT LIST ('AMOUNT OF FINE IS', N);

would cause AMOUNT OF FINE to be printed followed by the value of N.

Sample Program 7: ASSESS7

As an illustration of character data as output, the book fine calculation program, ASSESS1, could be modified as follows.

```
ASSESS7:  PROCEDURE OPTIONS (MAIN);
          DECLARE USER CHARACTER (25) VARYING, DAYS FIXED (2),
               RATE FIXED (2), FINE FIXED (3);
          GET LIST (USER, DAYS, RATE);
          FINE = DAYS * RATE;
          PUT SKIP LIST (USER, 'OWES THE LIBRARY', FINE,
               'CENTS FOR OVERDUE MATERIALS.');
          END ASSESS7;
```

4.6   Character Strings in the IF Statement

A common type of test in a search procedure involving character strings is to determine whether two strings match one another. The use of relational and logical operators (Section 2.3) acting upon character variables and constants to form conditional expressions offers a convenient method of comparison. The chief use of such conditional expressions is in IF clauses, and the type of test most often used with character strings is that of comparison for equality or inequality, although the other seven relational operators may also be used with character strings. In the latter case, because the comparisons are made on the internal representation of data in the computer, the result is machine dependent and may vary from one computer to another.

The character strings compared in an IF statement may be represented as constants, variables, or combinations of these concatenated together (see Section 5.1). If the strings are unequal in length, the shorter string is supplied with blanks on the right before the comparison is made. This may give rise to a condition of equality holding between two strings of different lengths.

Sample Program 8: CATALOG

As an illustration of the use of character strings in an IF statement, suppose we are searching in an author file for all of the books by a particular author. Let us assume that each record in the file contains the following information

> author's initials and last name
> title of book
> call number

We wish to search the file for books by A. D. Jones, and for each such book found in the file we want as printed output the title and the call number for this book.

```
CATALOG:  PROCEDURE OPTIONS (MAIN);
          DECLARE (NAME CHARACTER (20), TITLE
                 CHARACTER (30), CALLNO CHARACTER (10),
                 AUTHOR CHARACTER (20)) VARYING;
          GET LIST (AUTHOR);
          PUT LIST (AUTHOR);
SEARCH:   GET LIST (NAME, TITLE, CALLNO);
          IF NAME = '000' THEN GO TO STOP;
          IF NAME = AUTHOR THEN GO TO PRINT;
          GO TO SEARCH;
PRINT:    PUT SKIP LIST (TITLE, CALLNO);
          GO TO SEARCH;
STOP:     END CATALOG;
```

Observe that in the sample input data for the program above, in order to end the loop, the author file concludes with a dummy data card in which the data field for the name of an author appears as '000'.

Sample input data for the program is shown below.

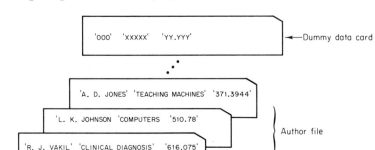

Internal Representation of PL/I Characters

To facilitate searching it is often desirable that a list of titles, a list of names, or a list of numbers be printed in alphabetical or numerical order. To create such a listing, PL/I allows the use of a sort method which is based on the direct comparison of two character strings to determine which of the two comes alphabetically or numerically first. The comparison of the two character strings is actually a comparison of the binary coded internal representations of the characters in those strings. These internal representations, which could have been arbitrarily selected, were actually chosen in such a way that the values of the internal representations of the letters of the alphabet are in ascending numerical order corresponding to alphabetical order. In other words, the value of the code for the letter A is smaller than the value of the letters B–Z, and the value of the code for the letter B is larger than the value for A but smaller than the value of the letters C–Z, and so on. A blank, comma, period, and all special characters have internal representations whose values are smaller than the value for any letter. Similarly, the digits 0–9 are assigned internal representation in ascending order. When two character strings of different length are compared, before the comparison is made the shorter of the character strings is padded with blanks on the right until it is of the same length as the longer string. For example, let us consider two identifiers having the values

$$\text{WORD1} = \text{`SMITH'}$$
$$\text{WORD2} = \text{`JOHNSON'}$$

When the IF statement

IF WORD1 < WORD2 THEN GO TO L1;

is used, the actual comparison is between the character strings 'SMITHƀƀ' and 'JOHNSON' because the shorter string is padded on the right. Table 4.1 shows the internal representation of the PL/I 60-character

TABLE 4.1

Internal Representation of Character Set

Character	ASCII representation	EBCDIC representation	Character	ASCII representation	EBCDIC representation
blank	01000000	01000000	T	10110100	11100011
0	01010000	11110000	U	10110101	11100100
1	01010001	11110001	V	10110110	11100101
2	01010010	11110010	W	10110111	11100110
3	01010011	11110011	X	10111000	11100111
4	01010100	11110100	Y	10111001	11101000
5	01010101	11110101	Z	10111010	11101001
6	01010110	11110110	@	10100000	01111100
7	01010111	11110111	–		01101101
8	01011000	11111000	#	01000011	01111011
9	01011001	11111001	.	01001110	01001011
A	10100001	11000001	,	01001101	01101011
B	10100010	11000010	:	01011010	01111010
C	10100011	11000011	;	01011011	01011110
D	10100100	11000100	+	01001011	01001110
E	10100101	11000101	–	01001100	01100000
F	10100110	11000110	*	01001010	01011100
G	10100111	11000111	/	01001111	01100001
H	10101000	11001000	<	01011100	11010000
I	10101001	11001001	=	01011101	01111110
J	10101010	11010001	>	01011110	11000000
K	10101011	11010010	&	01000110	01010000
L	10101100	11010011	|		01001111
M	10101101	11010100	¬		01011111
N	10101110	11010101	(	01001000	01001101
O	10101111	11010110	)	01001001	01011101
P	10110000	11010111	'	01000111	01111101
Q	10110001	11011000	%	01000101	01101100
R	10110010	11011001	$	01000100	01011011
S	10110011	11100010	?	01011111	01001010

set based on the Extended Binary-Coded-Decimal Interchange Code (EBCDIC) and the American Standard Code for Information Interchange (ASCII).

EXERCISES

1.   Modify the SAMPLE PROGRAM 7: ASSESS7 to include a loop so that the printout contains the names of more than one user who are assessed book fines.

2.   Modify the SAMPLE PROGRAM 8: CATALOG to include a loop so that the file may be searched for books by more than one author. Discuss how to avoid requiring multiple copies of the file as part of the input stream for the modified program.

CHAPTER **5**

Character Manipulation

In library data processing applications there is frequently a need to split, scan, measure, compare, and join character strings. Text editing requires many search and split operations, alphabetization is essential in making an index, and complex pattern matching problems arise in searching. The following six operations are useful in this connection.

5.1 Concatenation

The concatenation operator ‖ is useful in chaining together two or more strings. It behaves as follows.

> DECLARE (A, B, C, D) CHAR (80) VARYING;
> A = 'LIBRARY';
> B = 'ADMINISTRATION';
> C = ' ';
> D = A ‖ C ‖ B;

51

After this code is executed, D has the value 'LIBRARY ADMINISTRATION'. On the other hand, if we were interested in obtaining as a value of D the character string 'LIBRARY AND ADMINISTRATION', we would have written

$$D = A \| \text{' AND '} \| B;$$

Note that for the first value of D the variable C, which is a blank, was inserted between A and B. In the second assignment for D the conjunction AND is imbedded between two blanks.

5.2 The Substring Function

This built-in function of PL/I allows one to identify, isolate, and compare portions of strings. This function takes two, or optionally three, arguments as follows.

$$\text{SUBSTR (arg 1, arg 2, arg 3)}$$

where "arg 1" is the name of a character string, and "arg 2," "arg 3" can be any legitimate arithmetic expressions.

Operating on "arg 1," the given character string, SUBSTR reproduces that portion of the string named in "arg 1," starting with the position indicated by the integer specified in "arg 2" and continuing for the number of characters indicated by the integer obtained from "arg 3." Thus if A and B are declared as character variables, the statement

$$B = \text{SUBSTR } (A, 3, 4);$$

will pull out four consecutive characters from string A starting at the third position in A and assign this substring constant as the value of B.

Optionally, "arg 3" may be omitted, in which case as many consecutive characters in string A, starting at the third position, as remain in A will be assigned to B.

Observe that the SUBSTR function accepts as its first argument not only names of character variables, or identifiers, but also *values* of character variables, or character constants. For example, the statement

$$X = \text{SUBSTR ('IMMODERATION', 3, 4);}$$

will assign the string 'MODE' as the value of X (assuming X has been declared to be a character variable).

5.3   The INDEX Function

The INDEX function is useful when one wishes to search a string for a known substring. Its general form is

INDEX (arg 1, arg 2)

where "arg 1" is the name or value of the character variable to be examined, and "arg 2" is the name or value of the desired substring. In the vocabulary of information retrieval, "arg 2" is the *search argument*. The INDEX function will return a value of 0 if the search string "arg 2" does not exist as a substring of the given string "arg 1"; otherwise, its value is the position of the first character of the substring in the given string. If the substring appears more than once, only the leftmost occurrence of it in the given string is noted, since the search is from left to right.

EXAMPLES TO ILLUSTRATE THE INDEX FUNCTION

In matching of query terms against natural language text frequently a complete match is not required but only a matching of roots. For example, one may wish to consider the terms *information, informed, inform, informative, informational,* and so on as equivalents of *inform*.

Let us assume that the character string which is examined is 'INFORMATIVE'. Then we could use the INDEX function as follows.

L = INDEX ('INFORMATIVE', 'INFORM');

where a nonzero value of L would indicate a match. Since 'INFORM' is a substring of 'INFORMATIVE' beginning in position 1, the INDEX function will return a value of 1 and assign it to L, so that L = 1 after the execution of the statement.

If A is a character variable whose current value is the string constant 'INFORMATIVE' and B a character variable whose current value is 'INFORM', then the statement

L = INDEX (A, B);

will assign a value of 1 to L as in the previous example.

5.4   The LENGTH Function

The LENGTH function has the general form

LENGTH (arg 1)

where "arg 1" is a character string constant or the name of a character variable. LENGTH will return an integer value specifying the length of the character string currently specified in "arg 1". The LENGTH function is especially useful in work with character variables that have been assigned the VARYING attribute.

For example, if B is a character variable whose current value is the character string 'INFORMATION', then the assignment statement

$$x = 12 + \text{LENGTH (B)};$$

would assign the value 23 to x.

5.5   The TRANSLATE Function

The TRANSLATE function derives its name from the fact that it translates a given character string (arg 1) into another character string (the value returned by the function) by causing specified characters (arg 3) in the given string to be replaced by other specified characters (arg 2). The general form of the function is

TRANSLATE (arg 1, arg 2, arg 3)

where "arg 1" is the name of the character string to be translated, "arg 3" is a string that specifies the characters in arg 1 to be replaced, and "arg 2" represents the string of characters to replace those specified in arg 3. Arg 3 is called the *position* string and arg 2 the *replacement* string; together, they form a translation table in which each character in arg 3 that also appears in arg 1 is replaced in arg 1 by the corresponding character of arg 2. The correspondence is by position of the characters; that is, the first character in arg 3 is to be replaced by the first character in arg 2, the second in arg 3 by the second in arg 2, and so forth. Where arg 2 is shorter in length than arg 3, blanks are added on the right to extend its length. The value returned by the TRANSLATE function is a string identical in length and content to that of arg 1 except for the replacements carried out in accordance with the characters specified in arg 2 and arg 3. As usual, arg 1, arg 2, and arg 3 take as values either actual character strings or names of character variables. It should be noted that, like the other built-in string handling functions of PL/I, this one works equally well upon character strings and bit strings (discussion of bit strings is found in Section 11.1).

EXAMPLE

DCL AND CHAR (4) INIT('FFFT');
AND = TRANSLATE (AND, '10', 'TF');

This use of TRANSLATE causes any 'T' in AND to be replaced by '1' and any
'F' to be replaced by '0'. After the code is executed, the value of AND is
'0001'.

As we shall see in Chapter 9, it is convenient to define Boolean functions by means of *truth tables* in which the logical values "truth" and
"falsity" may be represented by the letter symbols 'T' and 'F' respectively,
or alternatively, by the binary digits '1' and '0', as shown:

X	Y	Z	X	Y	Z
F	F	T	0	0	1
F	T	F	0	1	0
T	F	F	1	0	0
T	T	T	1	1	1

The TRANSLATE function offers a convenient method of conversion between
such tables.

5.6 The VERIFY Function

The VERIFY function compares a given string against a second string,
called the *verification string*, to determine whether all of the characters of
the given string are among those of the verification string. The general form
of the function is

VERIFY (arg 1, arg 2)

where "arg 1" is the given string to be verified and "arg 2" is the verification string. The value returned by the function is 0 if every character in
arg 1 is contained in arg 2; otherwise, the value returned by the function
is the position of the leftmost occurrence of the first character in arg 1 not
contained in the verification string. Thus, if s1 is a string variable having
the value 'A121z' and s2 is the string of alphabetic characters A–Z, then

VERIFY (s1, s2)

returns the value 2, since the second position of s1 represents the leftmost occurrence of the first nonalphabetic character in s1. If s1 has the value 'BC' and s2 is the verification string 'ACBD', the VERIFY function returns the value 0, since every character in s1 is present in s2.

EXAMPLE

In a library circulation control system it is useful to provide a mechanism whereby a breakdown by classification of titles of the numbers of books in circulation can be obtained from other circulation data. For example, the system should provide knowledge about the number of books in circulation that deal with particular subject matters, say, statistics, astronomy, or biology. Such information not only serves to identify levels of usage among the different classes of the library's holdings, but it may also provide rudimentary guidelines for deciding new directions of growth in building and maintaining the collection based on past usage.

A simple illustration of how such information may be provided involves use of the VERIFY function. Suppose we wish to know the number of books currently in circulation that pertain to physics, mathematics, or chemistry. Let us assume that the books in the collection are cataloged in accordance with the Library of Congress classification system. The LC main subject headings for the above three science subclasses are given by the letter codes 'QC', 'QA', and 'QD', respectively. Thus, the LC call number of any book on physics, say,

QC

721

.F46

will always contain the combination 'QC' as the first two letters of the call number. If we assume that the input stream consists of the call numbers of all books currently in circulation:

... 'HF/5415.2/.G75' 'DF/222/.M5' 'QC/35/.M647L' 'B/3501/.H45' 'PR/2944/.G75/1970' 'JA/76/.A7513/1969' 'GB/661/.M514H' ...

then the following PL/I code provides us with a numerical count of the books in circulation whose main subject matter is physics, mathematics, or chemistry:

```
COUNTER = 0;
GET LIST (CALLNO);
IF VERIFY (SUBSTR (CALLNO, 1, 2), 'QACD') = 0
    THEN COUNTER = COUNTER + 1;
GET LIST (CALLNO);
```

It should be observed that the same logic can be written without use of the VERIFY function, employing instead OR logic in the IF statement. However, as can be seen, the coding is more cumbersome:

```
COUNTER = 0;
GET LIST (CALLNO);
IF ((SUBSTR (CALLNO, 1, 2) = 'QC') | (SUBSTR
    (CALLNO, 1, 2) = 'QA') | (SUBSTR
    (CALLNO, 1, 2) = 'QD'))
    THEN COUNTER = COUNTER + 1;
GET LIST (CALLNO);
```

Additional applications of the VERIFY function are possible in providing more detailed information about usage levels among LC classes of books in a library circulation system.

5.7 Use of SUBSTR as a Pseudo-Variable

As a special feature of PL/I, the SUBSTR function may be used on the left side of the equal sign in an assignment statement as if it were a variable name. The general form for such an assignment is

SUBSTR (arg 1, arg 2, arg 3) = expression;

When used in this context, SUBSTR is called a *pseudo-variable* because it specifies the destination in an assignment operation. Observe, however, that the function SUBSTR itself is not the destination; rather, it specifies a substring of the destination string.

As an example, suppose we have a 13-character variable D which currently contains 'CONCENTRATION'. The assignment statement

SUBSTR (D, 4, 5) = 'STERN';

would change the value of D to 'CONSTERNATION'.

An illustration of the use of SUBSTR as a pseudo-variable will be found in SAMPLE PROGRAM 13: REVERSE. In this program, which reverses the order of the letters appearing in a character string, SUBSTR appears as a pseudo-variable on the left side of the assignment statement immediately preceding the END statement.

It should be further noted that PL/I also provides the programmer with the flexibility to use pseudo-variables as members of a data list in a GET statement, so that part of an input character string can be read and stored. For example, consider the following code.

DECLARE DATE CHAR (6) INIT ((6)'0');
GET LIST (SUBSTR (DATE, 3, 2));

Suppose that the data in the input stream is the character string

'061371'

After the code is executed, DATE will have the value '001300'.

5.8 Programming Illustrations of Character-String Functions

We conclude the chapter with a brief account of two programming examples. The sample programs are intended to illustrate, at a rudimentary level, several major applications of the built-in functions in PL/I that facilitate string manipulation.

Sample Program 9: INVERT

The program below, called INVERT, accepts as input a file of names of individuals in which each surname appears first, separated by a comma, and followed by the first name and/or initials. The program inverts the order of each individual's full name so that the first name and/or initials appear first, followed by his surname last. The program assumes that the full names of individuals are separated by semicolons in both the input and output file.

```
INVERT:  PROC OPTIONS (MAIN);
         DECLARE (SURNAMEFIRST, SURNAMELAST, FIRST, LAST) CHAR (80)
             VARYING, COMMA CHAR (1) INITIAL (',');
  NEXT:  GET LIST (SURNAMEFIRST);
         IF SURNAMEFIRST = '000' THEN GO TO STOP;
         ADDCOM = INDEX (SURNAMEFIRST, COMMA);
         FIRST = SUBSTR (SURNAMEFIRST, ADDCOM + LENGTH (COMMA),
             INDEX (SURNAMEFIRST, ';') − (ADDCOM + LENGTH (COMMA)));
         LAST = SUBSTR (SURNAMEFIRST, 1, ADDCOM − 1);
         SURNAMELAST = FIRST || ' ' || LAST || ';';
         PUT SKIP LIST (SURNAMELAST);
         GO TO NEXT;
  STOP:  END INVERT;
```

An example of the input and output stream for INVERT is shown below.

(*INPUT*):   ...; 'JONES, JESSE H.;' 'RAFT IV, RIFT T.;' TIM, TINY;'
        'WILCOX JR., HARRY S.;' 'YERT, J.C.;' ...

(*OUTPUT*):   ...; JESSE H. JONES; RIFT T. RAFT IV; TINY TIM; HARRY S.
        WILCOX JR.; J.C. YERT; ...

Sample Program 10: PARSE

The program below, called PARSE, reads a title, prints out the title in full, and then prints each word in the title on separate lines. To separate each word out of the title, the program looks for blanks and stores in location w the character string between two blanks (one word). The program assumes that a semicolon is used to mark the end of the title.

```
PARSE:    PROC OPTIONS (MAIN);
          DECLARE (TITLE CHARACTER (80), W CHARACTER (10))
             VARYING;
          GET LIST (TITLE);
          PUT LIST (TITLE);
          M = −1;
          L = 1;
GETWORD:  M = M + L + 1;
          L = INDEX (SUBSTR (TITLE, M), ' ') − 1;
          /*FIND THE POSITION OF A BLANK*/
          IF L < = 0 THEN GO TO FINISH;
          /*TEST FOR LAST WORD IN TITLE*/
          W = SUBSTR (TITLE, M, L);
          /*STORE WORD IN W*/
          PUT SKIP LIST (W);
          GO TO GETWORD;
FINISH:   W = SUBSTR (TITLE, M);
          PUT SKIP LIST (W);
          END PARSE;
```

If the input data for Sample Program 10 were 'AUTOMATION AND LIBRARIES;' then the output of the program would be as follows.

        AUTOMATION AND LIBRARIES;
        AUTOMATION
        AND
        LIBRARIES;

EXERCISES

1. Write a PL/I program which accepts as input the truth table shown on the left and produces as output the truth table shown on the right:

X Y Z	X Y Z
0 0 1	F F T
0 1 1	F T T
1 0 0	T F F
1 1 1	T T T

2. *Sample Program 10*: PARSE fails to suppress as output the semicolon that is used to mark the end of a title. Write the code to suppress the semi-colon in the last line of output.

3. The PARSE program accepts as input data only *one* title. Rewrite the program to accept several titles as input data.

4. Rewrite the program to test whether a word in the title is an article, preposition, or conjunction (for example, THE, AN, OF, BY, AND, etc.). If so, ignore these words so that they do not appear in the word-by-word printout of the title on separate lines.

5. As a variation of the program in the preceding exercise, the input data for each title should include a document identification number. The output of the program should consist of a word-by-word printout of the title (excluding articles, prepositions and conjunctions) in which the full title and document number follow each word of the title that is printed, as shown below.

First word	Full title	Document number
Second word	Full title	Document number
Third word	Full title	Document number
⋮	⋮	⋮

It should be noted that the printout above resembles a KWOC (Key-Word-Out-of-Context) index except that the key words in the output will be in the order in which they appear in the title. In a true KWOC index, the terms appear in alphabetic order.

CHAPTER 6

Statement Label Data

6.1 Statement Label Constants

It is convenient to distinguish between *statement label constants* and *statement label variables*. A *statement label constant* is a name or identifier written as a prefix to a statement, thus allowing control to be transferred during program execution to that statement through reference to its label. A colon separates the statement from its label, and reference is made to the label by means of a statement such as the GO TO statement.

6.2 Statement Label Variables

A *statement label variable* is a special type of program control variable which assumes statement label constants as its values. Since storage must be allocated for such variables, they must always be explicitly declared in a declaration statement whose general form is

DECLARE name LABEL;

where the "name" assigned to a statement label variable may be any legitimate PL/I identifier. The LABEL attribute in the declaration specifies that the named variable(s) takes on statement label constants as values. It is not necessary to specify the length of the constants.

The content of a storage location represented by a statement label variable is usually determined by means of an assignment statement having the following form:

name = statement label constant;

The most obvious use of a statement label variable is to allow the possibility for a GO TO statement to have a variable destination. Instead of directing control to a particular statement having a specific label, the program can direct control to the statement whose label is currently the value of the statement label variable.

The following four PL/I conventions should be observed in connection with the use of statement label variables.

1.   Unlike the assignment of ordinary character constants in an assignment statement, the statement label constant is not required to be surrounded by single quotation marks.

2.   While statement label variables can be declared and appear in assignment statements, they cannot appear as items of GET and PUT statements. They cannot be read in or printed out. Nor will PL/I allow the placement of a label constant in a location previously occupied by a character string. For example, the assignment statement SYMBOL = ADDRESS; in the sequence of statements below represents an *invalid* PL/I statement.

```
       DECLARE ADDRESS LABEL, SYMBOL CHARACTER (20) VARYING;
STEP:  K = 10;
       ADDRESS = STEP;
       SYMBOL = ADDRESS;
       PUT LIST (SYMBOL);
```

3.   Once they are declared by use of the LABEL attribute in a declaration statement, statement label variables need not appear anywhere else in the program. However, if one occurs in the program as part of an assignment

statement, the statement label constant associated with that variable as a result of the assignment statement *must appear* as an actual label of a statement in the program.

4. It is possible to restrict the use of statement label variables to a particular set of label names by writing a declaration as follows.

DECLARE name LABEL (label 1, label 2, etc.);

where "label 1," "label 2," etc. represent a set of actual statement label constants used in the program. Each constant so listed *must appear* as an actual label of a statement in the program.

Sample Program 11: OVERDUE

The use of the statement label variable can be illustrated by the following program. Suppose a library wants a list of all borrowers who have failed to return books by a certain due date. The data for each book loan consist of

due date, name and address of borrower, and
title and author of book on loan

Moreover, upon return of the book the data pertaining to the loan of the book are discarded.

The program, called OVERDUE, processes each book loan. If the due date of the loan is earlier than the current date, the name and address of the borrower, as well as title and author of book, are printed. If not, the information is ignored, and the data of the next book loan are processed in a similar manner. The program terminates upon reading a dummy DUE DATE code of 000000.

```
OVERDUE:    PROCEDURE OPTIONS (MAIN);
            DECLARE (CURRENT_DATE, DUE_DATE) FIXED (6),
                (NAME, ADDRESS, TITLE, AUTHOR) CHARACTER
                (20) VARYING, ACTION LABEL;
            GET LIST (CURRENT_DATE);
            PUT LIST (CURRENT_DATE);
NEXT_LOAN:  GET LIST (DUE_DATE);
            IF DUE_DATE = 0 THEN GO TO FINISH:
            IF DUE_DATE > = CURRENT_DATE
                THEN ACTION = NEXT_LOAN;
            ELSE ACTION = PROCESS;
            GET LIST (NAME, ADDRESS, TITLE, AUTHOR);
            GO TO ACTION;
```

PROCESS: PUT SKIP LIST (NAME, ADDRESS, TITLE, AUTHOR);
                    GO TO NEXT_LOAN;
FINISH: END OVERDUE;

EXERCISES

1.   What are the values of L and X after the following code is executed?

```
            DCL L LABEL INIT (L3);
    L1:  X = 25;
            GO TO L;
    L2:  X = 30;
            GO TO L;
    L3;  X = 35;
            L = L4;
            GO TO L2;
    L4:  X = 40;
```

2.   Assume that the format of the data for CURRENT_DATE and DUE_DATE in SAMPLE PROGRAM 11: OVERDUE is

YYMMDD

where "YY" represents the last two digits of the year, "MM" the month, and "DD" the day of the month. Thus, if the current date is July 15, 1971, the value of CURRENT_DATE would appear as 710715. A value of 691128 would indicate a current date of November 28, 1969.

Determine the output of SAMPLE PROGRAM 11: OVERDUE if the input stream is

701231, 710115, 'J. DOE', 'RPO 4432', 'PHYSICS
TODAY', 'R. PLANO', 701215, 'F. SMITH', 'RPO 3729',
'MODERN MATH', 'C. SIMS', 000000;

3.   Write a PL/I program that (1) accepts as input data the names of English language journals; (2) suppresses all prepositions, articles, and conjunctions appearing in the names; and (3) prints out in inverted order abbreviated names of the journals in which subject words occur first, separated by commas from descriptive words that refer to the kind of journal publication.

Examples of names of journals that are to be accepted by the program as input, and the abbreviated names that the program is to produce as output, are

Input	Output
JOURNAL OF PHYSICAL REVIEW;	PHYSICAL REVIEW, JOURNAL;
TRANSACTIONS OF THE AMERICAN MATHEMATICAL SOCIETY;	AMERICAN MATHEMATICAL SOCIETY, TRANSACTIONS;
COMMUNICATIONS OF THE ASSOCIATION FOR COMPUTING MACHINERY;	ASSOCIATION COMPUTING MACHINERY, COMMUNICATIONS;
LIBRARY JOURNAL;	LIBRARY JOURNAL;
NEW JERSEY LIBRARIES;	NEW JERSEY LIBRARIES;

CHAPTER 7

The DO Statement

7.1 The DO Group

An important program control statement in PL/I is the DO statement. It is a powerful and flexible statement that provides the programmer with several options for causing a sequence of instructions to act as a single unit for possible repetitive processing.

In PL/I the DO statement may be used in either of two basic ways:

1. The DO statement may be used to signal the beginning of a sequence of commands to be executed as a single unit. When used in this manner, the sequence of statements is called a DO *group* and behaves much like a single statement.

2. The DO statement may also be used to define and specify control for a series of statements that are to be executed one or more times in repetitive

fashion before control moves on to the next statement following the group of statements. When the DO statement is used in this manner, the sequence of statements is called a DO *loop*.

In both the DO group and the DO loop, PL/I requires the sequence of statements to be concluded by an END statement. Insofar as the organization of the statements is concerned, the DO and END statements serve as parentheses to bracket the set of statements, thus defining its limits to the processor.

The DO group is often used as a THEN clause in an IF statement. When so used, all of the statements of the DO group are executed as a single statement before a jump is made, or all of the statements are ignored and the statement immediately following the END statement is executed. When a DO group is used as an ELSE clause, all of the statements of the group are ignored whenever the THEN clause is executed.

SAMPLE PROGRAM 13: SEARCH and SAMPLE PROGRAM 14: COUNT illustrate the use of DO groups as THEN clauses.

7.2   The DO Loop

In addition to causing a sequence of statements to be executed as a single statement, as in a DO group, it is often desirable to use the DO statement to specify that the sequence of statements is to be executed repeatedly a certain number of times. This is accomplished by the use of the DO loop.

When used in this manner the basic DO statement can be supplemented by a number of features that serve to specify the conditions under which repeated execution of the sequence of statements is to occur.

The general form of the DO statement when used to specify a DO loop is as follows.

DO index = specifications;

where "index" is an identifier supplied by the programmer which serves as the name of the storage location where the processor will keep track of the number of repetitions of the loop, and the "specifications" designate the number of times the set of statements in the loop is to be executed.

PL/I provides the programmer with several forms of the DO statement in which to write the specifications required for controlling a DO loop.

The following are some of the forms which the DO statement may take.

The TO Phrase

The statements in a DO loop can be executed any desired number of times by specifying the starting and limiting values of the index. This is accomplished by use of the TO phrase, whose appearance in the DO statement has the general form

DO index = starting value TO limit;

where "starting value" and "limit" may be a decimal integer or floating point constant or any legitimate arithmetic expression that may be evaluated as a decimal integer or floating point number. For example, the following DO statements are valid in PL/I.

DO I = 1 TO 8;
DO I = 4 TO 10;
DO X = 10.5 TO 20.5;
DO I = J TO K;

Multiple TO Phrases

The flexibility of the basic DO statement may be increased by including any number of TO phrases within the specifications. In some cases, however, it may be desirable to omit the TO phrase(s) and specify the values of the index individually. The values need not be in ascending order. The following examples illustrate these uses of the DO statement.

DO I = 2 TO 4, 6 TO 8, 10 TO 12;
DO I = 2, 3, 4, 6, 7, 8, 10, 11, 12;
DO I = 7, 2, 14, 8, 23;

In the last example above, I is assigned the values 7, 2, 14, 8, and 23 in the order specified. After the DO loop is executed with I = 23, control passes to the next statement following the loop.

The BY Phrase

The flexibility of the DO statement can be extended in yet another direction by varying the rate at which the index is changed for each traversal of the loop. In the preceding examples it was assumed that the initial value of the index is the starting value specified in the TO phrase,

and that the value of the index is increased by one each time the DO statement is executed until the index exceeds the limiting value for the first time,
at which point control is passed to the statement immediately following the
DO loop. Thus by a PL/I default option, when an increment is not specified
in a BY phrase, the processor simply adds one to the value of the index for
each repetition. However, any increment can be specified by the use of the
BY phrase. Its appearance in the DO statement may take either of two
general forms.

> DO index = starting value TO limit BY increment;
> DO index = starting value BY increment TO limit;

where the value of "increment" may be a decimal integer or floating point
number. For example,

> DO I = 2 TO 10 BY 2;
> DO X = 0 TO 10.4 BY 0.2;
> DO I = J TO K BY L;
> DO X = 0 TO 3.65 BY .1, 5.5 TO 7.43
> BY .03, 9.6, 11 TO 13.4 BY .6;

Negative Increments

It is possible within PL/I to specify DO loops in which the value of the
index is decreased rather than increased. When this is desired, the BY
phrase must be used and a negative number (or an expression that is
evaluated as a negative number) must be specified as the increment. In such
cases the limiting value must always be algebraically less than the starting
value. Examples of negative increments are

> DO I = 12 TO 1 BY −2;
> DO I = N TO 1 BY −1;

Remember that the BY phrase is always required when specifying a negative
increment. Thus the following PL/I statement is *invalid*.

> DO I = 12 TO 4;

SAMPLE PROGRAM 12:   REVERSE illustrates the use of the negative increment
in a DO statement.

The WHILE Clause

PL/I provides further flexibility in the execution of DO loops by allowing
external conditions to be specified which must be satisfied if execution of

the DO loop is to continue. This is done by using the WHILE clause, whose simplest form is

DO WHILE (condition);

where "condition" is any legitimate logical expression which takes the value true or false such as would appear in an IF clause.

A more general form of the WHILE clause is the following.

DO index = starting value TO limit BY increment WHILE (condition);

Illustrations of the two forms of the WHILE clause shown above are found in SAMPLE PROGRAM 13: SEARCH and SAMPLE PROGRAM 15: FREQ1.

To illustrate the flexibility available to the programmer, it should be noted that the following DO statements represent alternate but equivalent ways of specifying the values of the index I.

DO I = 1 TO 8;
DO I = 1 BY 1 TO 8;
DO I = 1, 2, 3, 4, 5, 6, 7, 8;
DO I = 1 BY 1 WHILE (I < = 8);

Inclusion of the DO Statement within Input/Output

PL/I provides a convenient way of specifying by means of the DO statement a sequence of data elements that differs from the ordinary sequence as provided by the GET or PUT statements. Examples of valid occurrences of the DO statement within an input/output statement are the following.

GET LIST ((X(J) DO J = 1 TO 10));
GET LIST ((Y(J) DO J = 3 TO 9));
GET LIST ((Y(I) DO I = 4 TO 10 BY 3));

Observe that an additional pair of parentheses is required whenever the DO statement appears in the specification of the list of elements of an input/output statement. The first statement above fetches the next 10 values from the input stream and places them in locations X(1)–X(10), respectively. The second statement fetches seven values from the input stream and stores them at Y(3)–Y(9), respectively, while the third GET statement fetches three values from the input stream and stores them at location Y(4), Y(7), and Y(10). Thus X and Y are called *array variables* in PL/I. Any particular element in the array is referenced by means of the subscript notation. Thus, the fourth element in the array X is X(4). We shall discuss array variables in more detail in Chapter 8.

7.3 Programming Illustrations of the DO Statement

Sample Program 12: REVERSE

This program reads a character string, reverses the order of the characters in the string, and prints out the reverse string of characters. The program illustrates the use of the negative increment in a DO statement as well as use of the SUBSTR function as a pseudo-variable.

```
REVERSE:  PROCEDURE OPTIONS (MAIN);
          DECLARE (STRING1, STRING2) CHARACTER (80) VARYING;
          GET LIST (STRING1);
          PUT LIST (STRING1);
          STRING2 = (80) ' ';
    L1:   DO I = LENGTH (STRING1) TO 1 BY -1;
          J = LENGTH (STRING1) + 1 - I;
          SUBSTR (STRING2, J, 1) = SUBSTR (STRING1, I, 1);
          END L1;
          PUT SKIP LIST (STRING2);
          END REVERSE;
```

If the value of STRING1 is a series of digits in ascendant order, such as

'0 1 2 3 4 5 6 7 8 9'

the value of STRING2 is the series of same digits in descendant order

'9 8 7 6 5 4 3 2 1 0'

REMARKS

The program handles character strings of *variable* length, up to a maximum of 80 characters. The program returns a reversed string of length equal to that of the original input string, thus ignoring possible blanks to the right of the original input string. This is assured by the fact that the VARYING attribute applies to STRING1 and STRING2, and LENGTH (STRING1) is the upper limit of the values assumed by both I and J in the DO loop in the program. It should also be noted that a character string can contain numeric data.

To improve the clarity of programs containing DO loops, it is often useful to attach statement labels to the DO statements and include the labels in the corresponding END statements. Although it is not particularly important when DO loops are short, this technique provides easy identification of the boundaries of DO loops within a program. The use of the statement label L1 in the above program illustrates the technique.

Sample Program 13: SEARCH

This program (1) reads an index word and an accompanying sentence, which represents the text to be searched, (2) scans the words of the text for occurrences of the index word, and (3) prints out the positions at which the index word occurs in the text and the total number of occurrences.

The program uses two forms of the DO statement. The first one illustrates the WHILE clause with a DO loop, and the second one illustrates the use of the DO group (as opposed to a DO loop) as the THEN clause of an IF statement. In the program the DO group is nested within the DO loop, and the statement labels L1 and G1 are used, respectively, to identify the boundaries of the DO loop and the DO group.

```
SEARCH:  PROCEDURE OPTIONS (MAIN);
         DECLARE (TEXT CHAR(80), (WORD, INDEX) CHAR (15))
             VARYING, LOCATION (0:20) FIXED;
         GET LIST (INDEX, TEXT);
         PUT LIST ('THE TEXT IS:', TEXT);
         PUT SKIP LIST ('THE INDEX WORD IS:', INDEX);
         LOCATION = 0;
         WORD = (15) ' ';
         M = 1; L = 0;
    L1:  DO I = 1 BY 1 WHILE SUBSTR (WORD, LENGTH (WORD), 1)
             ¬ = '.');
         M = M + L;
         L = INDEX (SUBSTR (TEXT, M), ' ');
         IF L = 0 THEN WORD = SUBSTR (TEXT, M);
         ELSE WORD = SUBSTR (TEXT, M, L − 1);
         IF (SUBSTR (WORD, LENGTH (WORD), 1) = '.') & (SUBSTR
             (WORD, 1, LENGTH (WORD) − 1) = INDEX) THEN GO TO G1;
         IF SUBSTR (WORD, LENGTH (WORD), 1) = ','|
             SUBSTR (WORD, LENGTH (WORD), 1) = ';'|
             SUBSTR (WORD, LENGTH (WORD), 1) = ':' THEN
                 WORD = SUBSTR (WORD, 1, LENGTH (WORD) − 1);
         IF WORD = INDEX THEN
```

G1: DO;
    LOCATION (0) = LOCATION (0) + 1;
    LOCATION (LOCATION (0)) = 1;
    END G1;
    END L1;
    PUT SKIP LIST ('THE NUMBER OF OCCURRENCES OF THE INDEX WORD
        IN THE TEXT, AND THEIR LOCATIONS, ARE RESPECTIVELY',
        LOCATION);
    END SEARCH;

REMARKS

The program SEARCH is similar in part to the SAMPLE PROGRAM 10: PARSE in that both programs pull apart sentences and examine their words one by one on an individual basis. However, it should be noted that there are minor differences between the present program and PARSE in the implementation of the algorithm for finding, one by one, the words in a text.

In the declaration statement in the program, LOCATION (0 : 20) refers to the fact that the variable named LOCATION is declared to be an *array variable* and (0 : 20) serves as a *dimension attribute* for the variable. The latter specifies the number of dimensions in the array and the bounds for each dimension. In this case, (0 : 20) specifies that LOCATION is a one-dimensional array and that there are 21 elements in the array which are to be identified in accordance with the following subscript notation.

LOCATION (0), LOCATION (1), LOCATION (2), ..., LOCATION (20)

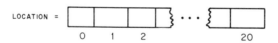

LOCATION =   0   1   2   20

The value of each element in LOCATION is initially set to 0 in the program, and after completion of the program the array contains as many nonzero elements as there are occurrences of the index word in the text. In addition there is one other nonzero element in the array, namely, LOCATION (0). In the program, LOCATION (0) is used both as a counter for tallying the total number of occurrences of the index word and as a subscript for identifying all other nonzero elements of the array. The two assignment statements that comprise the nested DO group labeled G1 in the program illustrate a common technique for treating an element of an array as an array subscript.

As mentioned earlier, array variables and dimension attributes will be discussed more fully in Chapter 8.

Sample Program 14: COUNT

This program (1) reads a text of arbitrary length (not exceeding 500 characters), (2) determines the number of sentences in the text, the average number of words in a sentence and the average number of characters in a word, and (3) prints the results. The program provides another illustration of a simple DO loop and a DO group nested within the DO loop. The main DO statement provides an illustration of the TO clause in which the limiting value of the index is specified by the expression LENGTH (TEXT) which takes on a decimal integer constant as its value.

```
COUNT:    PROCEDURE OPTIONS (MAIN);
          DECLARE TEXT CHAR (500) VARYING,
              SYMBOL CHAR (1),
              (STATEMENT_COUNT, WORD_COUNT,
              LETTER_COUNT) FIXED;
PROCESS:  GET LIST (TEXT);
          STATEMENT_COUNT, WORD_COUNT, LETTER_COUNT = 0;
    L1:   DO I = 1 BY 1 TO LENGTH (TEXT);
          SYMBOL = SUBSTR (TEXT, I, 1);
          IF SYMBOL = '.' | SYMBOL = '?' THEN
    G1:   DO;
          STATEMENT_COUNT = STATEMENT_COUNT + 1;
          WORD_COUNT = WORD_COUNT + 1;
          END G1;
          ELSE IF SYMBOL = ' ' THEN
              WORD_COUNT = WORD_COUNT + 1;
              ELSE LETTER_COUNT = LETTER_COUNT + 1;
          END L1;
          PUT SKIP LIST ('SENTENCE COUNT = ', STATEMENT_COUNT);
          PUT SKIP LIST ('AVERAGE WORD COUNT = ',
              WORD_COUNT / STATEMENT_COUNT);
          PUT SKIP LIST ('AVERAGE LETTER COUNT = ',
              LETTER_COUNT / WORD_COUNT);
          GO TO PROCESS;
          END COUNT;
```

REMARKS

Observe that PL/I allows the use of arithmetic expressions to specify items in the list specification of an output statement; for examples WORD_COUNT / STATEMENT_COUNT and LETTER_COUNT / WORK_COUNT. Thus in PL/I, arithmetic as well as character and logical operations may validly appear in the specification of an output statement. When the output statement is executed, the particular operations indicated in the expression (in the above case, the arithmetic operation of division) will be carried out, and the value of the expression will be computed and made ready for printout.

Sample Program 15:   FREQ1

This program reads a series of sentences as text and prepares a frequency table of the alphabetic characters which the text contains. The program illustrates a nest of DO loops in which the innermost DO loop is controlled by a simple WHILE condition.

```
FREQ1 :   PROCEDURE OPTIONS (MAIN);
          DECLARE ALPHA CHAR (26) INIT ('AB
              CDEFGHIJKLMNOPQRSTUVWXYZ'),
              TEXT CHAR (160) VARYING,
              LETTER CHAR (1),
              (COUNT, PREVIOUS_OCCUR, NEXT_OCCUR) FIXED;
PROCESS:  GET LIST (TEXT);
          PUT LIST (TEXT);
     L1:  DO I = 1 TO 26;
          LETTER = SUBSTR (ALPHA, I, 1);
          COUNT = 0;
          PREVIOUS_OCCUR, NEXT_OCCUR = INDEX (TEXT, LETTER);
          IF PREVIOUS_OCCUR = 0 THEN GO TO NEXT_LETTER;
     L2:  DO WHILE (NEXT_OCCUR ¬ = 0);
          COUNT = COUNT + 1;
          NEXT_OCCUR = INDEX (SUBSTR (TEXT,
              PREVIOUS_OCCUR + 1), LETTER);
          PREVIOUS_OCCUR = PREVIOUS_OCCUR + NEXT_OCCUR;
          END L2;
          PUT SKIP LIST (LETTER, ' = ', COUNT);
NEXT_LETTER:  END L1;
          GO TO PROCESS;
          END FREQ1 ;
```

REMARKS

Observe that the program is designed so that null frequencies are not printed for letters which do not appear in a given sentence. This is accomplished by inclusion of the IF statement

IF PREVIOUS_OCCUR = 0 THEN GO TO NEXT_LETTER;

where NEXT_LETTER is the name of the END statement associated with the outermost DO loop. When the THEN clause of this IF statement is executed, control passes immediately to the END statement of the outer DO loop, which causes index I to be advanced by 1 and the next letter of the alphabet to be placed in LETTER.

A most important statistical measure in processing natural language for information retrieval purposes is to analyze the frequency of words. In some automatic indexing methods the frequency of occurrence of words has been used as a means of determining the subject content of documents. Some researchers have used word frequency as a basis for the construction of a thesaurus.

To program this type of application, we have already seen that it is desirable to make use of array variables. In the chapter which follows the concept of arrays and their use in programming is discussed at greater length. SAMPLE PROGRAM 16: FREQ2 provides an illustration of this application.

EXERCISES

1.   The DO statement in SAMPLE PROGRAM 12: REVERSE could have been written as follows.

DO I = 1 TO LENGTH (STRING1);

What changes, if any, would this necessitate in the rest of the program?

2.   Determine the output of SAMPLE PROGRAM 13: SEARCH if the input stream is

'DO', 'IT IS BETTER TO DO AS I SAY, SAID HE, THAN DO AS I DO.'

3.   Assume that the second assignment statement in the nested DO group labeled G1 in SAMPLE PROGRAM 13: SEARCH is replaced by the following assignment statement.

LOCATION (LOCATION (0)) = M;

Determine the output of the modified program if the input stream remains as given in Exercise 2.

4. Determine the output of SAMPLE PROGRAM 14: COUNT if the input stream is

'NO, NO, NO, SAID SHE. SAID HE, WHAT AM I TO DO?'

5. Two drawbacks of SAMPLE PROGRAM 14: COUNT are that (1) punctuation symbols other than the period (.) and question mark (?) are included in the letter count, and (2) a bogus word count occurs following the encounter of a blank ( ) followed by a period (.). Rewrite the program to remove these drawbacks.

6. Determine the output of SAMPLE PROGRAM 15: FREQ1 if the input stream is the same as that given in Exercise 4.

7. Identify the statement in SAMPLE PROGRAM 15: FREQ1 that will always be executed last by the computer. If this situation is undesirable, explain how to modify it.

8. Modify SAMPLE PROGRAM 15: FREQ1 to provide as output the percentage of occurrence for each alphabetic letter appearing in the input text. For instance, each of the letters, D, H, I, N, and S occur with a 10 percent frequency in the text given in Exercise 4.

CHAPTER 8

Arrays and Structures

8.1 Arrays

In the examples we have used so far, each variable was assigned to a unique location in memory. In many instances, however, it is convenient to assign one name to a group of memory locations each of which contains a separate variable whose value can be changed at any time.

When the elements of a group of such variables have identical attributes they can be organized to form an _array_. For example, if a librarian wanted to build a shelflist in which the books are arranged according to their classification numbers, he can define the shelflist as an array. The array is given a name and the entire collection is treated as an entity. Each book in the collection becomes an item of the array and is referred to by giving its relative position in the array.

The advantage of using arrays is the capability of employing a single command for an operation to be performed on all of the members of the array and, at the same time, having the capability of handling each item in the array separately.

8.2 Declaration of Arrays

The following form of the DECLARE statement is used for the declaration of arrays.

DECLARE name (n, m, etc) attributes;

where "name" is an identifier for the array and "n, m, etc." are signed or unsigned integer constants that specify the dimensions of the array. A single integer would appear for a one-dimensional array, integers separated by a comma for a two-dimensional array, and so on. PL/I allows the use of as many as 32-dimensional arrays.

In addition to specifying the *number* of dimensions of an array it is also necessary to specify the beginning and end of each dimension, that is, the *bounds* of each dimension.

If only one integer is specified for each dimension, as in the above statement form, then the lower bound of each dimension is 1. Otherwise, the bounds of the dimension are expressed in the form i : j, where i and j are signed or unsigned integers such that $i \leq j$.

For example,

DECLARE name (5) attributes;

refers to a one-dimensional array whose lower bound is 1 and whose upper bound is 5. If, however, the lower bound of the array is not 1 but 3, then its value must be given in the following form.

DECLARE name (3 : 5) attributes;

where 3 represents the lower bound of the one-dimensional array and 5 represents its upper bound.

The statement form

DECLARE name (9, 16) attributes;

refers to a two-dimensional array in which the upper bound of the first dimension is 9, the upper bound of the second dimension is 16, and the lower bound of both dimensions is 1. If, however, the lower bound of the first dimension were -2 and that of the second were 10, then the statement would have the form

DECLARE name $(-2 : 9, 10 : 16)$ attributes;

but the upper bounds must always be greater than their respective lower bounds.

An example of a two-dimensional array is a document/term matrix representing a set of documents and the terms that are used to index them.

	Documents						
	1	2	3	4	5	...	m
Terms							
1		X	X		X		
2	X		X				
3	X						X
4		X	X		X	X	
5							
6	X	X			X		
7							
8			X	X			
⋮							
n				X	X		

Let us assume that the above matrix, called DOCUMENT, refers to a collection of 100 documents (m = 100) that are indexed using 300 terms (n = 300) and that both the numbering of the documents and that of the terms begin with 1 (that is, the lower bound of each dimension is 1). The statement to declare this matrix is

DECLARE DOCUMENT $(300, 100)$ CHARACTER(1);

where 300 is the upper bound of the first dimension (the number of rows in the matrix), and 100 is the upper bound of the second dimension (the number of columns in the matrix).

Other examples of declarations of arrays are

DECLARE DOCNO $(10 : 100)$ FIXED DECIMAL;
DECLARE TITLE (800) CHARACTER (80) VARYING;
DECLARE USER (200) FIXED INITIAL $((200) 0)$;
DECLARE PREPOSITION (5) CHARACTER (6) VARYING INITIAL
     ('FOR', 'OF', 'AND', 'BY', 'THE');

The first DECLARE statement will allocate 90 storage locations (10–100) for variables in decimal form all under the name DOCNO. The second DECLARE statement will reserve 800 locations for character strings of a maximum length of 80. The third statement will allocate 200 locations for decimal numbers all of which have 0 as their initial value, and in the last DECLARE statement the 5 locations that will be reserved will have as their initial value the character strings specified by the INITIAL attribute, as follows.

PREPOSITION (1) = 'FOR'
PREPOSITION (2) = 'OF'
PREPOSITION (3) = 'AND'
PREPOSITION (4) = 'BY'
PREPOSITION (5) = 'THE'

8.3 Operations on Arrays

As the preceding examples show, a member of an array can be identified through the use of *subscripts*. Subscripts specify the relative position of elements within an array. For example, if the one-dimensional array SHELF is declared as follows

DECLARE SHELF (8 : 14) CHAR (20) VAR;

then SHELF (10), the subscripted name, refers to a single element in the array, in this case the third element. When the name of the array is used without a subscript the name refers to the entire array. For example, the statement

PUT LIST (SHELF);

will print out all seven elements of the array SHELF. However, the statement

PUT LIST (SHELF (10));

refers only to the value of the element defined by the subscript, in this case the third element, and only this value will be printed out.

In the case of two-dimensional arrays, groups of elements of the array such as specified rows and columns can be referred to by substituting an asterisk (" * ") for a subscript. The first row of the array DOCUMENT can be referred to by the use of subscripts as

DOCUMENT (1, *)

and the first column of elements of the same array can be referred to by the form

DOCUMENT (*, 1)

It should be noted that the subscripted identifier DOCUMENT (1, *) may be considered as a one-dimensional array that includes the elements DOCU-MENT (1, 1), DOCUMENT (1, 2), DOCUMENT (1, 3), ..., DOCUMENT (1, 100).

Operations performed on arrays are done on an element-by-element basis. For example,

DECLARE CALLNO (6) CHAR (20) VAR INIT ('PN234', 'PH235', 'HD56');

will assign initial values to the first 3 elements of the array CALLNO in the following way

CALLNO (1) = 'PN234'
CALLNO (2) = 'PH235'
CALLNO (3) = 'HD56'

In two-dimensional arrays, data is first assigned to the elements of the first row of the array (from left to right), then to the second row and so on. Thus the right most subscript varies first in the assignment of data to a two-dimensional array. As an example let us consider the statement

DECLARE LIST (10, 20) CHAR (2) INITIAL ('2A', '3A', '4B');

This DECLARE statement will initialize the following elements of the first row of the array LIST.

LIST (1, 1) = '2A'
LIST (1, 2) = '3A'
LIST (1, 3) = '4B'

Arithmetic operations can also be performed on an entire array if the name of the array is used without a subscript. For example, consider the following set of statements.

DECLARE COMP (5) FIXED;
GET LIST (COMP);
COMP = COMP * COMP (1);
PUT LIST (COMP);

The GET statement reads in five items of data from the input string and assigns them to the array COMP. The arithmetic assignment statement then specifies that each element of the array is multiplied by the value of the first element. If the input values are

2, 5, 8, 12, 15

then after multiplication the printed values for the array COMP are

4, 10, 16, 24, 30

When an arithmetic operation is performed on more than one array, all the arrays involved must have identical bounds. Given the DECLARE statement

DECLARE A (3) FIXED, B (−5 : −3), C (1 : 3) FIXED DEC (6, 2);

it is correct to use the assignment statement

A = A + C;

but it is incorrect to use

A = A + B;

Although arrays A, B and C have the same *dimension* they do not have the same *bounds*. For arrays A and C, the bounds are 1 and 3 but for array B the bounds are −5 and −3.

Sample Program 16: FREQ2

As an illustration of the use of arrays, let us consider the following program that calculates the frequency of occurrence of words in a text. For purposes of illustration, the length of the text is restricted to 160 characters, and the number sign # is used as a special symbol to denote the end of the text. The program itself contains two basic loops called FIND and OCCUR. In the loop FIND, the input text is scanned character by character to locate punctuation symbols (including the space symbol) that identify the boundaries of words. The set of punctuation symbols used in FIND include the space (blank), comma, colon, semicolon, period, question mark, and the special end-of-text symbol (#). Words in the text are identified and stored sequentially as elements of a one-dimensional array called WORD, whose upper bound is arbitrarily specified not to exceed 100. The number of words in the text is similarly computed and stored in location I, which also serves as a subscript for the variable array WORD. In the loop OCCUR, each element of the array WORD is compared with all succeeding elements to determine matching occurrences of words. Where matching occurs, the higher subscripted element of the array is assigned blanks, and a count of the matching occurrence is noted. The number of occurrences for each word in the text is then printed. An alternative method of determining the occurrences of each word is to arrange the elements of the array alphabetically before any comparison is made. When this is done it is necessary to compare each element in the array only with the next element.

```
FREQ2:      PROCEDURE OPTIONS (MAIN);
            DECLARE (TEXT CHAR (160), WORD (100) CHAR (12))
                VARYING, COUNT INITIAL (1) FIXED;
            I = 0;
            GET LIST (TEXT);
            PUT LIST (TEXT);
FIND:       I = I + 1;
            DO L = 1 TO LENGTH (TEXT)
                WHILE (INDEX (',:;.?#', SUBSTR (TEXT, L, 1)) =
                0);
            END;
            /*FIND WORD BY LOCATING 'Ъ', ',', ':', ';', '.', '?',
                '#' IN THE TEXT*/
            WORD (I) = SUBSTR (TEXT, 1, L − 1);
            IF SUBSTR (TEXT, L, 1) = '#' THEN GO TO OCCUR;
            TEXT = SUBSTR (TEXT, L + 1);
            GO TO FIND;
            /*AT THIS POINT THE WORDS IN THE TEXT ARE STORED
                IN THE ARRAY 'WORD', AND THE NUMBER OF
                WORDS IS STORED IN I*/
OCCUR:      DO J = 1 TO I;
            IF WORD (J) = ' ' THEN GO TO NEXTWORD;
L1:         DO K = J + 1 TO I;
            IF WORD (J) = WORD (K) THEN
G1:         DO;
            WORD (K) = ' ';
            COUNT = COUNT + 1;
            /*WHERE WORD (K) MATCHES WORD (J), REPLACE
                EACH OCCURRENCE OF WORD (K) BY BLANKS AND
                COUNT SUCH OCCURRENCES*/
            END G1;
            END L1;
            PUT SKIP LIST (WORD (J), 'OCCURS', COUNT, 'TIMES');
            WORD (J) = ' ';
            COUNT = 1;
            /*REPLACE WORD (J) ITSELF BY BLANKS AND RESTORE
                COUNT TO 1*/
NEXTWORD:   END OCCUR;
            END FREQ2;
```

Sample Program 17: SHELFLIST1

The objective of this program is to augment the records of existing books in a library with additional records of newly arrived books in order to create a master list of all books in the library based on the order of their shelf classification number. The program reads an input string for each book in which the first six characters provide the classification number and the remaining characters represent the title of the book. An example of an entry for a book would be

510.78 MATHEMATICAL MODELS

The shelflist of existing books is stored in the one-dimensional array called OLDLIST and the data on newly arrived books is stored in another one-dimensional array called NEWLIST. By comparing the classification number of each new book with the classification number of one or more books in the OLDLIST, the proper place is found for the new book in the OLDLIST. If the classification number of a new book is such that it has to be inserted somewhere within the OLDLIST, the list is broken at this location and all succeeding classification numbers are pushed down one place in the list to make room for the data on the new shelf entry. If the classification number of a new book is greater than the last number in the OLDLIST, then its shelf data is placed at the end of the OLDLIST.

```
SHELFLIST1:  PROC OPTIONS (MAIN);
             DCL (OLDLIST (200), NEWLIST (100)) CHAR (80) VARYING
                 INITIAL ('AA'), (OLDCOUNT, NEWCOUNT) FIXED;
             DO I = 1 BY 1 WHILE (OLDLIST (I) ¬ = 'XX');
             /*OLDLIST (I) IS INITIALIZED TO A VALUE DIFFERENT THAN 'XX'
                 IN ORDER TO BEGIN THE DO LOOP WITH THE WHILE
                 CLAUSE*/
             GET LIST (OLDLIST (I + 1));
             END;
             OLDCOUNT = I − 1;
             /*THE NUMBER OF BOOKS CURRENTLY SHELVED IS STORED IN
                 LOCATION OLDCOUNT*/
             I = 1;
             DO WHILE (NEWLIST (I) ¬ = 'XX');
             GET LIST (NEWLIST (I + 1));
             I = I + 1;
             END;
```

```
                NEWCOUNT = I − 1;
                /*THE NUMBER OF NEW BOOKS TO BE ADDED TO SHELFLIST IS
                    STORED IN NEWCOUNT*/
                PUT LIST ('THIS IS THE OLD SHELFLIST:');
                PUT SKIP LIST ((OLDLIST (I) DO I = 2 TO OLDCOUNT));
                PUT SKIP LIST ('THIS IS THE SHELFLIST OF NEW BOOKS:');
                PUT SKIP LIST ((NEWLIST (I) DO I = 2 TO NEWCOUNT));
     UPDATE:    DO J = 2 TO NEWCOUNT;
    COMPARE:    DO I = 2 TO OLDCOUNT;
                IF (SUBSTR (OLDLIST (I), 1,6) > SUBSTR (NEWLIST (J),
                    1,6)) THEN GO TO MOVE;
                END COMPARE;
                /*'COMPARE' FINDS WHERE TO INSERT A NEW BOOK IN THE
                    SHELFLIST SO THAT IT REMAINS IN ASCENDING ORDER BY
                    CLASSIFICATION NUMBERS*/
                IF I = OLDCOUNT + 1 THEN OLDLIST (I) = NEWLIST (J);
                /*THE NEW ENTRY IS PLACED AT THE END OF THE SHELFLIST*/
                ELSE
     INSERT:    DO;
       MOVE:    DO K = OLDCOUNT TO I BY − 1;
                OLDLIST (K + 1) = OLDLIST (K);
                END MOVE;
                /*ROOM IS MADE IN THE SHELFLIST TO INSERT
                    ENTRY FROM THE NEW LIST*/
                OLDLIST (I) = NEWLIST (J);
                END INSERT;
                /*NEW ENTRY IS INSERTED IN THE SHELFLIST AT THE POSITION
                    POINTED BY VALUE OF I*/
                OLDCOUNT = OLDCOUNT + 1;
                /*THE SHELFLIST IS NOW LARGER BY ONE NEW ENTRY*/
                END UPDATE;
                PUT SKIP LIST ('THIS IS THE UPDATED SHELFLIST:');
                PUT SKIP LIST ((OLDLIST (I) DO I = 2 TO OLDCOUNT));
                END SHELFLIST1;
```

REMARKS

Observe that the upper bound of the OLDLIST is declared to be larger than the upper bound of the NEWLIST because the OLDLIST becomes the final list which includes all of the books recently acquired but not yet shelved. Since OLDLIST (1) and NEWLIST (1) are declared to have as their initial values the character string 'AA', storage of the input data actually begins at locations OLDLIST (2) and NEWLIST (2). This explains why the starting value of the index for several of the DO statements is 2. Finally, the input data that is to be stored in the arrays OLDLIST and NEWLIST should end with the dummy value 'XX'. This explains why in the two assignment statements

$$\text{OLDCOUNT} = \text{I} - 1;$$
$$\text{NEWCOUNT} = \text{I} - 1;$$

the value of I is decreased by 1 before storing in OLDCOUNT and NEWCOUNT.

Storage Allocation for an Array During Program Execution

An array variable in a PL/I program occupies the entire storage space assigned to it during execution of the program regardless of the number of elements actually used. For example, if an array is declared to have 100 elements, but only three of the elements actually contain data during the execution of the program the other 97 elements will still occupy their respective storage spaces and the space cannot be used to store other variables. In this case it is often desirable to allocate space only for those elements that will be used in a given execution of the program. Similar situations occur when the maximum number of elements for a given array is not known at the time the program is written, and when need for additional storage becomes apparent only during execution of a program.

To facilitate the solution of the type of problems just described, PL/I allows dynamic acquisition and release of storage area during program execution. By using the attribute CONTROLLED (abbreviated : CTL) in the declaration of an array variable, a dimension of the array may be varied during actual execution. An example of the use of this attribute is

```
DECLARE A(N) CONTROLLED;
GET LIST (N);
ALLOCATE A(N);
    ⋮
FREE (A);
```

In this example, the array A has an undefined dimension N, the value of which is not known when the program is written. During execution, the value of N is read from the input stream. After obtaining N, the execution of the instruction ALLOCATE A(N) assigns an area of storage to the array

A large enough to accommodate N elements. After processing of the data in array A is completed and if the data contained in array A is no longer needed, the storage space obtained with the ALLOCATE statement can be released by using the FREE statement. When the FREE statement is used, the values in array A are lost.

If several allocations are made for the same array variable, a "stack" of elements is created. If a second ALLOCATE were executed for array A before the FREE statement is executed, then the previous allocated elements would be "pushed down" and the new ones "stacked" above. A FREE statement, when executed, will release the most recent allocation (that is, the allocation on top of the stack) and the next allocation will be "pushed up." When this technique is used, all the data in the elements remaining in the "stack" is preserved, while data in the released elements is lost.

For example,

```
DCL BOOK (N) CHAR (6);
GET LIST (N);
ALLOCATE BOOK (N);
GET LIST (BOOK);
N = N + 2;
ALLOCATE BOOK (N);
GET LIST (BOOK);
PUT DATA (BOOK);
FREE BOOK;
PUT DATA (BOOK);
```

The first ALLOCATE statement assigns N location for the array BOOK, the second ALLOCATE saves N + 2 locations. The first PUT DATA (BOOK) prints N + 2 elements of the array BOOK because this was the last allocation. If we want to print the first N elements, then the FREE statement must be used and the second PUT DATA (BOOK) will print the values stored with the first allocation.

8.4   Structures

Arrays are collections of homogeneous data. If an array is declared as consisting of character strings of length 10, none of its elements can be assigned data having a different set of attributes. Yet it is often desirable to assign a collective name to a group of data with different attributes. For example, writing procedures to process library documents would be facilitated considerably if such document-related information as title, author, identification number, data of publication, and subject terms could be referred to by a single name. This type of heterogeneous data can be organized by use of the so-called *structure variable* (structure, for short) in PL/I.

While an array is an aggregation of data, a structure is a hierarchical collection of data. An instance of the latter is the outline for a book in which the material is divided into parts, and the individual parts are further sub-divided. For example, the material may be so organized as to reflect the following structure.

> I.
> > A.
> > > 1.
> > > 2.
> > B.
> II.
> > A.
> > B.

where each part is called a *level* and those levels which are not further subdivided are called *elementary levels*. Thus I.A.1 and I.A.2, as well as II.A and II.B, are elementary levels.

8.5   Declaration of Structures

In PL/I the DECLARE statement

```
DECLARE 1 DOCUMENT,
          2 TITLE CHAR (80),
          2 AUTHOR CHAR (80),
          2 ID FIXED (6),
          2 DATE,
            3 MONTH FIXED (2),
            3 DAY FIXED (2),
            3 YEAR FIXED (2);
```

establishes a structure called DOCUMENT with subservient levels TITLE, AUTHOR, ID, and DATE. In addition, DATE has as subservient levels MONTH,

DAY, and YEAR. Observe that the name of the structure DOCUMENT has no attributes because it merely represents the name of a group of data. The elementary levels are variables whose attributes have to be explicitly declared. The variables do not have to appear on separate lines, as shown above, but this is often done for clarity.

In order to be able to identify any component variable in a structure and assign a value to it, it is convenient to *qualify* the variable by preceding it with one or more variable names at a higher level of the structure. All such names are separated by a period. Thus, to assign a value to the variable named DAY in the above structure, any of the following qualified names may be used.

DOCUMENT.DATE.DAY

DOCUMENT.DAY

DATE.DAY

A name is qualified only to avoid ambiguity, and the level of qualification depends on the necessity to make it unique.

Any variable at any level within a structure, including the level 1 structure variable itself, can be dimensioned as an array variable (see Section 8.6). However, with an exception to be noted, attributes can be specified only for variables appearing at the elementary levels of a structure. The exception is the VARYING attribute, which cannot be specified for any variable in a structure.

8.6   Operations on Structures

In maintaining a list of library bibliographic records, for example, it is advantageous to group the structures representing the bibliographical information for each document in an array to form an ARRAY OF STRUCTURES. By using this method of organization, it is possible to refer to an entire collection of structures by a single name with a subscript. For example, if in the previous DECLARE statement DOCUMENT is replaced by DOCUMENT (800), this refers to a collection of 800 bibliographic records identically organized in which each individual item can be identified by DOCUMENT (I). In this case the qualified name DOCUMENT (93).DATE.YEAR refers to the last two digits that appear on the 93rd bibliographic record of the collection.

Sample Program 18: SHELFLIST2

Let us consider another version of SAMPLE PROGRAM 17: SHELFLIST1 where each book is declared as a structure containing such elements as classification number, title, author, and date of publication. If the sample input data for the OLDLIST is

373 , 'A HIGH SCHOOL CURRICULUM FOR LEADERSHIP',
'LAPATI, AMGRICO D.', 09, 12, 61,
378.13 , 'UNIVERSITY ADULT EDUCATION IN THE ARTS',
'GOLDMAN, FREDA H.', 06, 10, 61,
547.076, 'PROBLEMS IN ORGANIC CHEMISTRY',
'DANIELS, RALPH', 08, 25, 61,
00.0 , 'XX'

and sample input data for the NEWLIST is

510.78 , 'MATHEMATICAL MODELS', 'CUNDY, H.M.',
10, 13, 62,
512.8 , 'FUNDAMENTAL CONCEPTS OF HIGHER ALGEBRA',
'ALBERT, A.A.', 12, 10, 56,
00 , 'XX'

then SAMPLE PROGRAM 18 will print out the following.

OLD LIST CLASSIFICATION NUMBERS
373   378.13   547.076
NEW LIST CLASSIFICATION NUMBERS
510.78   512.8
THIS IS THE UPDATED SHELFLIST
373   A HIGH SCHOOL CURRICULUM FOR LEADERSHIP
          LAPATI, AMGRICO D. 09 12 61
378.13   UNIVERSITY ADULT EDUCATION IN THE ARTS
          GOLDMAN, FREDA H. 06 10 61
510.78   MATHEMATICAL MODELS
          CUNDY, H.M. 10 13 62
512.8   FUNDAMENTAL CONCEPTS OF HIGHER ALGEBRA
          ALBERT, A.A. 12 10 56
547.076   PROBLEMS IN ORGANIC CHEMISTRY
          DANIELS, RALPH 08 25 61

```
SHELFLIST2:  PROC OPTIONS (MAIN);
             DECLARE 1 OLD (200),
                       2 CLASS FIXED (6,3),
                       2 TITLE CHAR (80) INIT ('AA'),
                       2 AUTHOR CHAR (20),
                       2 DATE,
                         (3 MONTH, 3 DAY, 3 YEAR) FIXED (2),
                     1 NEW (100),
                       2 CLASS FIXED (6,3),
                       2 TITLE CHAR (80) INIT ('AA'),
                       2 AUTHOR CHAR (20),
                       2 DATE,
                         (3 MONTH, 3 DAY, 3 YEAR) FIXED (2),
                     (OLDCOUNT, NEWCOUNT) FIXED;
             I = 1;
             DO WHILE (OLD (I).TITLE ¬ = 'XX');
             GET LIST (OLD (I + 1));
             I = I + 1;
             END;
             OLDCOUNT = I - 1;
             I = 1;
             DO WHILE (NEW (I).TITLE ¬ = 'XX');
             GET LIST (NEW (I + 1));
             I = I + 1;
             END;
             NEWCOUNT = I - 1;
             PUT SKIP LIST ('OLD LIST CLASSIFICATION NUMBERS');
             PUT SKIP LIST ((OLD (I).CLASS DO I = 2 TO OLD COUNT));
             PUT SKIP LIST ('NEW LIST CLASSIFICATION NUMBERS');
             PUT SKIP LIST ((NEW (I).CLASS DO I = 2 TO NEW-
                 COUNT));
   UPDATE:   DO J = 2 TO NEWCOUNT;
   COMPARE:  DO I = 2 TO OLDCOUNT; IF (OLD (I).CLASS > NEW
                 (J).CLASS) THEN GO TO MOVE;
             END COMPARE;
             IF I = OLDCOUNT + 1 THEN OLD (I) = NEW (J);
             ELSE
   INSERT:   DO;
   MOVE:     DO K = OLDCOUNT TO I BY - 1;
             OLD (K + 1) = OLD (K);
```

```
          END MOVE;
          OLD (I) = NEW (J);
          END INSERT;
          OLDCOUNT = OLDCOUNT + 1;
          END UPDATE;
          PUT SKIP LIST ('THIS IS THE UPDATED SHELFLIST');
  PRINT:  DO I = 2 TO OLDCOUNT;
          PUT SKIP EDIT (OLD (I)) (F (6, 3), X (3), A (80),
            SKIP, X (9), A (20), X (2), (3) F (3, 0));
          END PRINT;
          END SHELFLIST2;
```

REMARKS

If in place of the complete bibliographic information we want only to print a list of authors and titles from the merged list, then the following output statement may be substituted for the DO loop labeled PRINT in Sample Program 18.

PUT LIST ((OLD (I).AUTHOR, OLD (I).TITLE DO I = 2 TO OLDCOUNT));

Observe that the statement GET LIST (OLD (I + 1)) in the program reads six items for each structure from the input data because the structure OLD is declared to contain six elements, three at the second level and three at the third level.

EXERCISES

1. Rewrite SAMPLE PROGRAM 17: SHELFLIST1 so that storage of the input data begins at locations OLDLIST (1) and NEWLIST (1) instead of OLDLIST (2) and NEWLIST (2).

2. Write a PL/I program which reads in a maximum of 30 words in any order, stores them in an array, and prints them in alphabetical order (see Table 4.1 for the internal representation of the alphabet).

3. Rewrite the program in Exercise 2 so that it accepts as input data a list of author names in the form

```
          last name, first name
          JONES, TOM
          SMITH, JOHN
              ⋮
```

and prints the list of authors in alphabetical order by their last name (see Table 4.1 for the internal representation of punctuation).

4.   Use the input data given in Exercise 2 of Chapter 7 and write a PL/I program which prints the following matrix

WORD	OCCURRENCES				
	1	2	3	4	5
IT	X				
IS	X				
BETTER	X				
TO	X				
DO			X		
AS		X			
I		X			
SAY	X				
⋮	⋮				

where the columns represent number of occurrences for each word and the rows list the words in the order in which they appear in the input text.

5.   Write a PL/I program to rearrange the list of words in the above matrix in Exercise 4 in alphabetical order.

6.   Write a PL/I program to transpose the matrix in Exercise 4 so that the columns list the words of the text and the rows represent the number of occurrences for each word (use edit-directed I/O).

7.   Write a program which performs the task described in Exercise 4 but uses a structure variable instead of an array variable to represent the matrix.

CHAPTER 9

Basic Concepts of Boolean Algebra

9.1 The Concept of Sets

The concept of sets is a basic one in document retrieval. It is also a familiar concept since any collection of objects can be regarded as being a set. Thus, the group of graduate students currently enrolled in Library Science at Rutgers constitute a set, as do the patrons of a library, or a collection of documents about air pollution. The objects of a set are called its *members* or *elements.*

The simplest way to define a set is to list all of its elements. To decide whether or not a given object belongs to the set, it is sufficient to examine the list of elements of the set. This procedure is called defining a set by *enumeration.*

A more useful way to define a set is by some property or combination of properties that all members of the set share in common. To decide whether or not a given object belongs to the set, it is sufficient to determine whether the object exhibits all the properties in question. Thus, to determine whether Mary Jane Smith is a member of the set of graduate students enrolled in Library Science at Rutgers, we could examine the list of all such students. However, we could also establish whether Mary Jane possesses the *defining properties* of the set. In some instances, where there are infinitely many members of a set, it is impossible to list all the members of the set. Thus, we cannot enumerate the set of all even integers, but we can always determine whether any given integer belongs to the set. On the other hand, there are sets for which it is difficult to produce the property or combination of properties, other than the property of belonging to the set, that defines precisely the set. An example is the three-element set consisting of Mary Jane Smith, the ninth floor of the United Nations building, and the year 876 B.C.

In document retrieval we deal with sets of documents that are defined by the properties that hold for the documents in the collection. The defining property may be the subject content of the document, its author(s), the journal in which the article was published, or some other characteristic.

A given document can belong to several different sets corresponding to the properties that are formally recognized in the particular retrieval system. For example, a document on air pollution caused by carbon monoxide published in 1970 by J. Jones could be viewed as a member of the following sets.

Set A = {Documents on air pollution}
Set B = {Documents on carbon monoxide}
Set C = {Documents whose author is J. Jones}
Set D = {Documents published in 1970}
Set E = {Documents published in 1970 by J. Jones}
Set F = {Documents published in 1970 by J. Jones on air pollution}
Set G = {Documents published in 1970 by J. Jones on air pollution caused by carbon monoxide}
Set H = {Documents published on air pollution in 1970}

.
.
.

Several of the sets given above are said to be *subsets* of another set. For example, set E, {documents published in 1970 by J. Jones}, is a subset of set D, {documents published in 1970}, as well as a subset of set C, {documents whose author is J. Jones}; and set G, {documents published in 1970 by J. Jones on air pollution caused by carbon monoxide}, is a subset of set C, {documents whose author is J. Jones}. In fact, set G is a subset of all of the sets listed above, including itself.

Thus, by inquiring whether or not the elements of a given set possess some *additional* property, we are led to the concept of a subset of a given set. When all the elements of a set X are also elements of a set Y, then X is said to be a subset of Y, and the relationship is expressed by the notation $X \subseteq Y$. By this definition a set can be regarded as being a subset of itself. When X is a subset of Y, and Y contains at least one element that does not belong to X (causing X to be *distinct* from Y), then X is called a *proper subset* of Y. This relationship is expressed by the notation $X \subset Y$.

In the example above, set E is a subset of set D so that $E \subseteq D$, since all documents published in 1970 by J. Jones are among the documents published in 1970. However, if the set D contains documents published in 1970 by authors other than J. Jones, then E is a proper subset of D, and we write $E \subset D$.

A set may also be defined by properties that are *not* possessed by the elements of the set, for example, the set of documents by J. Jones that are *not* on air pollution.

Operations on Sets

In document retrieval systems document sets are defined at the time of indexing and at the time of searching. The objective of searching is to select from the *universal set* (that is, from all the documents in the retrieval system) the particular set of documents that satisfy the query.

When highly structured vocabularies are used in a retrieval system, searching is facilitated by the fact that it is possible to define new sets and to formalize and make explicit their relationships to each other. In precoordinate systems formulation of the search query is limited to the sets that were defined at the time of indexing. In postcoordinate systems (coordinate indexing) a given query may be formulated by defining new sets that are logical combinations of those defined originally during indexing.

For example, let us assume that the following sets were originally defined at the time of indexing.

Set $A =$ {Documents on computer processing}
   (contains documents D_1, D_3, D_5)
Set $B =$ {Documents on library records}
   (contains documents D_2, D_4, D_5, D_6)
Set $C =$ {Documents by J. Jones}
   (contains documents D_7, D_8)
Set $D =$ {Documents on business records}
   (contains documents D_1, D_9, D_{10})

From these four original sets a new set could be defined to satisfy the query, "What documents deal with computer processing of library records?"

In this example the query calls for a set of documents that deal with computer processing of library records. No such set was defined originally during indexing. However, in a postcoordinate retrieval system the set can be defined by combining sets A and B to form a new set called the *intersection* of A and B, $A \cap B$, which consists of all elements belonging simultaneously to both A and B. The new set would consist of those documents that have the indexing terms *computer processing* and *library records* both assigned to them. These should be documents about computer processing of library records—a subject that is more specific than the subjects represented by either of the original index terms.

It is possible to combine two sets A and B so that the resulting set represents a subject that has the same specificity or is less specific than the subjects represented by either of the combined sets. The resulting set is called the *union* of A and B, $A \cup B$, and consists precisely of those elements which belong to A or to B or to both. Thus $A \cup B$ in the above example refers to the set of documents dealing with computer processing or library records or both.

The *complement* $\bar{A}$ of a set A is the set of all elements of the universal set which do *not* belong to A. In the example above, $\bar{A}$ refers to the set whose elements are D_2, D_4, D_6, D_7, D_8, D_9, and D_{10}; that is, those documents in the retrieval system not dealing with computer processing. It is possible to combine the complement and intersection of sets to form a new set that represents a subject that is more specific than the subjects represented by each of the combined sets alone. For example, the set $A \cap \bar{B}$ represents those documents dealing with computer processing except for computer processing of library records, which is a more specific subject than either computer processing or library records alone.

It is convenient to represent graphically the relationship among sets with the aid of so-called *Venn diagrams*. In Figure 9.1 the rectangle represents the universal set U (all documents in the retrieval system) and the two circles represent the sets A and B, respectively. The shaded regions in Figure 9.1 illustrate the concepts of complement, intersection, and union.

As the definition and above examples illustrate, complement is analogous to the Boolean operator NOT; to say that an object is a member of $\bar{A}$, the complement of A, means that it does *not* belong to the set A. Similarly, intersection is analogous to the Boolean operator AND; thus an element belongs to the intersection $A \cap B$ provided that the element belongs both to A *and B*. And, finally, union is analogous to the Boolean operator OR; an element belongs to the union $A \cup B$ if and only if it belongs to A *or* to B *or* to both. More complicated combinations of sets involving the Boolean operators and two or more sets can be defined to describe the documents satisfying a given query. Thus the compound set

$$((A \cap \bar{B}) \cap C) \cap \bar{D}$$

refers to those elements belonging to both A and C and outside each of B and D. This set would satisfy the query calling for those documents by J. Jones dealing with computer processing except for computer processing of library records and computer processing of business records. This is an instance of the *null* set since, $A \cap C$, the intersection of A and C,

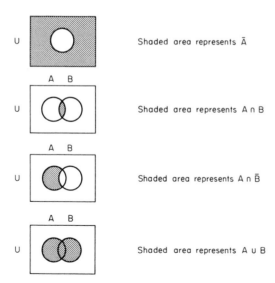

Figure 9-1

is empty. That is, there are no elements in common between sets A and C, since none of the documents by J. Jones deal with computer processing. The large number of combinations that are theoretically possible is, however, limited in practice by the intellectual limitations imposed by the subject matter of the document collection and by the operational limitations imposed by the system design.

Since the algebra of the subsets of a set is a Boolean algebra, we now turn to an extended discussion of the basic concepts of Boolean algebra.

9.2   Boolean Variables, Functions, and the AND, OR, NOT Operators

One of the important facts of Boolean algebra is that it is a *two-valued* algebra. What this means is that underlying the algebra are two mathematical symbols "0" and "1" which are not to be regarded as numbers of ordinary arithmetic but rather as *undefined terms*.

We may, if we choose to do so, *interpret* the symbols 0 and 1 as standing for the logical values *false* and *true*, respectively. Thus, when we say that a variable or expression assumes the value 1 or 0, we mean by this that it can take only the logical values true or false. Such variables may be thought of as denoting *propositions* or *statements*, hence the name propositional calculus or statement calculus.

A *letter* is a variable which assumes the value 0 or 1 only. We express the fact that x assumes the value 0 or 1 by writing $x = 0$ or $x = 1$, respectively.

Associated with each letter x is $\bar{x}$, called the *negation* of x, such that $\bar{x} = 1$ when $x = 0$ and $\bar{x} = 0$ when $x = 1$. The bar symbol above the letter denotes the Boolean operation NOT, and corresponds to the symbol $\neg$ in the PL/I character set. Thus $\bar{x}$ and $\neg x$ are equivalent ways of expressing the negation of x. Both x and $\bar{x}$ are called *literals* associated with the same letter.

x	$\bar{x}$
0	1
1	0

Note that we have in fact defined an *operation of negation* in terms of the symbols 0 and 1. The definition of negation is intended to illustrate among other things, that a special set of logical relationships holds between the symbols 0 and 1. One such relationship is expressed as follows

$$\bar{0} = 1, \qquad \bar{1} = 0$$

Given literals x_1 and x_2, then $x_1 + x_2$ is called a *sum* or *union*. Thus $x_1 + x_2 = 0$ if $x_1 = x_2 = 0$; otherwise $x_1 + x_2 = 1$. The symbol $+$ denotes the Boolean operation OR, and $x_1 + x_2$ is read "x_1 or x_2," where "or" is used in the inclusive sense to mean "x_1 or x_2 or both." The corresponding symbol in the PL/I character set is $|$, so that $(x_1 + x_2)$ becomes the PL/I expression $(x(1)|x(2))$. The operation OR is also called *disjunction* or *alternation*.

x_1	x_2	$x_1 + x_2$
0	0	0
0	1	1
1	0	1
1	1	1

By virtue of the above definition of OR we know that the following relationship holds between the symbols 0 and 1.

$$0 + 0 = 0, \qquad 1 + 0 = 0 + 1 = 1 + 1 = 1$$

Given literals x_1 and x_2, $x_1 x_2$ is called a *product* or *multiplication*. Thus $x_1 x_2 = 1$ if $x_1 = x_2 = 1$; otherwise $x_1 x_2 = 0$. Sometimes $x_1 x_2$ is written as $x_1 \cdot x_2$. The juxtaposition, or the symbol "$\cdot$", denotes the Boolean operation AND, and $x_1 x_2$ is read "x_1 and x_2." The corresponding symbol in the PL/I character set is $\&$, and $(x_1 x_2)$ becomes the PL/I expression $(x(1) \& x(2))$. The operation AND is also called *conjunction*.

x_1	x_2	$x_1 \cdot x_2$
0	0	0
0	1	0
1	0	0
1	1	1

Based on the above definition of AND, the following relationship is seen to hold between the symbols 0 and 1.

$$0 \cdot 0 = 0 \cdot 1 = 1 \cdot 0 = 0, \qquad 1 \cdot 1 = 1$$

TABLE 9.1

Sixteen Possible Functions of Two Literals

$x_1 x_2$	$F_0\,F_1\,F_2\,F_3$	$F_4\,F_5\,F_6\,F_7$	$F_8\,F_9\,F_{10}\,F_{11}$	$F_{12}\,F_{13}\,F_{14}\,F_{15}$
0 0	0 1 0 1	0 1 0 1	0 1 0 1	0 1 0 1
0 1	0 0 1 1	0 0 1 1	0 0 1 1	0 0 1 1
1 0	0 0 0 0	1 1 1 1	0 0 0 0	1 1 1 1
1 1	0 0 0 0	0 0 0 0	1 1 1 1	1 1 1 1

There are 16 possible functions of two literals, including the AND and OR functions. Table 9.1 lists these functions in tabular form. In Table 9.1 the two literals, x_1 and x_2, can take any one of four different combinations of values. For each combination the corresponding value for each function is listed. For example, if $x_1 = 1$ and $x_2 = 0$ (third row of table), the function $F_8(x_1, x_2) = x_1 x_2$ has the value 0, and the function $F_{14}(x_1, x_2) = x_1 + x_2$ has the value 1.

Table 9.2 lists the more common functions and identifies each operation by giving the name, symbol, and meaning associated with the usual interpretation of that function.

The above functions represent Boolean operations that are called *binary* because they always apply to a pair of variables or expressions serving as arguments of the function. A Boolean function need not be restricted to two arguments but may take a finite number of letters as arguments, provided that the function itself always assumes the value

TABLE 9.2

Names, Symbols and Meanings of Common Boolean Functions

Function	Name of operation	Symbol	Meaning
F_0	Universal falsehood	0	Logically false, contradictory
F_3	Negation	$\bar{x}_1$	Not x_1
F_6	Exclusive disjunction	$x_1 \oplus x_2$	x_1 or x_2 but not both
F_8	Conjunction	$x_1 x_2$	x_1 and x_2
F_9	Equivalence	$x_1 \equiv x_2$	x_1 if and only if x_2
F_{11}	Implication	$x_1 \supset x_2$	If x_1 then x_2
F_{13}	Converse implication	$x_1 \subset x_2$	Only if x_1 then x_2
F_{14}	Disjunction	$x_1 + x_2$	x_1 or x_2
F_{15}	Universal validity	1	Logically true, tautologous

0 or 1 for all possible assignments of truth values to the arguments. This means that there is no theoretical limitation to the number of index terms that can be used as arguments in a retrieval system. However, there are practical limitations inherent in document retrieval systems as it was pointed out in Section 9.1.

A Boolean function is said to be *inconsistent* or *invalid* if it assumes the value 0 for all possible assignments of values to all its letters. The simplest representation of an invalid Boolean function is expressed by F_0 in Table 9.2.

A Boolean function is said to be *consistent* if it assumes the value 1 for some but not all possible assignments of values to its letters.

Finally, a Boolean function is said to be universally *valid* (or tautologous) if it assumes the value 1 for *all* possible assignments. F_{15} in Table 9.2 expresses the simplest representation of any valid Boolean function.

9.3 Some Useful Equivalences

$$0 + x \equiv x, \qquad 0 \cdot x \equiv 0$$
$$1 + x \equiv 1, \qquad 1 \cdot x \equiv x$$
$$0 + 1 \equiv 1, \qquad 0 \cdot 1 \equiv 0$$
$$x + y \equiv \overline{(\bar{x} \cdot \bar{y})} \qquad \text{(DeMorgan's Law)}$$
$$x \cdot y \equiv \overline{(\bar{x} + \bar{y})} \qquad \text{(DeMorgan's Law)}$$

Observe that DeMorgan's Laws have the effect of defining the OR operation in terms of the operations of NOT and AND, and conversely, the AND operation can be defined in terms of the operations of NOT and OR. We shall see in the next section that it is possible to define any of the 16 two-valued binary functions appearing in Table 9.1 in terms of the operations of NOT, AND, and OR. However, by virtue of DeMorgan's Laws we see that even further reduction in the number of distinct basic logical operations is possible. These facts are of major importance in the application of Boolean algebra in the logical design of document retrieval systems.

Another important concept of Boolean algebra is that of *double negation*, or the complement of the complement of a set. If within the universal set of all documents represented in a given retrieval system, we define set A as follows

$$\text{Set } A = \{\text{Documents by J. Jones}\}$$

then the *complement* of set A, denoted by $\bar{A}$, is the set of all documents in the system whose author is other than J. Jones. The complement of the latter set $\bar{A}$, denoted by $\bar{\bar{A}}$, is then the set of all documents whose author is *not* other than J. Jones. In other words, the complement of the complement of A is the original set A itself. We express this fact symbolically as

$$\bar{\bar{A}} = A$$

In view of the fact that the *principle of double negation* (double complementarity) holds in Boolean algebra, that is,

$$\bar{\bar{0}} = 0, \qquad \bar{\bar{1}} = 1, \qquad \bar{\bar{f}} = f$$

DeMorgan's Laws may be rewritten as

$$\overline{x_1 + x_2} = \bar{x}_1 \cdot \bar{x}_2, \qquad \overline{x_1 \cdot x_2} = \bar{x}_1 + \bar{x}_2$$

Stated verbally, the above version of DeMorgan's Laws says that *the negation of a sum of terms is the product of the negations of the terms and the negation of a product of factors is the sum of the negations of the factors.*

DeMorgan's Laws are useful in forming the negation of a given expression. For instance, the negation of an expression containing NOT, AND, and OR operators can be formed by negating each nonnegated variable, removing the negation from each negated variable, and interchanging AND and OR operators throughout the expression. For example, applying DeMorgan's Laws yield the negation of $x_1 \bar{x}_3 + x_1 \bar{x}_2 x_4$ as

$$\overline{(x_1 \bar{x}_3 + x_1 \bar{x}_2 x_4)} = (\bar{x}_1 + x_3)(\bar{x}_1 + x_2 + \bar{x}_4)$$

We shall see later that an important application of DeMorgan's Laws occurs in the context of document retrieval systems whenever it is necessary to translate a given search query into a standard logical form containing only the operators AND, OR and NOT. Specific examples of standard logical forms are discussed in Section 9.4, and illustrations of how a given search request can be translated into these logical normal forms, using DeMorgan's Laws, are found in Section 10.4.

REMARKS ON DUALITY

DeMorgan's Laws also illustrate the existence of a *duality property* in the logic of Boolean functions. Observe that the equivalences presented at the beginning of Section 9.3 may be grouped in *dual pairs*, each member of a pair being obtainable from the other by replacing each of the operations OR and AND by the other and replacing each of the symbols 0 and 1 by the other, wherever they appear.

Thus, if in $0 + x = x$ we replace OR by AND and 0 by 1, we obtain $1 \cdot x = x$ as the dual of $0 + x = x$. In similar fashion other dual pairs can be formed.

To illustrate the duality property of Boolean algebra we group below as dual pairs all of the Boolean identities that have been considered so far.

$$
\begin{array}{ll}
\bar{0} = 1 & \bar{1} = 0 \\
0 + 0 = 0 & 1 \cdot 1 = 1 \\
0 + 1 = 1 & 1 \cdot 0 = 0 \\
1 + 0 = 1 & 0 \cdot 1 = 0 \\
1 + 1 = 1 & 0 \cdot 0 = 0 \\
0 + x = x & 1 \cdot x = x \\
1 + x = 1 & 0 \cdot x = 0 \\
\overline{x_1 + x_2} = \bar{x}_1 \cdot \bar{x}_2 & \overline{x_1 \cdot x_2} = \bar{x}_1 + \bar{x}_2
\end{array}
$$

Finally, $\bar{f} = f$ may be regarded as its own dual (self-dual) since the required interchange leaves it unaltered.

Now suppose that we are able to establish the validity of a certain Boolean identity. The *principle of duality* states that we may conclude the truth of the dual of that identity without adducing additional proof. In other words, if the principle of duality is accepted, one need concern oneself with adducing evidence for demonstrating the validity of only *one* member of a dual pair of Boolean identities. For instance, if the validity of the identity $0 + x = x$ has been established, then the validity of the dual identity, $1 \cdot x = x$, follows by the principle of duality.

Knowledge of this important principle often facilitates the application of Boolean algebra in the design of computer-based information handling systems.

9.4 Normal Form Expressions

A product (sum) of a finite number of literals in which no letter appears more than once is called a *fundamental product (sum)*. Thus $x_1 + \bar{x}_2$, $x_2 x_3$, $x_1 + x_4 + \bar{x}_6$, $\bar{x}_1 x_3 x_4$ are fundamental products and sums, whereas $x_2 x_2$, $x_3 \bar{x}_3$, $x_1 + x_1$, $x_2 + \bar{x}_2$ are not fundamental sums and products.

Of particular interest among the Boolean functions of n letters are the fundamental products (sums) containing all n of the letters as factors (terms), either negated or not. When $n = 1$, x_1 and $\bar{x}_1$ serve as such products (sums). When $n = 2$, these products (sums) are $\bar{x}_1\bar{x}_2$, $\bar{x}_1 x_2$, $x_1 \bar{x}_2$, and $x_1 x_2$ ($\bar{x}_1 + \bar{x}_2$, $\bar{x}_1 + x_2$, $x_1 + \bar{x}_2$, $x_1 + x_2$). Since each of the letters is chosen in negated or nonnegated form, the number of such products (sums) is 2^n. We call these products (sums) the *canonical products* (*sums*) of the n letters.

The characteristic property of a canonical product is that it takes on the value 1 for exactly one assignment of values of x_1 through x_n, namely the particular assignment which makes each literal of the product equal to 1.

For example, if $n = 2$, $x_1\bar{x}_2 = 1$ only when $x_1 = 1$ and $\bar{x}_2 = 1$, thus making $x_2 = 0$. If $n = 3$, $\bar{x}_1 x_2 \bar{x}_3 = 1$ only when $x_1 = 0$, $x_2 = 1$, and $x_3 = 0$. Similarly in other cases.

The characteristic property of a canonical sum is that it takes on the value 0 for exactly one assignment of values of the x's, namely the assignment which makes each literal of the sum equal to 0.

For example, if $n = 2$, $x_1 + \bar{x}_2 = 0$ only when $x_1 = 0$ and $\bar{x}_2 = 0$, thus making $x_2 = 1$. If $n = 3$, $\bar{x}_1 + x_2 + \bar{x}_3 = 0$ only when $x_1 = 1$, $x_2 = 0$, and $x_3 = 1$, and so forth.

With the above remarks serving as background, we next introduce the definitions of two basic concepts in Boolean algebra: *normal form* and *developed normal form*.

When a Boolean function is expressed as the sum (product) of a finite number of fundamental products (sums), the function is said to be expressed in disjunctive (conjunctive) *normal form*. Thus,

$$F = x_1 x_2 + \bar{x}_1 x_3 + \bar{x}_1 \bar{x}_2 x_3$$
$$G = \bar{x}_1 x_2 + x_1 \bar{x}_3$$

represent two Boolean functions that are expressed in disjunctive normal form, and

$$F = (x_1 + x_3)(\bar{x}_1 + x_2 + \bar{x}_3)(x_2 + x_3)$$
$$G = (\bar{x}_1 + \bar{x}_3)(x_1 + x_2)$$

represent the same two Boolean functions expressed in conjunctive normal form.

A disjunctive (conjunctive) normal form of a Boolean function is said to be a *developed normal form* if every fundamental product (sum) is a canonical product (sum). Thus,

$$F = x_1x_2x_3 + \bar{x}_1x_2x_3 + x_1x_2\bar{x}_3 + \bar{x}_1\bar{x}_2x_3$$

is the developed disjunctive normal form of the function one of whose disjunctive normal forms is $x_1x_2 + \bar{x}_1x_3 + \bar{x}_1\bar{x}_2x_3$, and

$$F = (x_1 + x_2 + x_3)(x_1 + x_2 + \bar{x}_3)(\bar{x}_1 + x_2 + \bar{x}_3)(\bar{x}_1 + \bar{x}_2 + \bar{x}_3)$$

is the developed conjunctive normal form of the same function.

The canonical products (sums) appearing in developed normal forms are sometimes called *canonical implicants* (*implicates*) of the functions under consideration. Thus $\bar{x}_1x_2x_3$ is a canonical implicant of the function F whose developed normal forms are shown above, and $\bar{x}_1 + x_2 + \bar{x}_3$ is a canonical implicate of the same function F.

This brings us to a remarkable theorem of Boolean algebra which has major significance for our study because of its applications in several fields including information handling and document retrieval. This is the so-called *Normal Form Theorem* of Boolean algebra.

THEOREM. *Every consistent Boolean function has at least one disjunctive (conjunctive) normal form.*

We now explain informally a procedure for converting any Boolean expression into a disjunctive (conjunctive) normal form. The procedure is as follows:

Step 1. Replace all logical operations other than AND, OR, and NOT in accordance with the following definitions.

$$x_1 \oplus x_2 = x_1\bar{x}_2 + \bar{x}_1x_2$$
$$x_1 \equiv x_2 = x_1x_2 + \bar{x}_1\bar{x}_2$$
$$x_1 \supset x_2 = \bar{x}_1 + x_2$$
$$x_1 \subset x_2 = x_1 + \bar{x}_2$$

Step 2. Apply DeMorgan's Laws and other equivalences to move the operations of NOT and AND (OR) inward so that NOT operates only on letters and AND (OR) operates only on letters and negations of letters.

Illustration

As an illustration of the procedure, consider the steps involved in converting the Boolean expression

$$(x_1 + \bar{x}_2) \supset (x_2 + \bar{x}_1)$$

into a disjunctive normal form. We proceed as follows:

Step 1. Replace the operation of implication in the expression in accordance with the appropriate definition to yield

$$\overline{(x_1 + \bar{x}_2)} + (x_2 + \bar{x}_1)$$

Step 2. Apply DeMorgan's Laws to move negation and AND operator inward as far as possible, yielding

$$\bar{x}_1 x_2 + x_2 + \bar{x}_1$$

Thus $\bar{x}_1 x_2 + x_2 + \bar{x}_1$ is a disjunctive normal form of $(x_1 + \bar{x}_2) \supset (x_2 + \bar{x}_1)$.

In similar fashion it can be shown that $\bar{x}_1 x_2$ is a disjunctive normal form of the expression

$$\bar{x}_1(x_2 + x_1 \bar{x}_2)$$

In the context of a document retrieval system the latter expression may be viewed as a search request that defines the following set of documents:

"All documents such that index term x_1 is absent from the document and either index term x_2 is present in the document or both index term x_1 is present and x_2 is absent."

Based on the fact that $\bar{x}_1 x_2$ is a disjunctive normal equivalent of the original expression, the search request could be shortened considerably as follows:

"All documents in which index term x_1 is absent and x_2 is present."

We now consider a second normal form theorem that, like the normal form theorem above, has equally wide import for its many applications in other fields of scientific activity. Insofar as library science is concerned, this second theorem provides the cornerstone for any development of the logic underlying information handling. Indeed, without the existence of this theorem, the concept of a coordinate index possessing the logical properties commonly ascribed to it would prove impossible since there would be no guarantee that any given document could always be described in terms of a unique function of the indexing terms. Moreover, without the existence of this theorem, there would be no guarantee that any given coordinate index itself represents a unique logical function, thus rendering invalid any search manipulation of the index. This is the so-called *Uniqueness Theorem* of Boolean algebra.

THEOREM. Let $x_1, x_2, \ldots, x_n$ be all the letters of the Boolean function F and let $p_0, p_1, \ldots, p_{2^n-1}$ be the 2^n canonical products obtainable by negating in all possible ways zero or more of the letters $x_1, x_2, \ldots, x_n$ in the product form $x_1 x_2 \cdots x_n$. The sequence $p_0, p_1, \ldots, p_{2^n-1}$ is so arranged that x_n is negated in alternate p's, x_{n-1} in alternate pairs, x_{n-2} in alternate groups of fours, and so on, as shown by

$$
\begin{array}{ll}
\bar{x}_1 \bar{x}_2 \cdots \bar{x}_{n-1} \bar{x}_n & p_0 \\
\bar{x}_1 \bar{x}_2 \cdots \bar{x}_{n-1} x_n & p_1 \\
\bar{x}_1 \bar{x}_2 \cdots x_{n-1} \bar{x}_n & p_2 \\
\quad \vdots & \vdots \\
x_1 x_2 \cdots x_{n-1} x_n & p_{2^n-1}
\end{array}
$$

Let $c_0, c_1, \ldots, c_{2^n-1}$ each be 0 or 1. Then for every consistent Boolean function F there is one and only one sequence $c_0, c_1, \ldots, c_{2^n-1}$ such that

$$
F = (c_0 p_0 + c_1 p_1 + \cdots + c_{2^n-1} p_{2^n-1}) \tag{9.1}
$$

We now offer two procedures for determining the right-hand side of Equation (9.1). The first is known as the "Method of Algebraic Expansion."

Method of Algebraic Expansion

The method is as follows:

1. First obtain a disjunctive normal form of F.
2. By means of the identity, $x_1 = x_1(x_2 + \bar{x}_2) = x_1 x_2 + x_1 \bar{x}_2$, expand the disjunctive form so that all letters of F appear in each of the terms, that is, expand the disjunctive form into a sum of canonical products.
3. Prefix each resulting canonical product with the symbol 1.
4. Supply all missing but possible canonical products, prefixed with 0. The result is the right-hand side of Equation (9.1).

Illustration

Let us illustrate the procedure by finding the right-hand side of Equation (9.1) for the function

$$
F = x_1 \bar{x}_2 + x_1 \bar{x}_3
$$

We begin by noting that the function is already expressed in disjunctive normal form. Next, we identify letters missing from each term (the letter

x_3 is missing from the first term and the letter x_2 from the second term). Using the identity $x_1 = x_1(x_2 + \bar{x}_2)$ as often as necessary, we rewrite the expression to include possible missing letters in each term, as

$$x_1\bar{x}_2(x_3 + \bar{x}_3) + x_1\bar{x}_3(x_2 + \bar{x}_2)$$

Expanding this expression into a sum of canonical products, and prefixing each with the symbol 1, we obtain

$$1x_1\bar{x}_2x_3 + 1x_1\bar{x}_2\bar{x}_3 + 1x_1x_2\bar{x}_3$$

Supplying missing canonical products, prefixed with 0, we finally have

$$F = 0\bar{x}_1\bar{x}_2\bar{x}_3 + 0\bar{x}_1\bar{x}_2x_3 + 0\bar{x}_1x_2\bar{x}_3 + 0\bar{x}_1x_2x_3$$
$$+ 1x_1\bar{x}_2\bar{x}_3 + 1x_1\bar{x}_2x_3 + 1x_1x_2\bar{x}_3 + 0x_1x_2x_3$$

The second method, called the "Method of Value Enumeration," consists of computing the sequence of c's by determining the value of the function for each of the possible 2^n assignments of values to all of the letters of the function.

Method of Value Enumeration

The method is as follows:

1.   Enumerate the 2^n possible substitutions of the values 0,1 for the letters $x_1, x_2, \ldots, x_n$ as

$$\xi_0, \xi_1, \ldots, \xi_{2^n-1}$$

2.   If ψ is any Boolean function of $x_1, x_2, \ldots, x_n$, denote by $\psi(\xi_k)$ the value of ψ for the substitution ξ_k.
3.   Determine the sequence of c's as follows.

$$c_0 = F(\xi_0)$$
$$c_1 = F(\xi_1)$$
$$\vdots$$
$$c_{2^n-1} = F(\xi_{2^n-1})$$

4.   Form the set of canonical products by replacing in each ξ_k all 0's by the negations of those letters taking the value 0 in ξ_k and replacing all 1's in ξ_k by those letters taking the value 1 in ξ_k. For instance, if $\xi_k = (0, 1, 0, 0)$, then the canonical product p_k associated with ξ_k is $\bar{x}_1x_2\bar{x}_3\bar{x}_4$. The sum of the combined products c_kp_k represents the desired result.

Illustration

To illustrate the method of value enumeration for determining the right-hand side of Equation (9.1), we consider the same function used in the previous illustration, namely,

$$F = x_1 \bar{x}_2 + x_1 \bar{x}_3$$

First we enumerate the eight possible substitutions of the values 0, 1 for the letters x_1, x_2, and x_3 as shown in column ξ_k of Table 9.3. Next, we compute the value of the function F for each of the eight assignments of values to the letters of F, as shown in column $F(\xi_k)$ of the table. The values which the function assumes for these assignments are shown in column c_k. Finally, column p_k displays the canonical products of F. With this information we are able to verify that F has the same expanded form as shown in the previous illustration, that is,

$$F = 0\bar{x}_1\bar{x}_2\bar{x}_3 + 0\bar{x}_1\bar{x}_2 x_3 + 0\bar{x}_1 x_2\bar{x}_3 + 0\bar{x}_1 x_2 x_3$$
$$+ 1x_1\bar{x}_2\bar{x}_3 + 1x_1\bar{x}_2 x_3 + 1x_1 x_2\bar{x}_3 + 0x_1 x_2 x_3$$

The right-hand side of Equation (9.1) is called the "developed disjunctive normal form of F" because it is a sum of canonical products.

In practice, we of course do not write down the canonical products whose coefficients c_i are 0 (since $0 \cdot x = 0$). Rather, we express as the developed disjunctive normal form of F the sum of exactly those canonical products whose coefficients c_j are 1 (deleting of course the c_j's since

TABLE 9.3

Method of Value Enumeration for $x_1\bar{x}_2 + x_1\bar{x}_3$

k	ξ_k (x_1, x_2, x_3)	$F(\xi_k)$ $F(x_1, x_2, x_3)$	$x_1\bar{x}_2 + x_1\bar{x}_3$	c_k	p_k
0	(0, 0, 0)	$F(0, 0, 0) = 0$	$1 + 0$	$1 = 0$	$\bar{x}_1\bar{x}_2\bar{x}_3$
1	(0, 0, 1)	$F(0, 0, 1) = 0$	$1 + 0$	$0 = 0$	$\bar{x}_1\bar{x}_2 x_3$
2	(0, 1, 0)	$F(0, 1, 0) = 0$	$0 + 0$	$1 = 0$	$\bar{x}_1 x_2\bar{x}_3$
3	(0, 1, 1)	$F(0, 1, 1) = 0$	$0 + 0$	$0 = 0$	$\bar{x}_1 x_2 x_3$
4	(1, 0, 0)	$F(1, 0, 0) = 1$	$1 + 1$	$1 = 1$	$x_1\bar{x}_2\bar{x}_3$
5	(1, 0, 1)	$F(1, 0, 1) = 1$	$1 + 1$	$0 = 1$	$x_1\bar{x}_2 x_3$
6	(1, 1, 0)	$F(1, 1, 0) = 1$	$0 + 1$	$1 = 1$	$x_1 x_2\bar{x}_3$
7	(1, 1, 1)	$F(1, 1, 1) = 1$	$0 + 1$	$0 = 0$	$x_1 x_2 x_3$

$1 \cdot x = x$). Thus, without loss of uniqueness, we may view the developed disjunctive normal form of a function F as the sum of the canonical products which correspond to the combinations of values of the letters at which F takes the value 1.

So viewed, the developed disjunctive normal form of the function considered in the preceding illustration becomes simply

$$F = x_1 \bar{x}_2 \bar{x}_3 + x_1 \bar{x}_2 x_3 + x_1 x_2 \bar{x}_3$$

9.5 Evaluation of Boolean Functions by Truth Tables

The method of value enumeration, as we just saw in Section 9.4, can be used to determine the developed disjunctive normal form of any Boolean function F. The method also provides the basis for the evaluation of Boolean functions by so-called *truth tables*. A Boolean function F is said to be evaluated whenever the truth value of the function is determined for each of the possible 2^n assignments of truth values to the letters of F. A truth table offers a purely mechanical means for expressing all possible combinations of values for the letters of the function and the resulting values of the function for each combination. The truth table for any function F is basically an adaptation of the columns shown in Table 9.3, and consists primarily of column ξ_k and column c_k. If the truth table technique is used to evaluate complicated functions, the construction of the truth table is best carried out in stages, in which case it may be desirable to include column $F(\xi_k)$ as an intermediate column of the truth table. The truth table for the evaluation of $x_1 \bar{x}_2 + x_1 \bar{x}_3$ is shown in Table 9.4.

If F and G are two Boolean functions of $x_1, x_2, \ldots, x_n$, the functions

TABLE 9.4

Truth Table for $x_1 \bar{x}_2 + x_1 \bar{x}_3$

x_1	x_2	x_3	$x_1 \bar{x}_2 + x_1 \bar{x}_3$
0	0	0	0
0	0	1	0
0	1	0	0
0	1	1	0
1	0	0	1
1	0	1	1
1	1	0	1
1	1	1	0

TABLE 9.5

Proof by Perfect Induction of
$\bar{x}_1(x_2 + x_1\bar{x}_2) = \bar{x}_1 x_2$

x_1	x_2	$\bar{x}_1(x_2 + x_1\bar{x}_2)$	$\bar{x}_1 x_2$
0	0	0	0
0	1	1	1
1	0	0	0
1	1	0	0

are said to be equivalent to one another if and only if they have the same truth value for all possible combinations of values for the n letters. The equivalence of two given Boolean functions may be ascertained by constructing and comparing their respective truth tables. Since equivalent functions have identical truth tables, if the resulting values for the two functions correspond, their equivalence is proved. This method of verification is known as *proof by perfect induction*. The technique is useful in document retrieval in determining whether or not the logical forms of two search requests are equivalent. Thus, in Section 9.4 we had occasion to consider two search requests whose logical forms were $\bar{x}_1(x_2 + x_1\bar{x}_2)$ and $\bar{x}_1 x_2$, respectively. Proof by perfect induction of their equivalence is shown in Table 9.5. In order to verify the validity of the assignment of the value 0 to $\bar{x}_1(x_2 + x_1\bar{x}_2)$ in the first row of the truth table, observe that $\bar{0}(0 + 0\bar{0}) = 1(0 + 01) = 1(0 + 0) = 1.0 = 0$. Similar considerations will verify the validity of the assignments shown in the other rows of the truth table, as follows.

$$\bar{0}(1 + 0\bar{1}) = 1(1 + 00) = 1(1 + 0) = 1.1 = 1$$
$$\bar{1}(0 + 1\bar{0}) = 0(0 + 11) = 0(0 + 1) = 0.1 = 0$$
$$\bar{1}(1 + 1\bar{1}) = 0(1 + 10) = 0(1 + 0) = 0.1 = 0$$

9.6 A Generalized Notation

It is sometimes convenient to introduce abbreviations for certain types of Boolean expressions. Thus when a Boolean letter x_i appears either negated or nonnegated in an expression, it is often useful to express this fact in a general way by the formula

$$x_i^{(\alpha)}$$

where $x_i^{(\alpha)}$ takes as its value either x_i or $\bar{x}_i$.

Next, when we wish to refer to the canonical product $x_1 x_2 \cdots x_n$, it is useful to express the product by the following general abbreviation

$$\prod_{i=1}^{n} x_i^{(\alpha)}$$

Similarly, we shall consider

$$\sum_{i=1}^{n} x_i^{(\alpha)}$$

to be an abbreviation for the canonical sum $x_1 + x_2 + \cdots + x_n$.

In those instances where the sum or product of letters is possibly noncanonical as for instance, $x_1 \bar{x}_2 x_4$ or $\bar{x}_2 + x_5$, we shall employ the notation

$$\prod_{i \in A} x_i^{(\alpha)}, \quad \sum_{i \in A} x_i^{(\alpha)}$$

where A is a subset of the integers $1, 2, \ldots, n$.

Finally, to indicate the general formula for an expression written in disjunctive normal form, such as the sum of products below,

$$F = \bar{x}_1 x_2 + x_1 \bar{x}_3$$
$$F = \bar{x}_1 x_2 x_3 + \bar{x}_1 x_2 \bar{x}_3 + x_1 x_2 \bar{x}_3 + x_1 \bar{x}_2 \bar{x}_3$$

we shall employ the notation

$$F = \sum_k \left(\prod_{i \in A_k} x_i^{(\alpha)} \right)$$

where $x_i^{(\alpha)}$ takes as its value x_i or $\bar{x}_i$, A_k is a subset of the integers $1, 2, \ldots, n$ and $k = 1, 2, \ldots, s$. In the formula, $\prod_{i \in A_k} x_i^{(\alpha)}$ signifies the kth product term in the disjunctive normal form of F, and $\sum_k$ for $k = 1, 2, \ldots, s$ indicates that there are s such products in the sum.

Whenever it is appropriate to employ them, these generalized abbreviations will be used in Chapter 10 in the presentation of the logical model underlying document retrieval.

EXERCISES

1. What is the defining property of the set whose elements are 2, 3, 5, 7, 11?

2. If

$$A = \{2, 3, 5, 7, 9\}$$
$$B = \{1, 3, 4, 6, 7\}$$
$$U = \{1, 2, 3, 4, 5, 6, 7, 8, 9, 10\}$$

list the members of the following sets:

(a) $\bar{A}$ (e) $A \cup \bar{B}$
(b) $\bar{B}$ (f) $\bar{A} \cap B$
(c) $A \cap B$ (g) $\overline{(A \cup B)}$
(d) $A \cup B$ (h) $\overline{(\bar{A} \cap \bar{B})}$

3. Apply DeMorgan's Laws to obtain the negations of the following expressions:

(a) $\overline{(x_1 + \bar{x}_2)} + (x_2 + \bar{x}_1)$
(b) $x_1 \bar{x}_2 \overline{(\bar{x}_1 + x_2)}$
(c) $\bar{x}_1 x_2 x_3 + x_1 \bar{x}_3$
(d) $(x_1 + \bar{x}_2)(x_1 + x_3)$
(e) $\bar{x}_1(x_2 + x_1 \bar{x}_2 x_3) + x_2 \bar{x}_3$

4. Establish that each of the pairs of identities appearing below represent a dual pair.

$$x + x = x \qquad\qquad\qquad x \cdot x = x$$
$$x_1(x_2 + x_3) = x_1 x_2 + x_1 x_3 \qquad x_1 + x_2 x_3 = (x_1 + x_2)(x_1 + x_3)$$
$$x_1 + \bar{x}_1 x_2 = x_1 + x_2 \qquad\qquad x_1(\bar{x}_1 + x_2) = x_1 x_2$$

5. Convert each of the following Boolean expressions into a disjunctive normal form:

(a) $(\bar{x}_1 + x_2) \equiv (x_1 \equiv \bar{x}_2)$
(b) $(x_1 \supset \bar{x}_2) \supset (x_1 \equiv \bar{x}_2)$

6. Use the method of algebraic expansion to derive the developed disjunctive normal form of the function below. Verify the result by using the method of value enumeration

$$F = (((x_1 \supset x_2) \supset x_3) \supset x_1 x_2)$$

7. Prove by perfect induction that

$$x_1 x_2 x_3 + x_1 \bar{x}_2 x_3 + x_1 x_2 \bar{x}_3 = x_1(x_2 + x_3)$$

8. Prove by perfect induction that

$$x_1 + \bar{x}_1 x_2 x_3 = (x_1 + x_2)(x_1 + x_3)$$

CHAPTER 10

A Logical Analysis of Document Retrieval

10.1 Introductory Remarks

In this chapter we describe a model, based on the logic of Boolean functions, that can be applied to the design and analysis of document retrieval systems. The model is generic in the sense that it validly depicts the logical structure of any document retrieval system based on coordinate indexing. Because of its universality and generality, the model may be viewed as an effort to formulate the basic principles underlying the logic of document retrieval.

As an indication of its scope, the model can determine from any conceivable logical formulation of the search request what document or documents are sought. More specifically, algorithmic procedures are described so that complete solutions can be obtained for search requests formulated in terms of the AND, OR, and NOT operators. Limitation to these operations, however, is not inherent in the formal model. Rather, this restriction is imposed on the model solely from a desire to conform to the requirements of *existing* large-scale document retrieval systems. Moreover, no effort is made to assess the potential effectiveness of this form of restricted Boolean implementation as a model for document retrieval. The general model presented herein allows for many different ways in which to implement the logic. The effectiveness of a particular implementation as a model for document retrieval depends in part on the logical form which the implementation takes. Other factors than purely logical considerations, of course, also enter into the evaluative criteria for judging document retrieval systems.

It should be noted that the present logical model is incomplete in that no account is taken of considerations of relevancy and recall. The incorporation into the model of these factors could proceed by the introduction of probability measures on the logical variables taken as Boolean sets. However, such extension of the model is beyond the scope of the present text, and the reader is referred to several excellent related articles which have appeared recently in the literature and are listed among the references at the end of the text.

As an illustration of the capability of the PL/I language for bit-string manipulation, a sample programming implementation of the model is described in Chapter 11.

The General Model

From a logical point of view document retrieval is basically concerned with devising a system of Boolean relationships among the following sets of entities:

1. A set of documents D whose subject contents are identifiable through indexing.
2. A set of index terms I for identifying the subject contents of member documents of D.
3. A set of query requests Q to be applied to the set I to produce subsets of D.

In document retrieval a request Q defines an arbitrary selection of subject contents that may or may not correspond to a description of some subset of documents of D. Thus Q can be expressed as a combination of index terms of I, and the problem is to find as the value of the request Q a subset of documents of D satisfying the combination of index terms specified by Q.

More precisely, we assume we have a set of documents D each of whose subject content is expressed as a combination of index terms from the set I. If there are n terms in our indexing vocabulary I, and m documents in D to index, the description of the subject content of each document is expressed as a Boolean function of the index terms, as

$$
\begin{aligned}
D_1 &= f_1(I_1, I_2, \ldots, I_n) \\
D_2 &= f_2(I_1, I_2, \ldots, I_n) \\
&\vdots \\
D_i &= f_i(I_1, I_2, \ldots, I_n) \\
&\vdots \\
D_m &= f_m(I_1, I_2, \ldots, I_n)
\end{aligned}
\tag{10.1}
$$

Next, we wish to retrieve from D those documents which satisfy a given request Q, where Q represents an arbitrary selection of index terms that may or may not correspond to a description of the subject contents of a subset of documents of D. In general Q may be expressed as

$$
Q = g(I_1, I_2, \ldots, I_n)
\tag{10.2}
$$

Logically speaking, the problem of document retrieval is to evaluate Q as a function of the sets of documents D. That is to say, given the system of simultaneous Boolean equations (10.1), and the additional Boolean constraint (10.2), we seek to satisfy the Boolean equation

$$
Q = h(D_1, D_2, \ldots, D_m)
\tag{10.3}
$$

So viewed, the problem of document retrieval is seen as a special instance of the more general problem of solving simultaneous Boolean equations. Let us now reformulate the problem in this broader context.

10.2   Solution of Simultaneous Boolean Equations

When restated as a problem of solving simultaneous Boolean equations, the problem of document retrieval becomes the following.

Consider a Boolean function

$$
F(D_1, D_2, \ldots, D_m; I_1, I_2, \ldots, I_n)
$$

We attempt to solve for

$$Q = g(I_1, I_2, \ldots, I_n)$$

as a function of $D_1, D_2, \ldots, D_m$, so that F will be universally valid; that is, find

$$Q = h(D_1, D_2, \ldots, D_m)$$

such that

$$F(D_1, D_2, \ldots, D_m; I_1, I_2, \ldots, I_n) = 1$$

It may be recognized that the solution of simultaneous Boolean equations is but a special instance of the more general case of solving simultaneous equations. Another instance is that of solving simultaneous *linear* equations. In all such instances the underlying problem remains the same. The problem is as follows: Given a system of equations which defines a set of dependent or function variables in terms of a set of independent or argument variables, to find an alternate set of equations in which the roles of the independent and dependent variables are reversed such that both systems of equations are satisfied.

As may be expected, techniques for the solution of systems of simultaneous equations differ generally, depending on whether the system is linear, quadratic, Boolean, a set of inequalities (linear programming), and so on. It is not the purpose of the present discussion to consider general logical techniques for the solution of simultaneous Boolean equations. Rather, suffice it to say that such general techniques do exist, but we shall confine attention here to a consideration of a specific logical technique which is to be applied to a specific form of implementation for the Boolean equations.

For the purposes of present discussion we choose to implement the Boolean equations in a manner that allows for their easy representation as binary vectors or bit strings. In this way we are able to illustrate in a useful manner some of the facilities for bit-string manipulation in PL/I for implementing document retrieval.

Before turning to a consideration of the logic required for representing Boolean equations as binary vectors, we emphasize that the logical model under discussion plays a fundamental role in retrieval systems based on coordinate indexing in the sense that it provides the underlying conceptual basis for the formulation and searching of indexing systems involving coordination of terms. We also emphasize the fundamental importance of the Uniqueness Theorem of Boolean Algebra, presented in Section 9.4, as the cornerstone of both the logical model and document retrieval itself.

10.3 Representation of Boolean Equations

Canonical Products and Boolean Equations

In the particular implementation of the logical model with which we shall be concerned, the subject content of each document will always be expressed in the form of a *canonical product* in n letters, each letter representing an index term or its negation. The advantage of recording the description of a document in this manner is that for each index term we can always tell whether it is present or absent in the document. However, as a matter of convenience we may on occasion shorten a canonical product by deleting all occurrences of negations of index terms. The abbreviated noncanonical product would thus contain only index terms which are affirmed to be present in the document and would omit explicit reference to index terms which are absent from the document.

To illustrate, suppose that our indexing vocabulary consists of six key terms,

aldehyde, carbohydrate, enzyme, ester, hydrocarbon, polymer

and we have four documents whose subject content is assumed to be indexed as

$$D_1 = \bar{I}_1 \ I_2 \ I_3 \ \bar{I}_4 \ I_5 \ \bar{I}_6$$
$$D_2 = I_1 \ \bar{I}_2 \ I_3 \ I_4 \ \bar{I}_5 \ I_6$$
$$D_3 = I_1 \ \bar{I}_2 \ \bar{I}_3 \ I_4 \ I_5 \ \bar{I}_6 \qquad (10.4)$$
$$D_4 = \bar{I}_1 \ I_2 \ I_3 \ \bar{I}_4 \ \bar{I}_5 \ I_6$$

The system of Boolean equations (10.4) is viewed as representing the outcome of indexing the four documents. As a result, one would know that document D_1, for instance, contains keywords "carbohydrate," "enzyme," and "hydrocarbon," but does not contain keywords "aldehyde," "ester," and "polymer." Similarly for documents D_2, D_3, and D_4.

If preferred, the result of indexing each document could have been expressed in the form of an abbreviated noncanonical product of index terms. In the place of the system of Boolean equations (10.4), the result of indexing the documents could have been expressed as

$$D_1 = I_2 \ I_3 \ I_5$$
$$D_2 = I_1 \ I_3 \ I_4 \ I_6$$
$$D_3 = I_1 \ I_4 \ I_5$$
$$D_4 = I_2 \ I_3 \ I_6$$

However, it should be understood that from the standpoint of the logical requirements of the model, any system of abbreviated Boolean equations such as the ones above must always be viewed as a shorthand notation for a system of full canonical products as shown in (10.4).

So far we have seen that for document retrieval the general form of the index is viewed as a system of m Boolean equations,

$$D_1 = f_1(I_1, I_2, \ldots, I_n)$$
$$\vdots$$
$$D_m = f_m(I_1, I_2, \ldots, I_n)$$

which in the present model of document retrieval takes the explicit logical form of a set of full canonical products, as follows.

$$D_1 = \prod_{i=1}^{n} I_{1_i}^{(\alpha)}$$
$$\vdots \qquad\qquad (10.5)$$
$$D_m = \prod_{i=1}^{n} I_{m_i}^{(\alpha)}$$

where $I_i^{(\alpha)}$ takes as its value either I_i or $\bar{I}_i$. (An explanation of $\prod$ notation is provided in Section 9.6.)

10.4   Search Requests as Normal Form Expressions

We have also seen that the formulation of a search request Q may involve any logical combination of index terms and so assumes the form of an arbitrary selection of index terms which may or may not correspond to the description of the subject content of a subset of documents of D. The search request, we have seen, is thus expressed in its most general form as

$$Q = g(I_1, I_2, \ldots, I_n)$$

where $g(I_1, I_2, \ldots, I_n)$ represents any well-formed Boolean function over the variables $I_1, I_2, \ldots, I_n$.

Without loss of generality, we shall require as a condition of the present model of document retrieval that the search request—no matter in what logical form it is originally formulated—always be converted to an expression in *disjunctive normal form*. That is to say, we shall always demand the translation of Q into the following explicit form.

$$Q = \sum_k \left(\prod_{i \in A_k} I_i^{(\alpha)} \right) \qquad (10.6)$$

where $I_i^{(\alpha)}$ takes as its value I_i or $\bar{I}_i$, A_k is a subset of the integers $1, 2, \ldots, n$ and $k = 1, 2, \ldots, s$. (An explanation of $\prod$ and $\sum$ notation is provided in Section 9.6.)

That no loss of generality is involved in making this requirement a part of the model for document retrieval follows from the well-known Normal Form Theorem of Boolean Algebra discussed in Section 9.4.

EXAMPLE OF A SEARCH REQUEST

Suppose we are to search the document file in order to retrieve those documents satisfying the following request Q:

"carbohydrate or enzyme, but the latter if and only if either hydrocarbon is included or polymer is excluded"

The logical structure of the search request is revealed more clearly when Q is expressed symbolically as

$$Q = I_2 + I_3(I_3 \equiv (I_5 + \bar{I}_6))$$

The problem is to convert Q into an equivalent logical expression in disjunctive normal form. Recall from Section 9.4 that this may be done as follows:

$$Q = I_2 + I_3(I_3(I_5 + \bar{I}_6) + \bar{I}_3\overline{(I_5 + \bar{I}_6)})$$
$$Q = I_2 + I_3(I_3 I_5 + I_3 \bar{I}_6 + \bar{I}_3 \bar{I}_5 I_6)$$
$$Q = I_2 + I_3 I_5 + I_3 \bar{I}_6$$

The bottom expression thus represents a logically equivalent form of the original search request, but it now conforms to the requirement of the document retrieval model that all search requests should be ultimately formulated in disjunctive normal form.

10.5   Evaluating Search Requests

We come to the crux of the document retrieval problem; namely, the evaluation of Q in terms of a subset of documents of D.

Given the coordinate index (that is, an $m \times n$ system of Boolean equations) in which each of m documents is expressed as a canonical product of n index terms and negations of index terms, and given a search request Q representing an arbitrary selection of index terms expressed in disjunctive normal form, the problem is to search through the coordinate index in order to evaluate Q in terms of possible subsets of documents in D which satisfy the selection of terms formulated in Q.

Or to state the problem in another way, we formulate a request Q in terms of an arbitrary selection of index terms, as

$$Q = g(I_1, I_2, \ldots, I_n)$$

and we seek a solution to the Boolean equation

$$Q = h(D_1, D_2, \ldots, D_m)$$

such that the solution does not violate any of the m canonical products in the coordinate index and yet satisfies the logic of the request Q as specified by the particular selection of index terms.

To illustrate the problem we use the 4×6 coordinate index appearing earlier in Equation (10.4) in connection with the index terms "aldehyde," "carbohydrate," and so on. Suppose that Q consists of a search request that defines the set of all documents on "aldehyde and ester but not polymer." Thus Q is expressed symbolically in disjunctive normal form as

$$Q = I_1 I_4 \bar{I}_6$$

Now we seek a solution to the Boolean equation

$$Q = h(D_1, D_2, \ldots, D_m)$$

Searching through the 4×6 coordinate index we see that this equation has only one solution which satisfies both the search request and the four canonical products comprising the coordinate index; namely,

$$Q = D_3$$

Any other solution, such as $Q = D_1 + D_2$, is invalid since it fails to satisfy simultaneously the given search request and the canonical products of the coordinate index. We shall return to this illustration in Section 10.7 for a closer look at some of its ramifications for the logical model.

For any solution to the Boolean equation

$$Q = h(D_1, D_2, \ldots, D_m)$$

to be useful within the framework of document retrieval, it will be convenient to assume that the solution takes the logical form of a *fundamental sum* over the letters $D_1, D_2, \ldots, D_m$. That is to say,

$$Q = \sum_{i \in A} D_i. \tag{10.7}$$

where A is any subset of the integers $1, 2, \ldots, m$.

10.6   General Formulation of the Problem

The problem of document retrieval can now be rigorously formulated as follows.

Given a coordinate index of $m \times n$ canonical products,

$$D_1 = \prod_{i=1}^{n} I_{1i}^{(\alpha)}$$
$$\vdots$$
$$D_m = \prod_{i=1}^{n} I_{mi}^{(\alpha)}$$
(10.5)

and given a search request Q,

$$Q = \sum_{k} \left(\prod_{i \in A_k} I_i^{(\alpha)} \right)$$
(10.6)

we seek to find a solution,

$$Q = \sum_{i \in A} D_i$$
(10.7)

such that

$$F(D_1, D_2, \ldots, D_m; I_1, I_2, \ldots, I_n) = 1$$
(10.8)

To continue with the discussion of the model, it remains for us to characterize $F(D_1, D_2, \ldots, D_m; I_1, I_2, \ldots, I_n)$ in Equation (10.8) in a way that will be meaningful in the context of the document retrieval problem. It should be recognized, however, that the characterization of F is by no means unique. What is required, from a logical point of view, is simply that $F(D_1, D_2, \ldots, D_m; I_1, I_2, \ldots, I_n)$, however characterized, should be *universally valid*. We shall offer one characterization of F. However, *it should be recognized that the multiplicity of valid forms of F imbues the model with degrees of freedom and accounts for why, on the surface at least, there seem to be different kinds of document retrieval systems all based on coordinate indexing.*

It should also be observed that a close connection exists between the form of characterization of F and solving Equation (10.7) in the sense that the logical form of F determines the method of solution for solving Equation (10.7). *This fact also serves to explain why in actual practice different document retrieval systems employ different methods of solution for evaluating the search request.*

Let us now turn to a particular characterization of F and determine the method of solution for evaluating search requests based on this characterization.

10.7   A Characterization of F and Method of Request Evaluation Based on F

We seek a characterization of F such that $F(D_1, D_2, \ldots, D_m; I_1, I_2, \ldots, I_n)$ will be universally valid. Such a characterization will provide a general method for solving the equation

$$Q = h(D_1, D_2, \ldots, D_m)$$

Needless to say, with an explicit method available for evaluating search requests, the model of document retrieval we have presented here will have assumed its final and most important determination.

In order to arrive at a valid characterization of F, let us first turn to the preceding illustration of the model presented in Section 10.5 and examine the logical relationship that holds between the subject content of the document(s) designated as the solution variable(s) and the search request. In that illustration the coordinate index consisted of four canonical products each containing six index terms, the search request was formulated as $Q = I_1 I_4 \bar{I}_6$, and the entry in the coordinate index corresponding to the solution variable $Q = D_3$ was given to be $I_1 \bar{I}_2 \bar{I}_3 I_4 I_5 \bar{I}_6$.

It can be seen from the illustration that the relationship holding between the description of document D_3, which is the solution variable, and the search request is one of *logical implication*. That is to say, D_3 logically implies Q as follows

$$[I_1 \bar{I}_2 \bar{I}_3 I_4 I_5 \bar{I}_6 \supset I_1 I_4 \bar{I}_6] = 1$$

Moreover, it is seen that this relationship holds only between the description of document D_3 and the search request Q, and between none of the other documents in the coordinate index and Q. From the standpoint of common sense this relationship should not be surprising since the request Q did specify documents containing keywords I_1 and I_4 and not containing I_6, and document D_3, and D_3 alone, does indeed contain precisely this combination of keywords among others. What would be truly surprising is that the relation of logical implication did not hold between D_3 and Q, or that it were to hold, say, between D_1 and Q!

It is this relationship (that is, logical implication), rooted in common sense as we have now seen, that forms the basis for our particular characterization of F. Moreover, the relationship meets the desired requirement that F be so characterized that $F(D_1, D_2, \ldots, D_m; I_1, I_2, \ldots, I_n)$ will be universally valid, since the operation of logical implication is itself universally valid.

With these considerations in mind we make the further observation, which can also be confirmed by common sense, that *every document whose description in the coordinate index logically implies the subject content of the search request is a solution variable satisfying the search request.* Conversely, for every document known to be a solution variable, its description in the coordinate index will logically imply the subject content of the search request.

We may express this symbolically by saying that for every document D_j that appears in the coordinate index as a solution variable satisfying Q, the following is the case.

$$\left[\prod_{i=1}^{n} I_{j_i}^{(\alpha)} \supset \sum_{k} \left(\prod_{i \in A_k} I_i^{(\alpha)} \right) \right] = 1 \qquad (10.9)$$

From Equation (10.9) it is possible to establish the following.

THEOREM.   A necessary and sufficient condition that equation $Q = \sum_{i \in A} D_i$ have a solution is that there exists at least one document D_j in the co-ordinate index such that the document description of D_j, namely, $\prod_{i=1}^{n} I_{j_i}^{(\alpha)}$, logically implies the search request $Q = \sum_k (\prod_{i \in A_k} I_i^{(\alpha)})$. That is to say, $Q = \sum_{i \in A} D_i$ will have a solution if and only if the following is the case.

$$\sum_{j=1}^{m} \left[\prod_{i=1}^{n} I_{j_i}^{(\alpha)} \supset \sum_{k} \left(\prod_{i \in A_k} I_i^{(\alpha)} \right) \right] = 1$$

By virtue of the equality $D_j = \prod_{i=1}^{n} I_{j_i}^{(\alpha)}$, we may substitute D_j for the antecedents in the above equation to obtain

$$\sum_{j=1}^{m} \left[D_j \supset \sum_{k} \left(\prod_{i \in A_k} I_i^{(\alpha)} \right) \right] = 1 \qquad (10.10)$$

Equation (10.10) is the characterization of F we seek in the model of document retrieval such that $F(D_1, D_2, \ldots, D_m; I_1, I_2, \ldots, I_n)$ will be universally valid.

With this characterization of F in hand, we next consider the method of solution for the evaluation of the search request based on the above characterization.

We begin with a formal statement of the problem, as follows: Given the coordinate index

$$D_1 = \prod_{i=1}^{n} I_{1_i}^{(\alpha)}$$
$$\vdots$$
$$D_m = \prod_{i=1}^{n} I_{m_i}^{(\alpha)}$$

and given the search request Q

$$Q = g(I_1, I_2, \ldots, I_n)$$

we wish to solve for

$$Q = h(D_1, D_2, \ldots, D_m)$$

such that

$$((D_1 \supset Q) + (D_2 \supset Q) + \cdots + (D_m \supset Q)) = 1$$

Fundamental to the method for solving the next-to-last equation above will be a means for testing whether D_1 logically implies Q, or D_2 logically implies Q, ..., or D_m logically implies Q, as required in the last equation above. A speedy and direct method will now be explained for testing for logical implication. The method makes use of some concepts defined in Section 9.4, a new definition and the following theorem.

DEFINITION. Given fundamental products φ and ψ, then φ *subsumes* ψ if the letters and negations of letters whose product is ψ are among the letters and negations of letters whose product is φ. For example, $I_1 \bar{I}_2 I_3 I_4 I_5 \bar{I}_6$ subsumes $I_1 I_4 \bar{I}_6$ and does not subsume $\bar{I}_1 I_5 I_6$.

THEOREM. Given fundamental products φ, ψ_1, ψ_2, ..., ψ_m, then φ logically implies a sum of products $\sum \psi_i$, that is,

$$(\varphi \supset \psi_1 + \psi_2 + \cdots + \psi_m) = 1$$

if and only if φ subsumes either ψ_1, or ψ_2, ..., or ψ_m. For example, $\bar{I}_1 I_2 I_3 \bar{I}_4 \bar{I}_5 \bar{I}_6$ logically implies $I_2 + I_3 I_5 + I_3 \bar{I}_6$; that is,

$$(\bar{I}_1 I_2 I_3 \bar{I}_4 \bar{I}_5 \bar{I}_6 \supset I_2 + I_3 I_5 + I_3 \bar{I}_6) = 1$$

since $\bar{I}_1 I_2 I_3 \bar{I}_4 \bar{I}_5 \bar{I}_6$ subsumes I_2 (it also subsumes $I_3 \bar{I}_6$).

Our logical model is now complete, and we may state a full method of solution for document retrieval based on coordinate indexing, as follows:

Step 1. For each document entry D_j in the index write the full canonical product of index terms and negations of index terms describing the subject content of the document.

Step 2. Write the search request Q in terms of the desired selection of index terms in disjunctive normal form.

Step 3. Construct for each D_j an auxiliary implicational formula whose antecedent is the canonical product of index terms describing the content of D_j and whose consequent is the search request Q; that is,

$$\prod_{i=1}^{n} I_{j_i}^{(\alpha)} \supset \sum_k \left(\prod_{i \in A_k} I_i^{(\alpha)} \right)$$

Step 4. Determine for each D_j whether its auxiliary implicational formula is universally valid.

Step 5. Select as solution variables satisfying the search request Q only those D_j's whose auxiliary implicational formulas are valid.

10.8   Illustration of the Method

Let us apply the procedure to several examples.

EXAMPLE 1

Suppose that our indexing vocabulary consists of the six keywords "aldehyde" through "polymer" as illustrated before, and that we have five documents whose subject content are indexed as follows.

$$D_1 = I_1 \, I_2 \, I_4$$
$$D_2 = I_2 \, I_3 \, I_5$$
$$D_3 = I_1 \, I_3$$
$$D_4 = I_4 \, I_5 \, I_6$$
$$D_5 = I_3 \, I_4 \, I_6$$

The file is to be accessed to provide a list of documents satisfying the following request:

"carbohydrate or enzyme, but the latter if and only if either hydrocarbon is included or polymer is excluded"

SOLUTION

Step 1. The index entries are rewritten as full canonical products as follows.

$$D_1 = I_1 \, I_2 \, \bar{I}_3 \, I_4 \, \bar{I}_5 \, \bar{I}_6$$
$$D_2 = \bar{I}_1 \, I_2 \, I_3 \, \bar{I}_4 \, I_5 \, \bar{I}_6$$
$$D_3 = I_1 \, \bar{I}_2 \, I_3 \, \bar{I}_4 \, \bar{I}_5 \, \bar{I}_6$$
$$D_4 = \bar{I}_1 \, \bar{I}_2 \, \bar{I}_3 \, I_4 \, I_5 \, I_6$$
$$D_5 = \bar{I}_1 \, \bar{I}_2 \, I_3 \, I_4 \, \bar{I}_5 \, I_6$$

Step 2. The search request, which in its original formulation takes the logical form

$$Q = I_2 + I_3(I_3 \equiv (I_5 + \bar{I}_6))$$

is translated into disjunctive normal form as

$$Q = I_2 + I_3 I_5 + I_3 \bar{I}_6$$

Steps 3 and 4. For each document entry in the index we construct the required auxiliary implicational formula and then test the formula by the method of subsumption to determine whether it is universally valid.

$$(I_1 I_2 \bar{I}_3 I_4 \bar{I}_5 \bar{I}_6 \supset I_2 + I_3 I_5 + I_3 \bar{I}_6) = 1$$
$$(\bar{I}_1 I_2 I_3 \bar{I}_4 I_5 \bar{I}_6 \supset I_2 + I_3 I_5 + I_3 \bar{I}_6) = 1$$
$$(I_1 \bar{I}_2 I_3 \bar{I}_4 \bar{I}_5 \bar{I}_6 \supset I_2 + I_3 I_5 + I_3 \bar{I}_6) = 1$$
$$(\bar{I}_1 \bar{I}_2 \bar{I}_3 I_4 I_5 I_6 \supset I_2 + I_3 I_5 + I_3 \bar{I}_6) = 0$$
$$(\bar{I}_1 \bar{I}_2 I_3 I_4 \bar{I}_5 I_6 \supset I_2 + I_3 I_5 + I_3 \bar{I}_6) = 0$$

Step 5. From the outcome of testing for validity above we see that D_1, D_2, and D_3 represent document entries in the index that satisfy Q; that is,

$$Q = D_1 + D_2 + D_3$$

EXAMPLE 2

The above file is to be accessed to provide a set of documents satisfying the following combination of index terms:

"carbohydrate or polymer, but not enzyme"

SOLUTION

Step 1. Same as in Example 1 above.
Step 2. $Q = (I_2 + I_6)\bar{I}_3 = I_2 \bar{I}_3 + \bar{I}_3 I_6$.
Steps 3 and 4. $(I_1 I_2 \bar{I}_3 I_4 \bar{I}_5 \bar{I}_6 \supset I_2 \bar{I}_3 + \bar{I}_3 I_6) = 1$
$$(\bar{I}_1 I_2 I_3 \bar{I}_4 I_5 \bar{I}_6 \supset I_2 \bar{I}_3 + \bar{I}_3 I_6) = 0$$
$$(I_1 \bar{I}_2 I_3 \bar{I}_4 \bar{I}_5 \bar{I}_6 \supset I_2 \bar{I}_3 + \bar{I}_3 I_6) = 0$$
$$(\bar{I}_1 \bar{I}_2 \bar{I}_3 I_4 I_5 I_6 \supset I_2 \bar{I}_3 + \bar{I}_3 I_6) = 1$$
$$(\bar{I}_1 \bar{I}_2 I_3 I_4 \bar{I}_5 I_6 \supset I_2 \bar{I}_3 + \bar{I}_3 I_6) = 0$$

Step 5. $Q = D_1 + D_4$.

Hence, documents D_1 and D_4 satisfy the request.

EXAMPLE 3

The same file is to be accessed on behalf of the following request:

"polymer only if ester; otherwise aldehyde but not hydrocarbon"

SOLUTION

Step 1.   Same as in Example 1.
Step 2.   The request is basically composed of two parts:

(i)   "polymer only if ester," and
(ii) if none of the documents should satisfy (i), then "aldehyde but not hydrocarbon."

Accordingly, we have

$$Q_1 = I_6 \supset I_4 = \bar{I}_4 \bar{I}_6 + I_4 \bar{I}_6 + I_4 I_6 \cong I_4 I_6$$
$$Q_2 = I_1 \bar{I}_5$$

where $\bar{I}_4 \bar{I}_6$ and $I_4 \bar{I}_6$ are omitted in the translation of Q_1 to disjunctive normal form, based on an assumption that the syntax of the request Q_1 suggests no interest in documents *not* containing the keyword "polymer."
Steps 3 *and* 4.

$$(I_1 I_2 \bar{I}_3 I_4 \bar{I}_5 \bar{I}_6 \supset I_4 I_6) = 0$$
$$(\bar{I}_1 I_2 I_3 \bar{I}_4 I_5 \bar{I}_6 \supset I_4 I_6) = 0$$
$$(I_1 \bar{I}_2 I_3 \bar{I}_4 \bar{I}_5 \bar{I}_6 \supset I_4 I_6) = 0$$
$$(\bar{I}_1 \bar{I}_2 \bar{I}_3 I_4 I_5 I_6 \supset I_4 I_6) = 1$$
$$(\bar{I}_1 \bar{I}_2 I_3 I_4 \bar{I}_5 I_6 \supset I_4 I_6) = 1$$

$$(I_1 I_2 \bar{I}_3 I_4 \bar{I}_5 \bar{I}_6 \supset I_1 \bar{I}_5) = 1$$
$$(\bar{I}_1 I_2 I_3 \bar{I}_4 I_5 \bar{I}_6 \supset I_1 \bar{I}_5) = 0$$
$$(I_1 \bar{I}_2 I_3 \bar{I}_4 \bar{I}_5 \bar{I}_6 \supset I_1 \bar{I}_5) = 1$$
$$(\bar{I}_1 \bar{I}_2 \bar{I}_3 I_4 I_5 I_6 \supset I_1 \bar{I}_5) = 0$$
$$(\bar{I}_1 \bar{I}_2 I_3 I_4 \bar{I}_5 I_6 \supset I_1 \bar{I}_5) = 0$$

Step 5.

$$Q_1 = D_4 + D_5$$
$$Q_2 = D_1 + D_3$$

In view of the phraseology of the request—" Q_1; otherwise Q_2 "—it could be argued that only documents D_4 and D_5 satisfy the request, and documents D_1 and D_3 should be considered only if $Q_1 = 0$.

EXERCISES

1. Given the set of simultaneous Boolean equations below

$$AB + XY = B(A + C)$$
$$\bar{C} + \bar{X} = \bar{B} + \bar{Y}\bar{C}$$
$$B + Y = X + A + C$$

show that $X = B$ and $Y = A\bar{B} + C$ represent a valid solution of these equations.

2. Given the set of simultaneous Boolean equations below

$$\bar{B}X = Y\bar{C}$$
$$\bar{A}X = \bar{A}BY$$
$$\bar{Y} + \bar{C}X = \bar{C}$$
$$X + Y + C = YC$$

show that $X = BC$ and $Y = C$ represent a valid solution of the equations.

3. Solve the set of simultaneous Boolean equations below for B

$$AB = 0$$
$$A + B = 1$$

4. Solve the Boolean equation below for B

$$AB + \bar{A}\bar{B} = C$$

5. Suppose that we have an abbreviated coordinate index as shown below.

$$D_1 = I_2 \ I_3 \ I_5$$
$$D_2 = I_1 \ I_3 \ I_4 \ I_6$$
$$D_3 = I_1 \ I_4 \ I_5$$
$$D_4 = I_2 \ I_3 \ I_6$$

Provide the set of documents having keywords I_1 and I_4 but not I_6.

6. Suppose that we have 15 documents whose subject content are indexed as follows:

D_1: City government, police protection, taxes
D_2: Congress, politics, taxes, welfare programs
D_3: City government, police protection, street lighting
D_4: Civil rights, city government, politics
D_5: City government, economics politics, welfare programs
D_6: Congress, education, taxes, welfare programs
D_7: Economics, street lighting
D_8: City government, police protection, politics
D_9: Congress, economics, welfare programs
D_{10}: Civil rights, city government, Congress
D_{11}: Street lighting, taxes
D_{12}: City government, police protection, politics
D_{13}: Economics, education, welfare programs
D_{14}: Congress, economics, education, taxes
D_{15}: Civil rights, Congress, economics

Construct a coordinate index for the documents and provide a list of the documents satisfying the following request:

"civil rights, and either city government or police protection"

7. Using the coordinate index in Exercise 6, provide a set of the documents satisfying the following combination of index terms:

"education or welfare programs, but if the latter only if either taxes or Congress is included"

8. Again using the coordinate index in Exercise 6, provide the set of documents satisfying the following request:

"Congress and police protection"

CHAPTER 11

Binary Vectors, Bit String Manipulation, and Document Retrieval

11.1   Bit Strings

PL/I has the ability to consider a combination such as "10101" not only as a character representation but also as a bit string. Since bit strings have the same properties as the character strings discussed in Chapter 4, some means must be provided to distinguish them from character strings. This distinction is made by defining a bit-string constant as a series of zeros and ones enclosed within single quotation marks and followed by the letter B. Following are examples of bit strings.

'1'B
'010101111'B
'11111'B
(5) '1'B

The third and fourth examples above represent two ways of writing the same bit-string constant. In the fourth example, the integer in parentheses specifies how many times the enclosed sequence of 0 and 1 digits is to be repeated.

The DECLARE statement for a bit-string variable is

DECLARE name BIT (8);

where "name" is an identifier representing an internal storage location for storing an eight-bit string constant.

One way of interpreting the bits in a string is to consider 0 as a state of a condition and 1 as another state. For example, if in a document retrieval system a bit string is associated with each index term and each bit in such a string represents a document in the file, then the binary digit (bit) 1 could correspond to those documents indexed by the term in question and the bit 0 would correspond to those documents in the file not so indexed by the given term. Thus, if the bit string for a given index term is

'101001'B

then the total number of documents in the file is 6, and documents 1, 3, and 6 are indexed by the given term and documents 2, 4, and 5 are not indexed by the particular term.

Alternatively, a document retrieval system could be organized so that a bit string is associated with each document in the file and each bit in such a string represents the presence or absence of an index term in the document. In this case, if the bit string for a given document is

'11010'B

then the total number of terms in the index is 5, and the given document is indexed under terms 1, 2, and 4 but the document does not contain index terms 3 and 5.

The approaches above represent two basic ways of organizing the coordinate index in a document retrieval system. In the latter case the coordinate index is said to be organized as a *direct file*. In the former case it is said to be organized as an *inverted file*. We shall have occasion to provide further comments on these two file organizations in Section 11.3.

11.2 BOOL, UNSPEC, and STRING Functions

The BOOL Function

The built-in functions LENGTH, SUBSTR, and INDEX, presented in Chapter 5, can also be used for bit strings. In addition to these functions, PL/I provides a very powerful function that is specifically intended for bit-string manipulation. This function is called BOOL and has the basic form

BOOL (arg 1, arg 2, arg 3)

where "arg 1" and "arg 2" are bit strings of arbitrary length (padded, if necessary, to ensure that their lengths are equal), and "arg 3" is a four-bit string which defines a Boolean operation that is applied to the strings of arg 1 and arg 2 to produce a new string equal in length to the larger of arg 1 and arg 2.

The BOOL function operates as follows. Corresponding bit positions of arg 1 and arg 2 are examined in accordance with the Boolean table that follows to determine whether a 0 or a 1 is generated in the corresponding bit position of the new string.

Ith bit of arg 1	Ith bit of arg 2	Ith bit of new string
0	0	First bit of arg 3
0	1	Second bit of arg 3
1	0	Third bit of arg 3
1	1	Fourth bit of arg 3

Whenever the ith bits of arg 1 and arg 2 are 0 and 0, respectively, the ith bit of the new string is the same as the first bit of arg 3; if the ith bits of args 1 and 2 are 0 and 1, the ith bit of the new string is the same as the second bit of arg 3; if the ith bits of args 1 and 2 are 1 and 0, the ith bit of the new string is the same as the third bit of arg 3; and finally, if the ith bits of args 1 and 2 are 1 and 1, the ith bit of the new string is the same as the fourth bit of arg 3.

As an illustration, consider the assignment statement

Z = BOOL (X, Y, '1001'B);

where X and Y are bit-string variables having the values

X = '101'B   Y = '11001'B

The assignment of a bit string for z proceeds in accordance with the following Boolean table.

x_i	y_i	z_i
0	0	1
0	1	0
1	0	0
1	1	1

As a result, the value of z becomes the bit string

$$z = \text{`10010'}\text{B}$$

An application of the BOOL function is provided in Section 11.4 in SAMPLE PROGRAM 19: RETRIEVE1.

The UNSPEC Function

UNSPEC is a built-in function used to obtain the internal bit representation of a given identifier. The general form of the function is

$$\text{UNSPEC (arg x)}$$

where " arg x " is any constant or identifier used in PL/I. For example, the coding

$$\text{B} = \text{UNSPEC (A)};$$
$$\text{PUT LIST (B)};$$

prints the internal bit representation of the variable A. If A is a one-character string variable having as its value the letter "A", then B has as its value an eight-bit string constant corresponding to the internal representation of the letter "A" (see Table 4.1 for the internal representation of PL/I characters).

The UNSPEC function can also be used as a pseudo-variable in a manner similar to that discussed in Section 5.7 for the SUBSTR function.

In computer installations having only uppercase print capability, the UNSPEC function can be used to convert data stored internally as upper- and lowercase characters to a uniform uppercase format ready for printing by uppercase printers. The conversion is accomplished by use of the Boolean operator OR and the internal representation of the blank symbol, since the internal representation of any uppercase character can be obtained by OR-ing the internal representations of the corresponding lowercase character and the blank symbol. For example, the EBCDIC representations for the symbol " blank " and the lowercase letter " a" are

$$a = 10\ 00\ 00\ 01$$
$$\not{b} = 01\ 00\ 00\ 00$$

OR-ing the EBCDIC representations of lower case " a " and " blank " yields an eight-bit string which is identical with the EBCDIC representation for the uppercase letter "A":

$$(a \,|\, \not{b}) = 11\ 00\ 00\ 01$$
$$A\quad = 11\ 00\ 00\ 01$$

The following code represents a simple illustration of how the UNSPEC function may be used with OR-logic to convert mixed-case alphanumeric character data to upper case character data for printout. The code also illustrates the use of UNSPEC as a pseudo-variable:

DECLARE TEXT CHAR (20) VAR, BLANK CHAR (20) VAR INIT ((20)' ');
UNSPEC (TEXT) = UNSPEC (TEXT) | UNSPEC (SUBSTR (BLANK, 1, LENGTH (TEXT)));
PUT SKIP LIST (TEXT);

The STRING Function

The STRING function concatenates the elements of an array or structure variable into a single string element. The general form of the STRING function is

STRING (arg x)

where " arg x " is one or more elements of an array or structure variable having as values strings composed entirely of character data or entirely of bit data. Like the SUBSTR and UNSPEC functions, the STRING function can also serve as a pseudo-variable. The following example illustrates the use of the STRING function.

DECLARE BOOKNO (3) CHAR (5) VAR;
GET LIST (BOOKNO);
PUT EDIT (STRING (BOOKNO)) (A);

If the input stream consists of the character strings

'PL13' 'PH12' 'PD145'

then the printed output of the coding above would be the concatenated character string

PL13PH12PD145

To accomplish the same effect without the use of the STRING function, longer coding would be required, as illustrated below.

DECLARE (BOOKNO (3) CHAR (5), LIST CHAR (20)) VAR;
LIST = ' ';
DO I = 1 TO 3;
GET LIST (BOOKNO (I));
LIST = LIST || BOOKNO (I);
END;
PUT LIST (LIST);

11.3 Organization of a Coordinate Index as Binary Vectors

To illustrate the use of the BOOL function, binary vectors, and bit-string manipulation, we consider how the logical model developed in Section 10.7 for the design and analysis of document retrieval systems may be implemented in terms of a PL/I program. It should be observed that the implementation of the model in terms of computer programming can take many different forms. Moreover, in ongoing operational systems of document retrieval, the number of documents to be indexed and the number of terms in the indexing vocabulary do not remain fixed, and provision must be made for enlarging the coordinate index. New documents continually enter the system and vocabulary building is an ongoing process.

For purposes of illustrating how binary vectors lend themselves to bit-string manipulation involving the BOOL function, we have chosen a particular form of implementation of the document retrieval model which is based on organizing the coordinate index as a *direct file*. As was suggested in Section 11.1, the file of document records may be organized in two basic ways, and it is obvious that the design of a document retrieval program must take into consideration the organization of the data base.

In a *direct file*, which is the type of file organization most frequently used for data bases stored on magnetic tape, each record corresponds to a document. As a minimum, each record includes a serial number to identify the document and the index terms that are associated with the document. Quite frequently in this type of file, records are arranged in random order on the tape and need to be searched sequentially.

In an *inverted file* each record corresponds to an index term and, as a minimum, includes the index term and the serial numbers of those documents to which the term was assigned in indexing. This type of file organization is most frequently used with direct-access storage media, particularly disk storage. Use of disk storage provides direct access to the term, and after the term is located, the search proceeds serially through the file of document numbers that are associated with the particular term.

The term/document matrix shown in Figure 11.1 helps to illustrate the two types of file organization just described. When the matrix is read horizontally, it reflects a direct file organization; when it is read vertically, it corresponds to an inverted file.

```
                              Terms

                    │  A B C D E F . . . . . . . . . .
                    │
        Documents  1│  X   X       X   .
                   2│    X         X
                   3│            X X
                   4│  X
                   5│  X     X   X
                   6│    X   X
                   7│  X     X X
                   8│    X X     X
                    │  .
                    │  .
                    │  .
```

Figure 11-1. *Term/Document Matrix.*

Some retrieval systems combine the two types of file within a single system. The inverted file is used to locate appropriate records initially and the full logic of the search is applied to the direct file. Currently there seems to be a trend toward inverted files on direct-access storage devices. Many large document retrieval systems are engaged in redesigning, or are planning to redesign, their files in this manner partly because of the tremendous increase in the size of their files and partly because of the increased availability and economy of disk storage devices.

The foregoing remarks represent several important practical considerations that must be taken into account in evaluating the effectiveness of the programming implementations of different large-scale document retrieval systems. For purposes of the present text, however, it will suffice to show how the logical model for document retrieval presented in Section 10.7 may be implemented as a PL/I program in which the coordinate index is organized as a simple direct file. The model is implemented in SAMPLE PROGRAM 19: RETRIEVE1.

The input data for SAMPLE PROGRAM 19: RETRIEVE1 consists of two sets of data structures: (1) a coordinate index; and (2) search requests. The coordinate index consists of document description profiles which are stored in memory as an array of structures. The array is called DOCUMENT and is dimensioned to contain 350 document profiles. Each element of the array is a structure variable, called DOCUMENT (I), which contains the profile of the ith document in the coordinate index. DOCUMENT (I) contains in its structure two elementary variables: CONTENT, which is a 20-bit string variable for describing the subject content of the ith document; and IDENT, which is a six-digit fixed decimal variable serving as the identification number of the ith document. Each position in the 20-bit elementary string variable DOCUMENT (I). CONTENT represents an index term, where a bit value 1 indicates the application of the index term to the ith document and a bit value 0 represents the absence of that index term from the ith document. For purposes of illustration only, the coordinate index accessed by SAMPLE PROGRAM 19 is based on a collection of 350 documents and a maximum of 20 index terms.

The data for each document is punched on a card with the binary representation of the subject content of the document appearing in columns 1–20 and the document identification number in columns 75–80. For instance, the data for document number 257 might be coded as follows.

$$10001001000000101000 \qquad\qquad 000257$$
$$\uparrow \qquad\qquad\qquad \uparrow \qquad\qquad \uparrow \quad \uparrow$$
$$\text{col 1} \qquad\qquad \text{col 20} \quad \text{col 75} \quad \text{col 80}$$

where the index terms 1, 5, 8, 15, and 17 have been assigned to document number 257.

11.4   Implementation of the Search Request

We now consider the implementation of the search requests. Suppose that search request number 237546, initiated by John W. Doe, when translated into disjunctive normal form, is

$$Q = I_{17} + I_3 \bar{I}_5 I_{11} + \bar{I}_8 I_{13} \bar{I}_{18} + I_4 \bar{I}_7 I_8 I_{10} I_{14}$$

In general, SAMPLE PROGRAM 19: RETRIEVE1 requires for each such search request a general data card citing the search request number, the name of the requestor, and a quasi-logical representation of the request, followed by a pair of data cards for each logical product term appearing in the request. A final pair of cards containing all 0's and 1's, respectively, is always included at the end of each request. SAMPLE PROGRAM 19 is written to evaluate several search requests.

In order to process the foregoing search request, it would be necessary to provide a set of eleven data cards: 1 general data card, 4 pairs of data cards corresponding to each of the four products in the search request, and a pair of "dummy" data cards signaling the end of the request. A final "dummy" general data card is included to signal the end of the evaluation of the final search request.

The format of the general data card for the request above would be

237546, 'JOHN W. DOE,' '17 + 3. ⌐ 5.11 + ⌐ 8.13. ⌐ 18 + 4. ⌐ 7.8.10.14'

The format of the pair of data cards for the first product, I_{17}, is

```
00000000000000001000        237546
11111111111111111111        237546
↑                  ↑         ↑    ↑
col 1           col 20    col 75  col 80
```

The format of the data cards for the second product, $I_3 \bar{I}_5 I_{11}$, is

```
00100000001000000000        237546
11110111111111111111        237546
↑                  ↑         ↑    ↑
col 1           col 20    col 75  col 80
```

The format of the data cards for the third product, $\bar{I}_8 I_{13} \bar{I}_{18}$, is

```
00000000000010000000        237546
11111110111111111011        237546
↑                  ↑         ↑    ↑
col 1           col 20    col 75  col 80
```

The format of the data cards for the fourth product, $I_4 \bar{I}_7 I_8 I_{10} I_{14}$, is

```
00010001010001000000        237546
11111101111111111111        237546
↑                  ↑         ↑    ↑
col 1           col 20    col 75  col 80
```

The format of the dummy data cards signaling the end of any search request is

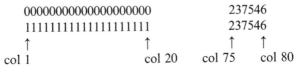

00000000000000000000   237546
11111111111111111111   237546
         ↑   ↑   ↑   ↑
      col 1   col 20   col 75   col 80

The format of the dummy *general data card*, which follows the data cards for the final search request, is

000000, 'xxxxx,' 'yyyyy'

Sample Program 19: RETRIEVE1

RETRIEVE1: PROCEDURE OPTIONS (MAIN);
            DECLARE 1 REQUEST (2), 2 CONTENT BIT (20), 2 IDENT
                FIXED (6), 1 DOCUMENT (350), 2 CONTENT BIT (20),
                2 IDENT FIXED (6), NUMBER FIXED (6), NAME
                CHARACTER (20) VARYING, FORM CHARACTER (54)
                VARYING;
            GET EDIT (DOCUMENT) (R (NAMELY));
NAMELY: FORMAT (B (20), X (54), F (6));
            /*350 CARDS REPRESENTING THE COORDINATE INDEX ARE
                READ IN AND STORED UNDER THE ARRAY NAMED
                'DOCUMENT'*/
NEWREQUEST: GET LIST (NUMBER, NAME, FORM);
            /*THE GENERAL DATA CARD FOR A SEARCH REQUEST IS
                READ*/
            IF NUMBER = 0 THEN GO TO STOP;
            /*TEST IS MADE FOR ADDITIONAL SEARCH REQUESTS*/
            PUT PAGE LIST ('THE DOCUMENTS LISTED BELOW SATISFY
                SEARCH REQUEST NO. ', NUMBER, 'WHICH WAS
                INITIATED BY ', NAME, 'AND SPECIFIES A
                COMBINATION OF INDEX TERMS AS FOLLOWS: ',
                FORM);
            SATISFY = 0;
            GET SKIP;
            /*PREPARE TO READ NEXT DATA CARD*/
CONTINUE: GET EDIT (REQUEST) (R (NAMELY));
            /*DATA FOR A PRODUCT TERM OF THE CURRENT SEARCH
                REQUEST IS STORED*/

IF BOOL (REQUEST (1).CONTENT, REQUEST (2).CONTENT,
         '0110'B) = (20) '1'B THEN GO TO CHECK;
/*TEST IS MADE FOR END OF THE CURRENT SEARCH
    REQUEST*/
I = 1;

NEXTDOCUMENT: IF BOOL (REQUEST (1).CONTENT, DOCUMENT (I).CONTENT,
         '1101'B) ⌐ = (20)'1'B THEN GO TO INCREMENT;
IF BOOL (DOCUMENT (I).CONTENT, REQUEST (2).CONTENT,
         '1101'B) ⌐ = (20)'1'B THEN GO TO INCREMENT;
/*TEST IS MADE TO DETERMINE WHETHER THE
    DESCRIPTION OF DOCUMENT (I) LOGICALLY IMPLIES
    THE PRESENT PRODUCT TERM OF THE SEARCH
    REQUEST*/
SATISFY = SATISFY + 1;
PUT SKIP LIST ('DOCUMENT NO. ', DOCUMENT (I).IDENT,
    'AS VERIFIED BY ITS ENTRY IN THE INDEX: ',
    DOCUMENT (I).CONTENT);
/*DOCUMENT (I) SATISFIES CURRENT SEARCH REQUEST*/

INCREMENT: IF I = 350 THEN GO TO CONTINUE;
/*IF ALL DOCUMENT ENTRIES IN COORDINATE INDEX
    HAVE BEEN TESTED FOR LOGICAL IMPLICATION WITH
    PRESENT PRODUCT TERM, THEN FETCH NEXT
    PRODUCT TERM IN SEARCH REQUEST*/
I = I + 1;
GO TO NEXTDOCUMENT;

CHECK: IF SATISFY = 0 THEN PUT SKIP LIST ('NONE OF THE
    DOCUMENTS LISTED IN THE INDEX SATISFY THE
    ABOVE REQUEST');
GO TO NEWREQUEST;

STOP: END RETRIEVE1;

11.5   Cyclic Retrieval

Cyclic retrieval is a method of multiple-step document retrieval in which use is made of the results of one retrieval operation to guide another. In cyclic retrieval the document file or data base is searched for an initial item of information. This selected item then provides information which is used as a guide in additional searches of the file to produce one or more items of information which are not directly available by the method of single access to the file. Access to the data file need not be limited to two passes. The essence of cyclic retrieval is, then, that repeated access to the data base is required in order to satisfy the original query posed by the user. SAMPLE PROGRAM 20: RETRIEVE2 provides an illustration of cyclic retrieval in which a dual access of the data file is required before an original query can be satisfied.

Sample Program 20: RETRIEVE2

RETRIEVE2 is a cyclic retrieval program in which an input query consisting of the title and author of a journal article is used to locate the entry of the article in the document data base. The program then abstracts from this entry certain key phrases describing the article, and accesses the data base a second time to locate all other articles whose entries also contain the set of selected key phrases describing the original article. Thus the output of the program is a list of entries of articles each of whose subject content is similar to that of an article known to the user only by its title and author.

The data base for RETRIEVE2 consists of a maximum collection of 5,000 technical papers, reports, and articles that have appeared in a particular published journal. The data base is assigned the structure name DOCUMENT in the program. Each article in the data base has an entry whose structure consists of these bibliographic items:

1 Document (I)
2 Reference number
2 Title
2 Author
2 Key phrases

As an illustration of an entry in the document data base, let us suppose that the complete bibliographic record for DOCUMENT (3974) appears as follows.

6811-2-72
VARIABLE LENGTH TREE STRUCTURES HAVING MINIMUM
AVERAGE SEARCH TIME
PATT, Y.
INFORMATION RETRIEVAL (4), FILE SEARCHING (5),
DOUBLE CHAINING (3), TREE STRUCTURES (4),
INVERTED LIST (3), DIRECT ACCESS MEMORY (2)

The reference number is a key to the year, volume, issue, and beginning page number of the article. Thus, the reference number for DOCUMENT (3974) is 6811-2-72 and indicates that the article appears in volume 11 (1968), issue number 2, beginning on page 72. The digit enclosed in parentheses following each key phrase refers to the weight assigned to that phrase. Weights range from 1 to 5, and higher weights signify greater relevance of the phrase. Thus, DOCUMENT (3974) has three key phrases with weights of 4 or greater.

In order to initiate action on a search request, the program accepts from the input stream a pair of data items which specify the title and author of an article whose entry is to be retrieved from the document data base for use later by the program. The title and author input data are required to have the same general format as their counterparts in the entries of the data base. With the title and author data in hand, the program searches the document data base for an entry whose title and author match the given title and author. The matching entry is then printed in its entirety. The program next determines and prints all key phrases in the matching entry which have a weight of 4 or greater. With this information as a guide, the program again searches the data base and prints out every entry which has among its key phrases the logical product of the phrases of weight 4 or greater found in the initial entry.

As an illustration of how the program operates, suppose that the search request consists of the following pair of title and author data.

> VARIABLE LENGTH TREE STRUCTURES HAVING MINIMUM
> AVERAGE SEARCH TIME
> PATT, Y.

A search of the document data base is made which results in the printout of the complete entry for DOCUMENT (3974) as shown earlier.

Among the key phrases listed for this entry, three have a weight of 4 or greater, and would be printed as follows.

> INFORMATION RETRIEVAL
> FILE SEARCHING
> TREE STRUCTURES

A second search is now made against the data base to produce a printout of all and only those entries which include among their respective lists of phrases the three key phrases shown above, regardless of the weights assigned to these terms in the respective lists.

The following is an example of a valid entry from the document data base that would be printed as a result of the second search.

> 6912-10-582
> A COMMENT ON OPTIMAL TREE STRUCTURES
> STANFEL, L. / KORFHAGE, R.
> INFORMATION RETRIEVAL (3), INVERTED LIST (4),
> DATA BASE (3), FILE SEARCHING (4), RANDOM
> SEQUENCING (3), TREE STRUCTURES (5)

For each pair of title and author data given as input, the program provides as output all entries from the data base satisfying the conditions illustrated above.

A dummy pair of title and author data cards serve to end the program.

```
RETRIEVE2:  PROCEDURE OPTIONS (MAIN);
            DECLARE 1  DOCUMENT (5000),
                       2 REFNO CHAR (11),
                       2 TITLE CHAR (160),
                       2 AUTHOR CHAR (80),
                       2 PHRASE CHAR (560),
                    (QTITLE, QAUTHOR) CHAR (160) VAR, TPHRASE CHAR
                    (560) VAR, QPHRASE (20) CHAR (30) VAR;
            /*NO ENTRY IN 'DOCUMENT' CAN CONTAIN MORE THAN 20
                    PHRASES. QUERY TITLE AND AUTHOR DATA ARE STORED
                    IN 'QTITLE' AND 'QAUTHOR'. 'TPHRASE' IS TEMPORARY
                    LOCATION FOR STORAGE OF PHRASES IN ENTRY MATCHING
                    TITLE AND AUTHOR DATA. 'QPHRASE' IS A 20-ELEMENT
                    ARRAY CONTAINING SUCH PHRASES WITH WEIGHTS
                    EQUAL TO OR LARGER THAN 4*/
            DO I = 1 BY 1;
            GET EDIT (DOCUMENT (I)) (A (811));
            IF REFNO (I) = '000' THEN GO TO QUERY;
            END;
            /*DOCUMENT DATA BASE IS STORED UNDER NAME 'DOCUMENT'.
                    END OF DATA BASE IS DENOTED BY DUMMY ENTRY WITH
                    REFNO = '000'*/
QUERY:      GET LIST (QTITLE, QAUTHOR);
            IF QTITLE = 'XXX' THEN GO TO STOP;
            PUT EDIT (QTITLE, QAUTHOR) (A, SKIP, A);
            /*QUERY DATA IS STORED AT 'QTITLE' AND 'QAUTHOR'*/
```

SEARCH1: DO J = 1 TO I − 1;

IF DOCUMENT (J).TITLE = QTITLE THEN IF DOCUMENT
(J).AUTHOR = QAUTHOR THEN GO TO MATCH;

ELSE;

END SEARCH1;

PUT LIST ('THE ABOVE CITATION IS NOT FOUND');

GO TO QUERY;

MATCH: PUT EDIT ('DOCUMENT NO. ', J, DOCUMENT (J)) (R(PRINT));

PRINT: FORMAT (SKIP, A, F (6, 0), SKIP, A (11), SKIP, A (160), SKIP,
A (80), SKIP, A (560));

/*DOCUMENT ENTRY MATCHING TITLE AND AUTHOR QUERY IS
PRINTED IN FULL*/

N = −1;

K, M = 1;

GETPHRASE: M = M + N + 1;

TPHRASE = SUBSTR (PHRASE (J), M);

TPHRASE = SUBSTR (PHRASE (J), M, INDEX (TPHRASE, ')'));

/*A PHRASE AND ITS WEIGHT IS STORED IN 'TPHRASE'*/

N = LENGTH (TPHRASE);

IF SUBSTR (TPHRASE, N − 1, 1) > = '4' THEN

DO;

QPHRASE (K) = SUBSTR (TPHRASE, M, N − 3);

PUT SKIP LIST (QPHRASE (K));

K = K + 1;

END;

/*STORE IN ARRAY 'QPHRASE' AND PRINT, WITHOUT ITS
WEIGHT, A PHRASE WHOSE WEIGHT IS > = 4*/

IF INDEX (SUBSTR (PHRASE (J), M), ',') = 0 THEN GO TO
SEARCH2;

/*TEST FOR FINAL PHRASE IN ENTRY MATCHING TITLE AND
AUTHOR DATA*/

GO TO GETPHRASE;

SEARCH2: DO J = 1 TO I − 1;

M = 0;

L1: DO L = 1 TO K − 1;

IF INDEX (PHRASE (J), QPHRASE (L)) = 0 THEN GO TO
NEXTENTRY;

M = M + 1;

END L1;

IF M = K − 1 THEN PUT EDIT ('DOCUMENT NO. ', J,
DOCUMENT (J)) (R (PRINT));
/*A DOCUMENT ENTRY IS PRINTED PROVIDED THAT IT
CONTAINS THE PHRASES STORED IN THE ARRAY
'QPHRASE'*/
NEXTENTRY: END SEARCH2;
           GO TO QUERY;
   STOP: END RETRIEVE2;

EXERCISES

1. What will be the value of z after the following code is executed?

$$X = \text{'0111'}B;$$
$$Y = \text{'110101'}B;$$
$$Z = \text{BOOL } (X, Y, \text{'1011'}B);$$

2. Given the following bit strings, write a BOOL assignment statement that computes the value of z from x and Y.

$$X = \text{'10110101'}B$$
$$Y = \text{'01100111'}B$$
$$Z = \text{'11010010'}B$$

3. Given bit strings x1 and x2, write a BOOL assignment statement for computing the value of $(x1 \supset x2)$ (see Tables 9.1 and 9.2 for definition of $\supset$).

4. Let R denote a search request, and D1 and D2 represent two document descriptions, as follows.

$$R = \bar{I}_2 I_3 \bar{I}_6 \quad D1 = I_1 \bar{I}_2 I_3 I_4 \bar{I}_5 \bar{I}_6 \quad D2 = \bar{I}_1 \bar{I}_2 I_3 I_4 \bar{I}_5 I_6$$

It was shown in Section 10.8 that R satisfies D1 but does not satisfy D2, since D1 logically implies R while D2 does not; that is,

$$(D1 \supset R) = 1$$
$$(D2 \supset R) = 0$$

SAMPLE PROGRAM 19: RETRIEVE1 illustrates an implementation of the foregoing logic by the use of two BOOL expressions in which R, D1, and D2 are represented by the binary vectors

$$R1 = \text{'001000'}B$$
$$R2 = \text{'101110'}B$$
$$D1 = \text{'101000'}B$$
$$D2 = \text{'001101'}B$$

Compute the values of the following BOOL expressions and explain how they establish that D1 logically implies R while D2 does not.

    (a) BOOL (R1, D1, '1101'B)
    (b) BOOL (D1, R2, '1101'B)
    (c) BOOL (R1, D2, '1101'B)
    (d) BOOL (D2, R2, '1101'B)

5. Convert the coordinate index in Exercise 5 of Chapter 10 into the form of an *inverted file* and from it provide the set of documents satisfying the search query

$$Q = I_1 \bar{I}_2 I_4$$

6. Using the inverted file in Exercise 5, show that documents D1 and D4 satisfy the search request $Q = I_2 I_3 \bar{I}_4$ by explaining the logic underlying the following code.

    (a) I2ANDI3 = BOOL (I2, I3, '0001'B);
    (b) NOTI4 = BOOL (I4, I4, '1100'B);
    (c) I2ANDI3ANDNOTI4 = BOOL (I2ANDI3, NOTI4, '0001'B);

7. Rewrite SAMPLE PROGRAM 19: RETRIEVE1 so that the coordinate index is in the form of an inverted file and the search logic is based on considerations presented in Exercise 6.

CHAPTER 12

_____

Program Organization

12.1 Introduction

The programs presented in the text so far have consisted of a single block of programming statements called a *main procedure*. When an application involves the processing of large amounts of data requiring a lengthy and complex program, it is sometimes advantageous to divide the program into several blocks or procedures. This approach facilitates the development of the program as well as its debugging because the procedures can be written, compiled, and tested separately, and then executed as a single program.

PL/I allows the use of several types of procedures, each of which has specified features and all of which require beginning and concluding statements necessary for their identification by the compiler. Since a PL/I procedure consists of a single block of programming statements, it is sometimes called a *procedure block*. In addition to procedure blocks, there is a second type of block in PL/I called the BEGIN *block*. We shall say more about BEGIN blocks in Section 12.5.

12.2   PL/I Procedures

A procedure or procedure block in PL/I is a group of statements that begins with the statement PROCEDURE and ends with the statement END:

label: PROCEDURE;
:
END label;

All procedures must have labels because it is through the name of the procedure that control is transferred to the procedure. A label in the END statement is optional; however, if it does appear, it must be the same as the label identifier used with the PROCEDURE statement to name the procedure.

The first procedure of a PL/I program is always the main procedure, and it is necessary to specify the OPTIONS (MAIN) attribute in its PROCEDURE statement. This provides information to the computer so that control is automatically transferred to the main procedure at the time of execution of the program. For programs consisting of several procedures, control does not automatically pass from one procedure to the next. Instead, control is selectively transferred from one procedure to another. The procedure initiating the transfer of control is known as the *invoking* or *calling procedure*, and the procedure to which control is transferred is referred to as the *invoked* or *called procedure*. The statement in the calling procedure which results in the transfer of control is called the *point of invocation*, and is usually a CALL statement (see Section 12.3) or an assignment statement containing the name of the invoked procedure (see Section 12.4). After completion of the invoked procedure, control is returned to the calling procedure, and the next statement to be executed is the one immediately following the point of invocation.

Procedures are classified in PL/I as *external procedures* and *internal procedures*. All main procedures are external procedures. As the name implies, an external procedure is separate from other procedures, is complete in itself, and can be compiled independently from other procedures. An internal procedure, on the other hand, is always nested in another internal procedure or an external procedure and is compiled with the external procedure which contains it.

```
SORT:   PROCEDURE OPTIONS (MAIN);
        ⋮
        END SORT;
ORDER:  PROCEDURE;
        ⋮
        END ORDER;
LIST:   PROCEDURE;
        ⋮
        END LIST;
```

Figure 12-1.   Diagram of external procedures.

Figure 12.1 shows a diagram of a program consisting of several external procedures. The program consists of three *external* procedures, all separate from one another. SORT is the main procedure of the program, and the two other external procedures, ORDER and LIST, are known as *subprograms*. Since control does not automatically pass to them, provision must be made for invoking the two subprograms. This may be done in a variety of ways, since SORT can invoke either or both of them and they may invoke one another. Finally, control returns to SORT, and execution of the program is completed upon execution of the END SORT statement.

The diagram in Figure 12.2 illustrates how the same program can be

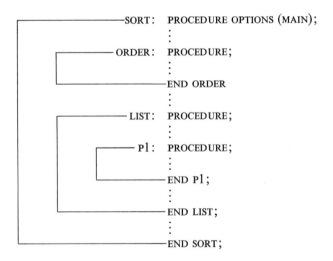

Figure 12-2.   Diagram of nested procedures.

organized so that the subprograms ORDER and LIST operate as internal procedures within the main procedure SORT. The diagram also illustrates that an external procedure may contain more than one internal procedure, either as separate procedures or as nested procedures. Thus, ORDER and LIST are contained in SORT as separate internal procedures, whereas the subprogram Pl is an internal procedure nested within the internal procedure LIST. As in the case of the diagram in Figure 12.1, SORT can invoke either or both of the subprograms ORDER and LIST, both of which may invoke one another or another external procedure. Similarly, the subprogram Pl can invoke another external procedure. However, neither SORT nor ORDER can directly invoke Pl; only LIST can invoke Pl. This is because in nested procedures only the procedure immediately containing another procedure can invoke that procedure.

A nested procedure must be wholly contained within its containing procedure. Moreover, two procedures which are separate with respect to one another cannot contain statements of one another; that is, none of the statements of the one procedure can appear between the PROCEDURE and END statements of the other procedure. The diagram in Figure 12.3 represents an *invalid* organization of the subprograms ORDER and LIST as separate internal procedures nested under the main procedure SORT. Although ORDER and LIST are procedures wholly contained within SORT, they fail to be separate from one another since some statements of the

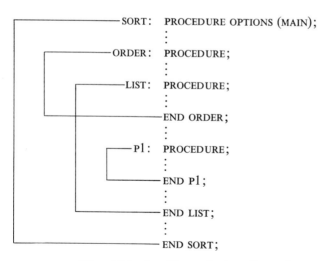

Figure 12-3. Invalid organization of internal procedures.

one procedure appear between the PROCEDURE and END statements of the other procedure.

12.3   Subroutines

Every PL/I program has one main procedure, which is an external procedure. Some PL/I programs have several procedures, in which case all procedures except the main procedure are called *subprograms*. In our treatment of subprograms so far, we have restricted ourselves to considering external procedures and internal procedures. We shall now discuss subprograms from another standpoint; namely, that PL/I recognizes two types of subprograms: *subroutines* and *function procedures* (or *functions*). A subroutine is a procedure which is invoked by means of a CALL statement, and a function procedure is invoked by use of the function name in an assignment statement. We shall discuss subroutines in this section and function procedures in Section 12.4.

The general format of the CALL statement is

CALL name (arg 1, arg 2, etc.);

where " name " refers to the name of the subroutine, and " arg 1," " arg 2," and so on designate an argument list consisting of variable names, constants, and expressions which are drawn from the invoking procedure.

The subroutine itself begins with a PROCEDURE statement labeled with the name of the subroutine and ends with an END statement which may also contain the subroutine name:

name: PROCEDURE (para 1, para 2, etc.);
        :
        END name;

where " para 1," " para 2," and so on refer to a list of parameter variables that are matched, one for one, with the arguments " arg 1," " arg 2," and so on in the CALL statement invoking the subroutine.

The purpose of matching a parameter list in the subroutine with an argument list in the CALL statement is to allow the subroutine to perform operations on data values whose names may be known only within the invoking procedure. The variable names in the argument list in the CALL statement, " arg 1," " arg 2," and so on, are said to be *passed* to the subroutine and, in effect, replace the parameters "para 1," "para 2," and so on everywhere in the subroutine during its execution. Upon completion of the subroutine, the argument names are *returned* to the invoking procedure. By this means, a subroutine can obtain values from the procedure that invoked it and, upon termination, can assign values to variables in that procedure. Moreover, because the subroutine contains a general parameter list and not a specific argument list known only to a given procedure, the subroutine can be invoked at different times by several procedures to perform the same operations on data values whose names may be known only within the individual invoking procedures.

Arguments must be passed for every parameter appearing in the parameter list of the subroutine, and the arguments must appear in the same order as the corresponding parameters in the parameter list. Moreover, the attributes of arguments appearing in a CALL statement must be identical to the attributes of the corresponding subroutine parameters. Hence, the programmer must exercise care to assure that the attributes are properly declared for each parameter within the subroutine—through the use of a declaration statement, default rules, or other standard PL/I conventions.

As an illustration of how a subroutine is programmed and used, let us consider the following example. Suppose that in a library application a procedure is wanted which tests for the occurrence of a subject phrase in a piece of catalog data and computes the boundaries of the phrase within the data item. Thus if the catalog data is the book title

'MY BROTHER WAS AN ONLY CHILD'

and the subject phrase is 'BROTHER', the procedure computes the values (4, 10), since the first and last characters of the subject word occupy the fourth and tenth positions within the title. If, on the other hand, the subject phrase is 'SOUL BROTHER', the procedure computes the value (0, 0). Subroutine SCOPE shows how this computation can be done:

```
SCOPE:   PROCEDURE (A, B, I, J);
         DCL (A, B) CHAR (100) VAR;
         I = INDEX (A, B);
         IF I = 0 THEN J = 0;
         ELSE J = I + LENGTH (B) − 1;
         RETURN;
         END SCOPE;
```

In some other procedure, SCOPE could be invoked as follows.

```
DELETE1 :   PROCEDURE (TEXT, PHRASE);
            DCL (TEXT, PHRASE, L, R) CHAR (100) VAR;
            CALL SCOPE (TEXT, PHRASE, II, JJ);
            IF II = 0 THEN RETURN;
       G1 : ELSE DO;
            L = SUBSTR (TEXT, 1, II − 1);
            R = SUBSTR (TEXT, JJ + 1);
            TEXT = L ‖ ‘ *** ’ ‖ R;
            END G1;
            RETURN;
            END DELETE1;
```

One method of transferring control to a subroutine, we saw earlier, is to specify the name of the subroutine in a CALL statement in the invoking procedure, as illustrated above. When the CALL statement is executed, control is transferred to the PROCEDURE statement of the subroutine, which serves as the primary entry point for the subroutine. When so invoked, the statements of the subroutine are executed in their normal order. However, it is possible to transfer control to subroutines at secondary entry points by the inclusion of one or more ENTRY statements in the subroutine. The general format of the ENTRY statement is

label: ENTRY (parameter list);

where "label" is the name of the statement and "parameter list" contains the parameters used by the subroutine when invoked at this point of entry. In order to invoke a subroutine at a secondary point, the label of the corresponding ENTRY statement must be specified in the invoking CALL statement. When control passes to a subroutine at a secondary entry point, the first statement to be executed in the subroutine is the one immediately following the ENTRY statement. SAMPLE PROGRAM 21: CONCORDANCE illustrates the use of ENTRY statements in a subroutine.

In the discussion of external and internal procedures in Section 12.2, it was pointed out that an internal procedure can be invoked only by the procedure that immediately contains it and none other. Thus the procedure P1 in Figure 12.2 can be invoked only by the procedure LIST which immediately contains it; neither of the procedures SORT nor ORDER can invoke P1. However, by use of the ENTRY statement, subroutine P1 can be made available to either SORT or ORDER, or any other external procedure. This is illustrated in Figure 12.4, where ORDER and LIST are both internal

```
SORT:      PROCEDURE;
           :
           CALL GETP1;
           :
ORDER:     PROCEDURE;
           :
           CALL GETP1;
           :
           END ORDER;
           :
LIST:      PROCEDURE;
           :
GETP1:     ENTRY;
           CALL P1;
P1:        PROCEDURE;
           :
           END P1;
           END LIST;
           :
           END SORT;
```

Figure 12-4. Use of ENTRY statement to call nested internal procedures.

to the procedure SORT but external with respect to each other, and LIST has two entry points labeled LIST and GETP1. When LIST is invoked at GETP1, the first statement executed invokes P1. Thus the invoking procedure (it can be ORDER, SORT, or another external procedure) has, in effect, called a procedure which is immediately contained in another procedure. Upon completion of P1, control returns to the END LIST statement, which immediately returns control to the original invoking procedure, namely, ORDER, SORT, or whatever.

One method of returning control from a subprogram to its invoking procedure is through use of the END statement. However, as was illustrated earlier in the subprogram DELETE1, it is sometimes desirable to return control before the END statement is reached. Another method of returning control is by executing the statement

RETURN;

which operates like the END statement to return control to the statement in the invoking procedure immediately following the point of invocation.

A RETURN statement may also be used in a main procedure to terminate the execution of the program by returning control to the operating system. As the subprogram DELETE1 illustrates, a subprogram or main procedure may contain any number of RETURN statements.

A GO TO statement may be used in internal procedures to transfer control to any containing procedure (see SAMPLE PROGRAM 21) but, generally, a GO TO statement cannot be used to transfer control from a containing procedure to any of its contained procedures. Similarly, a GO TO statement cannot be used to transfer control between external procedures.

SAMPLE PROGRAM 21: CONCORDANCE provides a detailed illustration of many of the salient points in the discussion of PL/I subprograms.

Sample Program 21: CONCORDANCE

The program reads a text as input and examines each word to determine whether it is a principal word. Words that (1) are not included in a stop-list, (2) are longer than four characters, and (3) have not occurred previously in the text are stored as an array of principal words and printed as output.

The program consists of three procedures: the main procedure is called CONCORDANCE; and the other two, called PROSCRIBE and PRINT, are internal procedures contained in the main procedure. The subroutine PROSCRIBE has a secondary entry called CHECK. PROSCRIBE is invoked at its primary entry point only once: at the beginning of the program when it is necessary to read from the input stream the words in the stop-list. A maximum of 200 words is allowed in the stop-list. PROSCRIBE is invoked at its secondary entry point, CHECK, each time a word in the text is examined for its length and possible inclusion in the stop-list. The PRINT subroutine prints the principal words that have not occurred previously in the text. The program imposes an upper limit of 100 distinct principal words in the text.

```
CONCORDANCE:  PROCEDURE OPTIONS (MAIN);
              DECLARE (TEXT CHAR (200), WORD CHAR (15)) VARYING;
              GET LIST (TEXT);
              PUT LIST (TEXT);
```

```
            CALL PROSCRIBE;
            /*NO ARGUMENTS ARE REQUIRED TO BE PASSED WHEN
                'PROSCRIBE' IS FIRST INVOKED*/
GETWORD:    DO L = 1 TO LENGTH (TEXT) WHILE (SUBSTR
                (TEXT, L, 1) ¬ = ' ');
            END GETWORD;
            IF INDEX (', ; : . ?', SUBSTR (TEXT, L − 1, 1)) = 0
                THEN WORD = SUBSTR (TEXT, 1, L);
            ELSE WORD = SUBSTR (TEXT, 1, L − 1);
            TEXT = SUBSTR (TEXT, L + 1);
            IF TEXT = '#' THEN GO TO FINISH;
            /*THE END OF THE TEXT IS DENOTED BY '#'*/
            CALL CHECK (WORD);
            /*'WORD' IS PASSED AS AN ARGUMENT TO THE SUBROUTINE
                'PROSCRIBE' AT ENTRY POINT 'CHECK'*/
            CALL PRINT (WORD);
            GO TO GETWORD;
PROSCRIBE:  PROCEDURE;
            DECLARE (W, STOPLIST (200)) CHAR (15) VARYING;
     L1:    DO I = 1 BY 1;
            GET LIST (STOPLIST (I));
            IF STOPLIST (I) = 'XXX' THEN GO TO GETWORD;
            /*STOPLIST ENDS WITH DUMMY SYMBOL 'XXX'*/
            IF I = 200 THEN
     G1:    DO;
            PUT SKIP LIST ('THE MAXIMUM NUMBER OF WORDS ALLOWED
                IN THE STOPLIST HAVE BEEN READ');
            GO TO GETWORD;
            END G1;
            END L1;
CHECK:      ENTRY (W);
            IF LENGTH (W) < = 4 THEN GO TO GETWORD;
     L2:    DO J = 1 TO I;
            IF STOPLIST (J) = W THEN GO TO GETWORD;
            END L2;
            END PROSCRIBE;
PRINT:      PROCEDURE (W);
            DECLARE (W CHAR (15), TERM (100) CHAR (15)
                INIT ((15)' ')) VARYING, COUNT FIXED BINARY INIT (1);
```

```
L3:    DO K = 1 TO COUNT;
       IF TERM (K) = W THEN GO TO GETWORD;
       /*IF CURRENT WORD IS ALREADY IN LIST OF PRINCIPAL
           WORDS THEN FETCH NEXT WORD*/
       END L3;
       TERM (COUNT) = W;
       PUT SKIP LIST (W);
       COUNT = COUNT + 1;
       /*ADD NEW WORD TO LIST OF DISTINCT PRINCIPAL WORDS,
           INCREMENT COUNT OF SAME, AND PRINT WORD*/
       IF COUNT > 100 THEN
G2:    DO;
       PUT SKIP LIST ('THE UPPER LIMIT OF 100 DISTINCT
           PRINCIPAL WORDS IN THE TEXT HAS BEEN REACHED');
       GO TO FINISH;
       END G2;
       END PRINT;
FINISH:  END CONCORDANCE;
```

REMARKS

The subroutines PROSCRIBE and PRINT illustrate the use of a GO TO statement to transfer control from a nested internal procedure to a containing procedure.

The END PROSCRIBE and END PRINT statements are used not only to indicate the end of the two subroutines but also to return control to the invoking procedure, namely, CONCORDANCE. In the case of END PROSCRIBE, control is returned to the statement immediately following the CALL CHECK statement rather than the statement following CALL PROSCRIBE. This is because CALL CHECK invokes the subroutine at a point which allows for a normal termination of the subroutine by execution of the END PROSCRIBE statement, whereas CALL PROSCRIBE invokes the subroutine at a point which does not allow for normal return of control.

12.4   Function Procedures

PL/I recognizes another type of subprogram, similar to a subroutine, called a *function procedure* or *function*. A function procedure differs from a subroutine in the way it is invoked. A subroutine is invoked by a CALL statement. A function subprogram is invoked by the occurrence of its name, together with an argument list, in an expression. Called a *function reference*, the expression commonly appears in an assignment statement, but it may appear anywhere in a PL/I program that a valid expression can legitimately appear. When invoked by a function reference, the subprogram computes a *single value* for the function based on the data values passed to it through the argument list, and returns the value to the function name for use in the invoking expression. As in the case of a subroutine, the arguments drawn from the invoking procedure can be variable names, constants, and expressions.

The function subprogram begins with a PROCEDURE statement labeled with the function name and ends with an END statement which may also contain the function name:

> function name: PROCEDURE (para 1, para 2, etc.);
> :
> RETURN (expression);
> END function name;

As in the case of a subroutine, the PROCEDURE statement contains a list of parameter variables " para 1," " para 2," and so on, which must equal the number of arguments in the function reference for replacement by them on a matching basis in the subprogram. It is also necessary, as in the case of subroutines, for the attributes of the function arguments in the invoking procedure to agree with those of the corresponding function parameters in the subprogram.

It may be noted that a special form of the RETURN statement is used to return control from a function subprogram to the procedure that invoked the function. The keyword RETURN is followed by an expression in parentheses that specifies the function value to be returned to the invoking procedure. Since a function subprogram can return only a *single* value, the expression in a RETURN statement must be an arithmetic or string expression that represents a single value. As in the case of subroutines, a function subprogram may contain more than one RETURN statement.

As an illustration of how a function subprogram can be used to define and evaluate a function for use in a program, let us consider the following example. Suppose that in a library application there is need for a special function which tests for the inclusion of a search string in a given character string and returns a value 0 if the search string is not included; otherwise the value of the function is the position within the given string of the *last* character of the search string. The function is similar to the built-in function INDEX provided by PL/I as part of the compiler, except that INDEX returns the position of the *first* character of the search string. If we assign the name LAST to this function, the following subprogram shows how this function can be defined.

```
LAST:  PROCEDURE (A, B);
       DECLARE (A, B) CHAR (100) VAR;
       I = INDEX (A, B);
       IF I = 0 THEN RETURN (0);
       ELSE I = I + LENGTH (B) − 1;
       RETURN (I);
       END LAST;
```

In some other procedure, LAST could be invoked as shown below.

```
DELETE2:  PROCEDURE (TEXT, PHRASE);
          DECLARE (TEXT, PHRASE, L, R) CHAR (100) VAR;
          J = LAST (TEXT, PHRASE);
          IF J = 0 THEN RETURN;
    G1:   ELSE DO;
          L = SUBSTR (TEXT, 1, J − LENGTH (PHRASE));
          R = SUBSTR (TEXT, J + 1);
          TEXT = L ‖ '***' ‖ R;
          END G1;
          RETURN;
          END DELETE2;
```

TEXT and PHRASE are declared as character-string variables in the invoking procedure DELETE2 and serve as arguments to be passed to the function procedure LAST. In the function subprogram LAST, A and B are the parameters corresponding to TEXT and PHRASE, and they are also declared as character-string variables. The values of the arguments TEXT and PHRASE are used as the values of the parameters A and B when the function subprogram is invoked by DELETE2. Finally, the value assigned to LAST in the expression LAST (TEXT, PHRASE) is the value computed for I in the subprogram and returned to the invoking expression. I and J are, by the first-letter rule (Section 3.2), identifiers for a fixed binary function value and require no explicit declaration.

Observe that in the function subprogram LAST, parameters A and B are declared as character strings of length 100. If the same function is to be invoked by a procedure whose argument strings exceed the length of 100, an error will occur. It is possible to avoid this situation by replacing the DECLARE statement in the function subprogram LAST with the statement

DECLARE (A, B) CHARACTER(*);

Like an ordinary argument variable, a function name has attributes. These attributes must be declared, either explicitly or by default, in the procedure that invokes the function and in the function subprogram itself. In the absence of other specifications, the first-letter rule may be applied to determine function attributes. However, to define function attributes explicitly, it is necessary to use the RETURNS attribute in a DECLARE statement in the invoking procedure, and the RETURNS option in the PROCEDURE statement in the subprogram.

As an illustration of this let us assume that in the preceding example the function was assigned the name FINAL instead of LAST. LAST has the attributes FIXED BINARY in the invoking procedure, since there is no explicit declaration of attributes for the function and the first-letter rule holds. LAST has the same attributes in the subprogram, because no attributes are specified for it in the PROCEDURE statement. If the function name is changed from LAST to FINAL and the function has the attributes FIXED BINARY, then the following changes must be made: (1) add the DECLARE statement below to DELETE2:

DECLARE FINAL RETURNS (FIXED BINARY);

and (2) change the PROCEDURE statement in the subprogram to

FINAL: PROCEDURE (A, B) RETURNS (FIXED BINARY);

An important advantage of function procedures is that the same procedure might be invoked from several points in the program with different arguments being passed. For this reason function procedures should be as general as possible. We have seen that PL/I provides a number of *built-in functions* (LENGTH, INDEX, SUBSTR, BOOL, VERIFY, and so on). The programmer need not write special procedures for these functions, since they are part of the language and may be invoked merely by a function reference. Through the use of function subprograms, additional functions may be defined by the programmer which can be similarly invoked by a function reference.

12.5   BEGIN Blocks

The BEGIN block was first discussed in Section 12.1 as one of two *block types* in PL/I. The other is the *procedure block*. Every main procedure and every subroutine or function subprogram is a procedure block.

As we shall explain, BEGIN blocks have many properties in common with procedure blocks, so it is appropriate to discuss BEGIN blocks now in more detail.

A BEGIN block is a set of statements bounded by a BEGIN statement and an END statement. For the sake of convenience, it is usually desirable to label the BEGIN statement and to assign the same label in the corresponding END statement:

label: BEGIN;
        ⋮
        END label;

A BEGIN block is closely akin to an internal procedure block, yet differs from it in important ways. A BEGIN block, however, cannot be an external block. It must be contained in a procedure, and it may contain other BEGIN blocks or procedures.

Like an internal procedure, a BEGIN block has an ability to share variables with a procedure that contains it. This can present a pitfall in the sense that a programmer might use a variable that is undeclared in a BEGIN block, thinking that the scope of the variable extends only to the BEGIN block, whereas the variable is shared throughout the containing block or procedure. This could result in an unintentional loss of a data value since there could be a single shared variable in a program where the programmer thought there were two. The way to avoid this situation is to declare in the internal procedure or BEGIN block every variable that need not be shared outside of that block.

As in the case of an internal procedure, if a variable is declared inside a BEGIN block, then the variable is known only inside the block; it cannot be shared with the containing procedure. This is illustrated in Figure 12.5, where the variable A declared in the main procedure P and the variable A declared in the BEGIN block B1 are distinct variables. In the main procedure, A is assigned the attribute CHAR (20), and in the BEGIN block B1, A is assigned the attribute BIT (8). After the END B1 statement is executed, A is again assigned the attribute at the beginning of the program, namely, CHAR (20). Storage for the second variable A is not allocated until the BEGIN block is entered, and the storage is released when control passes from the block.

A major difference between a procedure block and a BEGIN block is the way in which control passes to the block. Control passes to a subroutine or function subprogram by means of a CALL statement or a function reference. Control passes to a BEGIN block through execution of the normal

```
P:    PROCEDURE OPTIONS (MAIN);
      DECLARE A CHAR (20);
      :
B1:   BEGIN;
      DECLARE A BIT (8);
      :
      END B1;
      :
      END P;
```

Figure 12-5. Declaration of variables in a BEGIN block.

sequence of statements. That is, control passes to the BEGIN statement after the statement immediately preceding it has been executed, or after execution of a GO TO statement containing its label. The label of a BEGIN statement cannot appear in a CALL statement. Control passes from a BEGIN block by execution of either the END statement or a GO TO statement.

The primary use of the BEGIN block is to restrict the declaration and allocation of variables through a block of sequentially executed statements.

EXERCISES

1. If *before* execution of the procedure DELETE1 in Section 12.3,

    TEXT = 'THE VOICE OF THE TURTLE IS HEARD IN THE LAND'
    PHRASE = 'THE TURTLE'S VOICE'

what are the values of TEXT, PHRASE, II and JJ *after* execution of DELETE1 ?

2. If *before* execution of the procedure DELETE2 in Section 12.4,

    TEXT = 'THE PRESENT KING OF FRANCE IS ALIVE AND WELL'
    PHRASE = 'KING OF FRANCE'

what are the values of TEXT, PHRASE, and J *after* execution of DELETE2 ?

3. For the purposes of this exercise let us assume an on-line library circulation system which in addition to computing fines (if any) for returned books will also handle the reserve procedure. The list of reserves includes the author and title of books that have been reserved along with the names and telephone numbers of the users who requested them. When several users request the same book, their names are entered in the reserve list in the order in which the requests were made.

When a book is returned to the circulation desk, the program must check whether it is overdue and if so, calculate the fine. Next, the program must check the reserve list to determine whether the book was reserved by another user. If the book was reserved, the program is to print the author and title of the book and the name and telephone number of the user who was first to request the book.

The input data for the program should include (1) the current date and the rate per day for overdue books; (2) the author, title, due date, and the name of the borrower for each book returned; (3) the reserve list: a list of users requesting books in circulation including for each user his name and telephone number and the author and title of the book he requested.

CHAPTER 13

File Data Management

13.1 Introduction

The programming applications presented so far have dealt mainly with the facilities available in PL/I for the logical manipulation and processing of data. In this chapter we shall describe some of the capabilities of PL/I for the organization and management of data. A thorough discussion of this topic would be too long for an introductory textbook, so we shall restrict ourselves to a limited view of the subject.

A collection of data external to a PL/I program is called a *data set*. The symbolic representation of a data set in PL/I is a *data file* or *file*. A file has significance only within the context of a PL/I program as the name of a data set and does not exist as a physical entity external to the program. PL/I offers extensive attribute and I/O capabilities for the organization and transmission of data files between the external and internal storage devices of the computer. A file can be associated with different data sets at different times during the execution of a program (see the TITLE option in Section 13.3). As a result, a PL/I program can be written without knowledge of the I/O devices that will be used when it is executed. For this reason PL/I is called a device-independent language.

Data sets are stored on such external storage devices as punched cards, reels of magnetic tape, magnetic disks, magnetic drums, and punched paper tape. The data items within a data set are commonly arranged in distinct physical groupings called *blocks*. Each block may consist of one or more logical subdivisions, called *records*, each of which contains one or more data elements.

As we saw in Section 3.4, two different types of data transmission are available in PL/I for use with data sets: *stream oriented* and *record oriented*. With stream-oriented transmission, the data set is treated as a continuous stream of data without regard to record boundaries. Specifically, card boundaries in input and line boundaries in output have no special significance in stream-oriented transmission of data. With record-oriented transmission, the data is treated as a collection of physically separate records; and each record, containing one or more data elements, is transmitted intact to or from internal storage and an I/O device.

13.2   File Attributes

The following form of the DECLARE statement may be used for the declaration of a data file.

DECLARE name FILE file attributes;

where "name" is any valid PL/I identifier, the keyword FILE informs the compiler that "name" stands for the file name of a data set, and "file attributes" describe the attributes explicitly assigned to the data file. When attributes are explicitly assigned, it is not necessary to include the word FILE in the declaration. Any number of file names may be declared in a DECLARE statement along with any other variable names. For example, in the statement

DECLARE WORD CHARACTER (20) VARYING, (IN, OUT) FILE, COUNT LABEL;

the identifiers IN and OUT are declared to be the file names of two data sets.

The file attributes INPUT, OUTPUT, and UPDATE are used to specify the direction of data transmission permitted for a file. The INPUT attribute applies to a file that is to be read only, the OUTPUT attribute applies to a file that is to be written only, and the UPDATE attribute describes a file that is to be used for both input and output.

As we indicated earlier, the statement

DECLARE BOOKLOAN FILE INPUT;

may be written simply as

DECLARE BOOKLOAN INPUT;

because the file attribute INPUT informs the compiler that BOOKLOAN is a *file* name used only for input of data.

The file attributes STREAM and RECORD specify that the type of data transmission to be used in accessing a file during I/O operations is stream oriented or record oriented, respectively. For example, in the statements

DECLARE DUEDATE STREAM INPUT;
DECLARE BOOKFINE RECORD OUTPUT;

DUEDATE is declared to be the name of an input file whose data is to be transmitted to the computer in the form of a continuous input stream, and BOOKFINE is the name of an output file which is to receive data as a collection of physically separate records.

The PRINT attribute, when specified for a file that also has the STREAM and OUTPUT attributes, indicates that the file is to be printed.

Transmission of data from or to STREAM files is accomplished by use of the GET and PUT statements. Input and output of RECORD files, on the other hand, require the use of the READ and WRITE statements.

In PL/I there are two *standard* files, called SYSIN and SYSPRINT, to which the STREAM attribute is applied automatically. SYSIN is the standard PL/I file for card input, and SYSPRINT is the standard file for high-speed printer output. By default, a GET statement that does not include any reference to a file name is assumed to refer to the standard SYSIN file. Similarly, a PUT statement that omits any reference to a file name is assumed to refer to the SYSPRINT file.

The file attributes SEQUENTIAL and DIRECT KEYED apply only to RECORD files and refer to how their content is to be accessed. Files in which records are to be accessed in the order of their physical appearance, as in the case of data sets stored on magnetic tape, are said to have the SEQUENTIAL attribute. The opposite of a sequential file is a direct file, such as a data set stored on a magnetic disk. The DIRECT and KEYED attributes specify that the records in the file are to be accessed directly by means of an identifying key for each record. In this manner any record in the file may be read or written in any order by specifying the proper key in the READ or WRITE statement.

In order to take advantage of the difference between the time required for transmission of data and for internal processing of data, many computing systems are designed to allow I/O operations to take place concurrently with internal processing. Thus while a previous record is being processed, a new record may be read. The storage area in which records are kept while others are being processed is called a *buffer*. The buffer may be a part of the central storage area which is set aside for this purpose, or it may be an independent storage device. Buffers may be used for both input and output, and if they store only one record at a time they are called *single buffers*. By default, all files in PL/I which are declared to be RECORD SEQUENTIAL are assigned the BUFFERED attribute. When the records of a sequential file need not be stored in a buffer but may be assigned directly to the variables specified in a READ/WRITE statement, it is necessary to declare the file to have the UNBUFFERED attribute.

Table 13.1 provides a summary of the major file attributes in PL/I that apply to stream-oriented and record-oriented transmission of data.

TABLE 13.1

Summary of Major PL/I File Attributes

Stream-oriented transmission		Record-oriented transmission	
FILE	OUTPUT	FILE	SEQUENTIAL
STREAM	UPDATE	RECORD	DIRECT
INPUT	PRINT	INPUT	KEYED
		OUTPUT	BUFFERED
		UPDATE	UNBUFFERED

13.3　File Processing

In order to be able to process data associated with a file, it is necessary to perform certain preparatory operations known as *opening* and *closing* files.

Although there are many ways of opening a file, perhaps the most straightforward is the use of the OPEN statement. The general form of the statement is

OPEN FILE (name) attributes;

where "name" is the identifier designated by the programmer to denote the file name and "attributes" refer to a list of attributes describing the file.

If the file is also assigned a list of attributes in a DECLARE statement, they are merged with the attributes listed in OPEN statement; that is, a file attribute may be specified in the one statement or the other but not in both, and of course, there must not be any conflict in the assignment of attributes. The following example illustrates the merging of attributes.

> DECLARE SHELFLIST FILE;
> OPEN FILE (SHELFLIST) INPUT RECORD SEQUENTIAL;

A file is said to be opened *explicitly* when the opening occurs as the result of the execution of an OPEN statement. However, a file may be opened *implicitly*. An implicit opening of a file occurs when one of a group of statements, such as GET, PUT, READ, WRITE, or REWRITE, is executed for a file whose name does not appear in an OPEN statement which has already been executed.

When a program refers to more than one file, it is good practice to open all files in a single OPEN statement to improve the speed of operation. The same is true in closing files.

When the execution of a program is completed, any files that were opened during program execution are automatically deactivated at the conclusion of the program. However, to enable the programmer to deactivate files during the execution of a program, PL/I provides use of the CLOSE statement:

> CLOSE FILE (name);

Observe that it is not necessary for the programmer to specify any attributes in the CLOSE statement.

Through the use of the TITLE option in the OPEN statement, a programmer is allowed to choose dynamically, at the time of opening a file, one among several data sets to be associated with a particular file name. In this manner, a file name can, at different times, represent entirely different data sets. The TITLE option appears in an OPEN statement in the form

> OPEN FILE (name) TITLE (expression);

where "expression" is a character string indentifying the name of a particular data set representing a specific collection of data.

It is a practice among some programmers to consider the first item in a file as the header label by which identification of the file may be established. To accommodate this practice, the so-called IDENT option is available for use in the OPEN statement:

OPEN FILE (name) IDENT (label);

where "label" is a character-string variable standing for the name of the location in which the header label is stored.

Use of the TITLE option and the IDENT option is illustrated in the following coding.

DECLARE DATASET (3) CHARACTER (1) INITIAL ('1', '2', '3'), KWOC FILE
    INPUT, HEADER CHARACTER (20) VARYING;
DO I = 1 TO 3;
OPEN FILE (KWOC) TITLE ('INDEX' ‖ DATASET (I)) IDENT (HEADER);
PUT SKIP LIST ('THE HEADER LABEL FOR THE DATA SET CALLED INDEX',
    DATASET (I), 'IS ', HEADER);
CLOSE FILE (KWOC);
END;

In this example, the TITLE option associates the file KWOC with one of three data sets, INDEX1, INDEX2, and INDEX3, each time I is incremented in the DO loop. When KWOC is opened during the first iteration of the DO group, the IDENT option stores the contents of the header label of INDEX1 in location HEADER, and the PUT LIST statement prints the label for the data set INDEX1. The file is then closed, dissociating the file name KWOC from INDEX1. During the second iteration of the loop, KWOC is opened again and associated with INDEX2, whose header label is then printed. Similarly during the final iteration of the DO group, KWOC is associated with the data set INDEX3, and its header label is printed. The example illustrates how it is possible to identify by content a group of data sets that are stored on magnetic tape, assuming that each data set is described by a header label as its first item. It should be observed that the IDENT option fetches only a specified part of the contents of a file. Statements which transmit data to or from the file are, of course, the GET, PUT, READ, WRITE, and REWRITE statements.

The general formats of the GET and PUT statements for stream-oriented transmission of data are

GET FILE (name) LIST (data list);
PUT FILE (name) LIST (data list);
GET FILE (name) DATA (data list);
PUT FILE (name) DATA (data list);
GET FILE (name) EDIT (data list) (format list);
PUT FILE (name) EDIT (data list) (format list);

When the two standard SYSIN and SYSPRINT files are to be used, the file names need not be explicitly stated in GET and PUT statements. In other words, abbreviated GET and PUT statements in which no file names appear, such as

GET LIST (data list);
PUT EDIT (data list) (format list);

are equivalent, by default, to

GET FILE (SYSIN) LIST (data list);
PUT FILE (SYSPRINT) EDIT (data list) (format list);

Since all of the programming examples presented previously in the text have assumed card input and high-speed printer output, only the abbreviated forms of GET and PUT statements have been presented in the text.

In place of the FILE option, which is concerned with the transmission of data to and from an *external* medium, PL/I provides the STRING option for use in GET and PUT statements for strictly *internal* transmission of data. The use of the STRING option is best illustrated by several examples. Consider the following GET statement, which utilizes the STRING option.

GET STRING (CATALOG) EDIT (AUTHOR, TITLE, CALLNO) (A (10),
X (2), A (30), X (2), F (6));

Upon execution of the GET statement above, the character string CATALOG, which is already stored *internally* in the computer, is scanned, and the first ten characters of the string are assigned to AUTHOR, the next two characters are ignored, the next 30 characters are assigned to TITLE, the next two characters are ignored, the next six characters are converted to a fixed-point decimal number and assigned to CALLNO, and the remaining characters of the string, if any, are ignored.

Consider the following set of statements.

DCL PUBLDATE CHAR (20) VAR, (VOL, YR) FIXED DEC, MONTH CHAR (3);
PUBLDATE = '15(FEB1970)593–597';
GET STRING (PUBLDATE) EDIT (VOL, MONTH, YR) (F (2), X (1), A (3), F (4));

After this code is executed, VOL has the value 15, MONTH has the value 'FEB', and YR has the value 1970.

Although the STRING option can be used with list-directed, data-directed, or edit-directed transmission of stream data, the edit-directed mode is the most useful of the three modes. As illustrated above, the format list of edit-directed I/O provides greater editing facilities under the STRING option since individual items in the string need not be separated by commas or blanks.

Probably the most useful feature of the STRING option with the GET statement is that input data can be read and reread repeatedly under a choice of different formats. Consider the following code.

```
DECLARE X BIT (8), Y CHAR (8);
GET EDIT (X) (B (8));
Y = TRANSLATE (X, 'TF', '10');
GET STRING (Y) EDIT (X) (A (8));
```

If the data in the input stream is '11010010'B, after the foregoing code is executed, X has the value 'TTFTFFTF'.

The general formats of the READ, WRITE, and REWRITE statements for record-oriented transmission of data are

```
READ FILE (name) INTO (location);
WRITE FILE (name) FROM (location);
REWRITE FILE (name) FROM (location);
```

where "location" is declared as a character-string or bit-string variable of a length that is sufficient for the storage of a full record from the file. On input, the READ statement causes a single record to be transmitted into "location" exactly as it is recorded in the data set. On output, the WRITE statement causes a single record to be transmitted from "location" exactly as it is recorded internally.

When the length of the records in a file varies, it is possible to find the length of a record by declaring "location" as a character string whose length is the same as the length of the longest record, and using the built-in function LENGTH. The following code illustrates how this may be done.

```
DCL IN FILE INPUT, ABSTRACT CHAR (2000) VAR;
READ FILE (IN) INTO (ABSTRACT);
PUT LIST ('THE CURRENT ABSTRACT HAS: ',
    LENGTH (ABSTRACT), 'CHARACTERS');
```

The READ ... INTO statement can be used to access any INPUT or UPDATE file. The WRITE ... FROM statement is used to write into any OUTPUT or DIRECT UPDATE file. The REWRITE statement can be used to cause a record to be replaced in any UPDATE file. For SEQUENTIAL UPDATE files, the REWRITE statement causes the last record read from the file to be rewritten. That is, a record must be read before it can be rewritten in a

SEQUENTIAL UPDATE file. For DIRECT UPDATE files, any record can be rewritten regardless whether it has first been read.

For DIRECT KEYED files in which records are assigned unique keys, the following statements may be used.

READ FILE (name) INTO (location) KEY (variable);

WRITE FILE (name) FROM (location) KEY (variable);

where "variable" is a character string representing the key assigned to each record. A DIRECT KEYED file in which records are placed in ascending order by their keys allows records to be processed sequentially and accessed directly. This type of file can be printed sequentially when declared as SEQUENTIAL KEYED OUTPUT and can be updated when declared with the attributes DIRECT KEYED UPDATE.

Frequently when data is read from a file, there is no indication of how many records are in the file or what the content of the last record is. This leads to the problem of determining when to stop execution of the READ statement. If a PL/I program attempts to read beyond the boundaries of a file, normally an ON condition code is set and execution of the program stops. By means of the ON ENDFILE statement, however, it is possible to specify how the program should continue when this condition is encountered. The following code illustrates how the ON ENDFILE statement may be used to determine how many records are in a file and what the content of the last record is.

```
        ON ENDFILE (TITLES) GO TO PRINT;
        DO I = 1 BY 1;
        READ FILE (TITLES) INTO (TITLE (I));
        END;
PRINT:  PUT LIST ('THERE ARE ', I, 'TITLES IN THE CURRENT FILE.
        THE LAST TITLE IS: ', TITLE (I));
```

Sample Program 22: COPY

Let us assume that an index file for a group of documents, called INDEX1, is stored on magnetic tape and contains such bibliographic information as title, author(s), source of publication, abstract, and a set of subject terms. The file contains variable-length records, each of which describes the bibliographic data for a single document. The maximum length of a record is 8000 characters. In each record of INDEX1, the abstract is preceded by a string of six characters composed of two blanks, the digits '50', and two blanks, as shown:

' 50 '

The set of subject terms is headed by a six-character string consisting of two blanks, the digits '60', and two blanks:

'   60   '

SAMPLE PROGRAM 22: COPY reads sequentially into internal storage one record at a time from the index file called INDEX1, copies onto a second magnetic tape all of the bibliographic information contained in the record, except the abstract, and prints out the reduced record in the form of hard copy. The abbreviated version of INDEX1, which is also stored on magnetic tape, is called INDEX2. A record in INDEX1 is called FULLENTRY, and a record in INDEX2 is called SHORTENTRY. The program terminates when an ON ENDFILE condition is detected for INDEX1.

```
COPY:   PROCEDURE OPTIONS (MAIN);
        DECLARE INDEX1 FILE INPUT RECORD, INDEX2 FILE OUTPUT
            RECORD, (FULLENTRY, SHORTENTRY) CHARACTER (8000)
            VARYING;
        OPEN FILE (INDEX1, INDEX2);
        ON ENDFILE (INDEX1) GO TO STOP;
BEGIN:  DO I = 1 BY 1;
        READ FILE (INDEX1) INTO (FULLENTRY);
        SHORTENTRY = SUBSTR (FULLENTRY, 1, INDEX (FULLENTRY,
            '  50  ')) ‖ SUBSTR (FULLENTRY, INDEX (FULLENTRY,
            '  60  '));
        WRITE FILE (INDEX2) FROM (SHORTENTRY);
        PUT SKIP LIST (SHORTENTRY);
        END BEGIN;
STOP:   END COPY;
```

Sample Program 23:   POST

SAMPLE PROGRAM 23 illustrates how monographic cataloging data recorded in machine-readable MARC II format may be entered in a computer-based bibliographic file. The file, called CATALOG, is stored on disk as a DIRECT KEYED file, and each record in the file consists of a subject heading and a list of books, by author and title, which have been cataloged by the Library of Congress under that subject heading. The source for all entries in the file is the MARC II tape, which is prepared by the Library of Congress and distributed regularly to all interested libraries on a subscription basis.

Begun in 1966, the MARC program (MAchine-Readable Cataloging project) represents a major undertaking by the Library of Congress in centrally producing cataloging data in machine-readable form for distribution to libraries in the field. With the introduction of a revised format several years ago, MARC II records are presently distributed to participating libraries on a weekly basis and currently contain cataloging information for English-language monographs.

Each MARC record describes a single monograph and includes information normally found on a Library of Congress catalog card as well as additional data to facilitate machine processing. The MARC II record† is a variable-length record made up of fixed fields and variable fields and includes the following major elements.

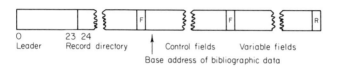

| 0 | 23 24 | | | | | |
| Leader | Record directory | | Control fields | Variable fields | | R |

Base address of bibliographic data

Each field in a MARC record, with the exception of the leader, terminates with a field terminator (F), and each record terminates with a record terminator (R). Figure 13.1 provides an illustration of the MARC II record format in detail.

The *leader* is fixed in length and contains 24 characters. The first five characters represent the length of the record and the thirteenth through seventeenth characters (numbered 12 to 16 because the first character position is designated as 0) provide the base address of the data. For example, the Leader shown in Figure 13.1 refers to a record that contains 441 characters and in which the base address of the data is 133.

24 Characters

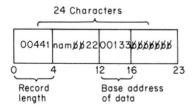

| 0 | 4 | 12 | 16 | 23 |
| Record length | | Base address of data | | |

† A detailed description of the MARC II format is found in *MARC Manuals Used by the Library of Congress*, Chicago, American Library Association, 1969.

Leader	Record directory
00441 n a m ƀƀ 2 2 00133 ƀƀƀƀƀƀƀ 001001300000 008004100013 050001600054	
0	23

082001300070 100003500083 245008900118 260004800207 300001900255 650003400274 ⨍

LC card number   Fixed length data elements

ƀƀƀ 64 008443 ƀ ⨍ 681001 s 1964 ƀƀƀƀ nyu ƀƀƀƀ ƀ ƀ ƀƀƀƀ ƀ00100ƀ eng 0 ƀ ⨍

LC call number   Dewey number   Main entry

0ƀ $aPS614$b.L75 ⨍ ƀƀ $a811.5082 ⨍ 10 $aLowenfels,ƀWalter,$d1897-$eed. ⨍

Title

1ƀ $aPoetsƀofƀtoday;$baƀnewƀAmericanƀanthology.$cWithƀaƀprologueƀpoemƀbyƀ

Imprint

LangstonƀHughes. ⨍ 0ƀ $aNewƀYork,$bInternationalƀPublishers$c [1964] ⨍

Collation   Subject heading

ƀƀ $a143ƀp.$c21ƀcm. ⨍ ƀ0 $aAmericanƀpoetry$y20thƀcentury ⨉

ƀ=blank   ⨍= field terminator   ⨉ = end of record

Lowenfels, Walter, 1897–   ed.
    Poets of today; a new American anthology. With a pro-
logue poem by Langston Hughes. New York, International
Publishers [1964]
    143 p.   21 cm.

       1. American poetry—20th cent.   I. Title.

PS614.L75   811.5082   64–8443

Library of Congress   ◯   [5]

Figure 13-1. Sample Library of Congress card in the MARC II format.

For the purpose of determining character positions a MARC record is divided into two basic parts. The first part consists of the leader and the record directory, and character positions in this part are numbered sequentially beginning with the first character position as 0. The second part of the record contains the remainder of the data, and character positions in this part are numbered sequentially starting with the base address of the data as position 0. The *base address* of the data corresponds to the character position immediately following the field terminator of the record directory.

The *record directory* is an index to the location of the various fields in the record and is made up of fixed-length entries, 12 characters each, with the last entry followed by a field terminator. Each group of 12 characters corresponds to a field in the record and provides the field's identification tag (the first three characters), its length (the next four characters), and its starting position (the last five characters) with respect to the base address. For example, in Figure 13.1, the record directory entry refers to the field whose identification tag is 245, whose length is 89 characters, and which begins in character position 118 starting from the base address of the data (character position 133) as position 0. The numeric tag 245 identifies the field as the title field.

Tag Length Starting position

```
| 245 | 0089 | 00118 |
```

The *control fields* contain such alphanumeric data elements as the Library of Congress card number, language, and country of publication, many of which are of fixed length.

The *variable fields* are made up of variable-length alphanumeric data such as main entry, title, imprint, collation, and subject heading.

Variable fields in the record include one or more data elements, and *subfield codes* are used to identify a particular data element in a field. The following subfield codes occur in the *title field* in Figure 13.1.

$a   Short title (" Poets of today; ")
$b   Remainder of title (" a new American anthology.")
$c   Remainder of title page transcription (" With a prologue poem by Langston Hughes.")

It should also be noted that each variable field starts with two *indicators* that are immediately followed by the delimiter (subfield) code for the first data element in the field. An indicator is a code which supplies additional information about the field and can be different from field to field. For example, an indicator for the main entry field may be used for sorting according to library filing rules, and an indicator in the title field could show that the title has an added entry.

In SAMPLE PROGRAM 23, the record directory is searched only for those tags that define the main entry, title, and subject heading fields, and the indicators in each of these fields are ignored.

Depending on the type of entry involved, the tag for the main entry field may be one of the following

> 100   Personal name
> 110   Corporate name
> 111   Conference or meeting
> 130   Uniform title heading

The title field also has several possible tags to differentiate among various types of titles. However, SAMPLE PROGRAM 23 considers only numeric tag 245. For the subject heading field only tag 650 (topical) is considered in SAMPLE PROGRAM 23.

SAMPLE PROGRAM 23 searches the record directory of each MARC record for a subject heading identified by tag 650. When such a record is found, the title, main entry, and subject heading fields are retrieved from it. These fields are stored in CATALOG in such a way that main entry and title fields having a common subject heading are grouped together using the common subject heading as a key. The process results in the following record structure.

> subject heading $A main entry $T title $A main entry $T title . . . $A
> main entry $T title

where $A and $T are characters inserted by the program to separate main entries from titles.

The program assumes that CATALOG is an existing file which is to be updated whenever a new MARC tape is received. Using the subject heading field as a key, the program examines each subject heading on the MARC tape and determines whether or not it appears in CATALOG. When a subject heading already appears in the file, the program will update the record headed by it. When a subject heading is a new one (representing a new key), then the program will add the corresponding new record to the file.

Adding a new record is accomplished by using the ON KEY statement. The ON KEY statement consists of two parts: the KEY condition and the on-unit. The latter represents an action, defined by either the programmer or the system, to be taken when an interrupt results from the occurrence of the KEY condition. It can be either a single unlabeled statement or an unlabeled BEGIN block. In SAMPLE PROGRAM 23 the on-unit consists of a BEGIN block which defines the action to be taken when a KEY condition appears during execution. A KEY condition is raised when a WRITE statement attempts to add a duplicate key to a DIRECT KEYED file. When a record of CATALOG has as a key a subject heading that is already in the file, the WRITE statement is not executed and the program passes control to the on-unit BEGIN block associated with the ON KEY statement.

The programmer can sometimes identify the type of error condition which may occur when writing or reading files by using the ONCODE built-in function as a debugging aid. This function returns a numeric value that identifies the type of error condition that caused the interruption of the normal execution of the program. Since the numeric codes returned by the ONCODE function are implementation dependent, the programmer should consult the documentation for the PL/I system he uses.

Another built-in function which may be used in a similar fashion to ONCODE is the ONKEY function. The value returned by this function is a varying-length character string giving the value of the key for the record that caused the input/output error condition to be raised.

As an illustration of the utility of the ONCODE and ONKEY built-in functions as program debugging aids, the statement

PUT DATA (ONCODE, ONKEY);

could be included in the BEGIN block which serves as the on-unit of the ON KEY statement in SAMPLE PROGRAM 23: POST.

```
POST:  PROC OPTIONS (MAIN);
       DECLARE MARC FILE SEQUENTIAL INPUT RECORD, MARCREC
       CHAR (2600) VARYING, CATALOG FILE RECORD DIRECT
       KEYED UPDATE, (CATREC, OLDREC) CHAR (7200) VAR,
       SUBJ CHAR (72), (MAINENT, TITLE) CHAR (300) VAR,
       TAG CHAR (3), AU CHAR (2) INIT ('$A'), TI CHAR (2)
       INIT ('$T'), (BASE, STPOS, POS) FIXED BIN, DIR CHAR
       (240) VAR;
       OPEN FILE (CATALOG), FILE (MARC);
       ICTR = 0;
       /*ICTR COUNTS THE NUMBER OF RECORDS FROM THE MARC
       FILE USED TO UPDATE CATALOG*/          [continued]
```

```
READ:   READ FILE (MARC) INTO (MARCREC);
        BASE = SUBSTR (MARCREC, 13, 5);
        L = BASE − (24 + 1);
        /*L IS THE LENGTH OF THE RECORD DIRECTORY*/
        DIR = SUBSTR (MARCREC, 25, L);
  L1:   DO I = 1 TO L BY 12;
        IF SUBSTR (DIR, I, 3) = '650' THEN GO TO SAVE;
        /*SEARCH FOR TAG 650 IN THE RECORD DIRECTORY*/
        END L1;
        GO TO READ;
SAVE:   LENFIELD = SUBSTR (DIR, I + 7, 5);
        /*LENFIELD CONTAINS THE LENGTH OF THE SUBJECT
            HEADING*/
        STPOS = SUBSTR (DIR, I + 3, 4);
        /*STPOS IS THE STARTING CHARACTER POSITION OF THE
            SUBJECT HEADING RELATIVE TO THE BASE ADDRESS*/
        POS = BASE + STPOS;
        POS = POS + 2;
        /*POS IS THE ABSOLUTE STARTING CHARACTER POSITION OF
            THE SUBJECT HEADING RELATIVE TO THE BEGINNING
            OF THE RECORD. THE 2 CHARACTERS ADDED TO POS
            CORRESPOND TO THE INDICATORS AT THE BEGINNING
            OF EACH FIELD*/
        SUBJ = SUBSTR (MARCREC, POS, LENFIELD);
  L2:   DO I = 1 TO L BY 12;
        IF SUBSTR (DIR, I, 1) = '1' THEN GO TO GETAUTHOR;
        IF SUBSTR (DIR, I, 3) = '245' THEN GO TO GETTITLE;
        END L2;
 ERR:   PUT LIST ('ERROR − NO MAIN ENTRY, NO TITLE');
        PUT SKIP LIST (MARCREC);
        GO TO READ;
        ON ENDFILE (MARC) GO TO CLOSE;
        ON KEY (CATALOG)
        BEGIN;
        READ FILE (CATALOG) INTO (OLDREC) KEY (SUBJ);
        CATREC = OLDREC ‖ MAINENT ‖ TITLE;
        REWRITE FILE (CATALOG) FROM (CATREC) KEY (SUBJ);
        ICTR = ICTR + 1;
        GO TO READ;
        END;
```

```
GETAUTHOR:   LENFIELD = SUBSTR (DIR, I + 7, 5);
             /*LENFIELD CONTAINS THE LENGTH OF THE MAIN ENTRY*/
             STPOS = SUBSTR (DIR, I + 3, 4);
             /*STPOS CONTAINS THE STARTING CHAR POSITION FOR THE
               MAIN ENTRY*/
             POS = BASE + STPOS + 2;
             MAINENT = AU ‖ SUBSTR (MARCREC, POS, LENFIELD);
             I = I + 12;
             IF SUBSTR (DIR, I, 3) = '245' THEN GO TO GETTITLE;
             GO TO ERR;
             /*TITLE IS THE NEXT FIELD AFTER MAIN ENTRY IN THE
               RECORD DIRECTORY*/
GETTITLE:    LENFIELD = SUBSTR (DIR, I + 7, 5);
             STPOS = SUBSTR (DIR, I + 3, 4);
             POS = BASE + STPOS + 2;
             TITLE = TI ‖ SUBSTR (MARCREC, POS, LENFIELD);
             CATREC = SUBJ ‖ MAINENT ‖ TITLE;
             WRITE FILE (CATALOG) FROM (CATREC) KEYFROM (SUBJ);
             ICTR = ICTR + 1;
             GO TO READ;
CLOSE:       CLOSE FILE (CATALOG), FILE (MARC);
             PUT EDIT ('THE NUMBER OF RECORDS RETRIEVED FROM THE
               MARC FILE IS: ' , ICTR) (SKIP, A, F (6, 0));
             END POST;
```

SAMPLE PROGRAM 23: POST illustrates two important programming applications in library operations relating to bibliographic control: (1) the process of updating a catalog file by taking into account pertinent information about newly acquired materials which is extracted from a comprehensive source-cataloging data base (such as the MARC II data base), and (2) the transfer of such bibliographic information from a data base whose records are organized as a *direct* file (the MARC file) to one whose records are organized as an *inverted* file (the CATALOG file).

Sample Program 24: SEARCH1

In the next two programming illustrations in the text, SAMPLE PROGRAMS 24 and 25, we show how some of the basic techniques of file data management may be employed in order to implement simple search strategies involving document retrieval files. In SAMPLE PROGRAM 24: SEARCH1 the retrieval file is organized as a *direct* file (see Section 11.3) in which each record corresponds to a document and includes the set of index terms associated with the document. In SEARCH2, the retrieval file is organized as an *inverted* file (see Section 11.3) in which each record corresponds to an index term and contains a list of the documents indexed by the term in question.

In SAMPLE PROGRAM 24: SEARCH1, the retrieval file is named DOCUMENT and each record in the file is described by a structure variable called DOCREC whose parts consist of a document accession number, title, author, and a set of index terms not exceeding ten in number. The last index term in each document record is always a dummy term called 'ENDTERM'. The file DOCUMENT is characterized by the attributes SEQUENTIAL, RECORD, and INPUT and can be used with data stored on magnetic tape or disk. A maximum of 30 query (search) terms are read in from cards, and the last query term is always a dummy term called '$STOP'. A match of a query term with an individual index term is defined as a "hit" and results in the retrieval of the corresponding document record.

```
SEARCH1:  PROCEDURE OPTIONS (MAIN);
          DECLARE QUERY (30) CHAR (40) VAR INIT ('XX'), DOCUMENT
              FILE SEQUENTIAL RECORD INPUT, HIT (30) CHAR (9000)
              VAR INIT (' '), 1 DOCREC, 2 DOC# CHAR (4), 2 TITLE
              CHAR (100), 2 AUTHOR CHAR (100), 2 TERM (10) CHAR
              (40);
          J = 1;
   FETCH: GET EDIT (QUERY (J)) (A (40), A (40));
      L1: DO WHILE (QUERY (J) ⌐ = '$STOP');
          J = J + 1;
          GO TO FETCH;
          END L1;
          ON ENDFILE (DOCUMENT) GO TO PRINT;
 NEXTREC: READ FILE (DOCUMENT) INTO (DOCREC);
  SEARCH: DO I = 1 BY 1 WHILE (TERM (I) ⌐ = 'ENDTERM');
          DO K = 1 TO J − 1;
          IF TERM (I) = QUERY (K) THEN HIT (K) = HIT (K) ‖ DOCREC.
              DOC# ‖ DOCREC.TITLE ‖ DOCREC.AUTHOR;
          /*A DOCUMENT ONE OF WHOSE TERMS MATCHES A QUERY IS
              ADDED TO THE LIST OF DOCUMENTS SATISFYING THAT
              QUERY.*/
          END;
          END SEARCH;
          GO TO NEXTREC;
```

```
PRINT:  DO I = 1 TO J − 1;
        PUT LIST ('THE FOLLOWING DOCUMENTS SATISFY THE TERM ',
          QUERY (I));
        PUT SKIP LIST (HIT (I));
        END PRINT;
        END SEARCH1;
```

It should be remarked that SEARCH1 allows multiple queries to be searched against each record in the document file. This approach is advantageous because it allows the file to be opened and closed only once. If each record in the file were searched separately for each query, the file would have to be opened and closed as many times as there are queries to be processed, and the search for each query would require a full pass of the file. Although in the sample program each query consists of a single index term, the method of multiple searching used in SAMPLE PROGRAM 24 is equally applicable to queries consisting of Boolean combinations of index terms.

Sample Program 25: SEARCH2

A retrieval file in which each record corresponds to an index term followed by a list of references representing documents indexed by the term is called an *inverted* file. In the next sample program to be considered in the text, an inverted file is searched for documents that satisfy individual query terms that are read from cards. For each query that matches an index term in the file, the corresponding file record is retrieved and printed.

In SEARCH2 the retrieval file is named INDEX and is organized as an inverted file in which the index term serves as the key for each record. Each record in the file is described by a structure variable called ENTRY. The file INDEX is declared with the attributes RECORD KEYED INPUT, and by use of the KEY option the READ statement will access directly the record whose index term corresponds to the query specified in the KEY option. Because the file is KEYED, it must be used with a direct-access device, such as a magnetic disk or drum.

```
SEARCH2:  PROCEDURE OPTIONS (MAIN);
          DECLARE INDEX FILE RECORD INPUT DIRECT KEYED, QUERY
            CHAR (40), 1 ENTRY, 2 TERM CHAR (40), 2 DOCUMENTS
            CHAR (1000);
          ON ENDFILE (SYSIN) GO TO STOP;
          ON KEY (INDEX)
          BEGIN;
```

```
                    PUT SKIP LIST ('NONE OF THE DOCUMENTS IN THE FILE SATISFY
                        THE TERM ', QUERY);
                    GO TO SEARCH;
                    END;
         SEARCH:    GET LIST (QUERY);
                    READ FILE (INDEX) INTO (ENTRY) KEY (QUERY);
                    PUT SKIP LIST ('THE FOLLOWING DOCUMENTS SATISFY THE
                        TERM ', QUERY);
                    PUT SKIP LIST (ENTRY.DOCUMENTS);
                    GO TO SEARCH;
         STOP:      END SEARCH2;
```

Because the records in the file labeled INDEX are accessed through their keys, SAMPLE PROGRAM 25 does not include search statements per se, as was the case in SAMPLE PROGRAM 24. Instead, searching is accomplished by use of the READ statement in conjunction with the ON KEY statement. In executing the READ statement, the PL/I system checks the key for each record and retrieves only those records whose key is specified. Each record is checked for the content of the key and is read only when the content of the key matches the content of the variable specified in the KEY option of the READ statement. This results in the retrieval of the desired record containing the list of documents satisfying the query term. On the other hand, the KEY condition is raised whenever the system searches for a key specified in the KEY option of the READ statement which does not exist in any record of the file. When this occurs, the on-unit of the ON KEY statement is executed. Since the on-unit is a BEGIN block, a message is printed that none of the documents listed in the file satisfy the query term, and control is passed to the GET LIST statement for fetching the next query term.

It should be pointed out that the retrieval file in SAMPLE PROGRAM 25 could contain copious amounts of redundant data. The complete bibliographic information for each document is repeated in the file as many times as index terms are assigned to a document. A more economical way of organizing an inverted file retrieval system is to include only document accession numbers in each record and to store the corresponding bibliogaphic information in a separate file (see Exercise 1 at the end of this chapter).

SAMPLE PROGRAMS SEARCH1 and SEARCH2 are intended to illustrate basic techniques of file manipulation and file processing as applied to document retrieval systems. No attempt was made, however, to incorporate Boolean search strategies into the two programs, since SAMPLE PROGRAMS 19 and 20: RETRIEVE1 and RETRIEVE2 in Chapter 11 have dealt adequately with the subject of implementing the logic of document retrieval. Taken together, the four SAMPLE PROGRAMS 19, 20, 24, and 25—RETRIEVE1, RETRIEVE2, SEARCH1, and SEARCH2—provide the basic programming fundamentals for illustrating how the facilities of PL/I can be used for the implementation of large-scale document retrieval systems.

EXERCISES

1. Using the approach illustrated in SAMPLE PROGRAM 25: SEARCH2, write a program which will read from an inverted file the document accession numbers as four-character numbers and use the numbers as keys to retrieve documents from a direct file containing the full document records arranged in order of their accession numbers.

2. Write a program consisting of a single procedure which creates a file as a keyed sequential file containing ten records and then reads from it as a direct keyed file.

3. Write a program which performs the task described in Exercise 2 but uses two procedures instead of one.

CHAPTER 14

Based Variables for List Processing

In PL/I there are four types of storage classes for variables: automatic, static, controlled, and based. The storage class of a variable indicates how storage is allocated to the variable during execution of the program. In general, if the storage class is not defined explicitly by an attribute, the PL/I compiler assigns by default *automatic* storage. This class of storage is allocated at the time when the block in which the variables are declared is activated, and released when control of the program leaves the block. *Static* storage is allocated when the object program is loaded in the computer memory. Allocation of storage can be made dynamically at run time by inclusion of certain statements in the program. In Chapter 8 we discussed how the ALLOCATE and FREE statements can be used to allocate *controlled* storage. We now discuss *based* storage, its allocation by means of the foregoing statements, and some of its major uses, especially for list processing.

14.1 Based Storage and Pointer Variables

Declaration of based storage for variables involves use of the BASED attribute and specification of a set of associated variables called *pointers*. Pointer variables may be declared explicitly by use of the POINTER (abbreviated: PTR) attribute, or they may be named contextually in the declaration of based variables, as illustrated:

DECLARE X BASED, P POINTER;

DECLARE X BASED (P);

where X is a based variable and P is its associated pointer variable.

The significance of associating pointer variables with based variables is that based variables, unlike other storage-class variables, do *not* have specific storage locations assigned to them once and for all by the compiler. Based variables can, in effect, be located anywhere in memory. Hence, before any reference can be made to a based variable, it is necessary to be able to determine its address. This is accomplished by means of a convention in PL/I that the value of the pointer variable is always the storage address in memory of the based variable.

A based variable is said to be *qualified* by the pointer variable associated with it. Since any pointer variable can be used to qualify any based variable, some nomenclature is required to identify the pointer variable that qualifies a given based variable. *Implicit* qualification occurs when the pointer variable is named contextually in the declaration of the based variable, as in the following case.

DCL X BASED (P), Y BASED (Q);

In this instance, the based variables X and Y are implicitly qualified by the pointer variables P and Q, respectively, whereas in

DCL (X, Y) BASED, (P, Q) PTR;

X, Y and P, Q are declared to be based and pointer variables, respectively, but no qualification of X and Y occurs. The arrow notation

P → X

is used to denote *explicit* qualification of a based variable by a pointer variable, and reads "the based variable X whose address is given by the pointer variable P." The following pairs of statements produce the same effect:

> DCL (X, Y) BASED, (P, Q) PTR;
> P → X = Q → Y + 5.0;
>
> DCL X BASED (P), Y BASED (Q);
> X = Y + 5.0;

where explicit qualification of the based variables occurs in the first pair of statements but not in the second. *It is the responsibility of the programmer to insure that based variables are properly qualified.*

14.2   Allocation of Based Storage

Several methods are available for the assignment of values to pointer variables. One way is by use of the ALLOCATE statement (Section 8.3), which has the following format when used with based variables.

> ALLOCATE name SET (pointer);

where "name" is the identifier for a based variable and "pointer" is the identifier for a pointer variable. The statement causes (1) allocation of storage to the based variable and (2) assignment of the address of that storage as the value of the pointer variable. If the based variable is previously qualified, then the SET clause can be omitted. Consider the code

> DCL X BASED (P), Y BASED (Q), R PTR;
> ALLOCATE X;
> X = 5.0;
> ALLOCATE Y SET (R);
> R → Y = X;

After this code is executed, storage is allocated for X, and the address of that storage is assigned to P, since X is qualified by P. Storage is also allocated for Y, and the address of that storage is assigned to R. The pointer variable Q, which also qualifies Y, is not assigned any value. It would be an error to refer to Q → Y before Q is assigned a value.

To release based storage, the FREE statement used for controlled variables (Section 8.3) may be used as follows.

> FREE X;
> FREE R → Y;

A second way in which values can be assigned to pointer variables is to assign to one pointer variable the value of another.

Another way of assigning values to pointer variables is by use of the built-in functions ADDR and NULL. The function ADDR takes a single argument, and the value returned by ADDR is the absolute address of the variable serving as the argument of ADDR. For example, the assignment statement

$$P = \text{ADDR} (x);$$

stores in P the absolute storage address of x. The built-in function NULL takes no argument and returns a null address that is different from any storage address in memory. For example, the statement

$$P = \text{NULL};$$

clears the value of P. The NULL function can be used to test for unallocated storage. It is also used to assign the null value to the last pointer in a list as an end-of-list indicator (see Figure 14.2).

14.3   Some Applications of Based Storage

One of the advantages of based storage is that storage can be allocated to a based variable over and over again, with the result that several generations of the variable may exist concurrently and can be available for use at one time. This fact explains the usefulness of based storage for list processing. Consider the code

```
DCL BOOK BASED (M), (N, O) PTR;
ALLOCATE BOOK;
GET LIST (BOOK);
ALLOCATE BOOK SET (N);
GET LIST (N → BOOK);
ALLOCATE BOOK SET (O);
GET LIST (O → BOOK);
```

After this code is executed, there are three generations of BOOK, the first addressed by the pointer variable M, the second by N, and the third by O. A reference to BOOK (that is, to M → BOOK) is to the first generation, N → BOOK to the second, and O → BOOK to the third. All of the generations are available at any time. This contrasts with the repeated use of ALLOCATE statements for controlled variables. Only the most recent generation of a controlled variable is available at any time.

Because all of the generations of a based variable are available at any time, based storage provides a convenient way of avoiding wasteful allocation of storage. This is illustrated by the code

```
            DCL BOOK CHAR (80) BASED, (P (1000), Q)PTR;
            ON ENDFILE (SYSIN) GO TO RELEASE;
    L1:     DO I = 1 TO 1000;
            ALLOCATE BOOK SET (P (I));
            Q = P (I);
            GET EDIT (Q → BOOK) (A (80));
            END L1;
    RELEASE:    FREE Q → BOOK;
```

The advantage of using based storage is that after this code is executed, there are as many generations of BOOK as there were data cards to be read in. Thus if the actual number of cards which are read turns out to be substantially less than 1000, no additional allocation of storage is needed beyond the number of cards actually read. Addresses of the cards are retained in a pointer array P in such a way that P (I) points at the Ith card. If only 650 cards are read, the value of P (I) for $I \geq 651$ is the null address. The FREE statement releases the storage already allocated for an input card when the end-of-file condition was encountered. Pointer Q is used as a temporary location for P (I), because the pointer qualifying a based variable cannot be subscripted.

Let us now look at a simple example that illustrates some of the principles of based storage. In Exercise 3 at the end of Chapter 8, we posed the problem of writing a basic sort routine using array variables. We now show how the program can be written using based variables. For purposes of illustration we assume that a maximum of five names are to be sorted alphabetically.

```
    SORT_BS:    PROCEDURE OPTIONS (MAIN);
                DCL NAME CHAR (10) BASED, (P(5), TEMP, P1, P2) PTR;
                ON ENDFILE (SYSIN) GO TO SORT;
    L1:         DO I = 1 BY 1;
                ALLOCATE NAME SET (P (I));
                TEMP = P (I);
                GET EDIT (TEMP → NAME) (A (10));
                END L1;
```

```
SORT:    FREE TEMP → NAME;
  L2:    DO J = 1 TO I − 2;
         DO K = J + 1 TO I − 1;
         P1 = P (J);
         P2 = P (K);
         IF P1 → NAME > P2 → NAME THEN
  G1:    DO;
         TEMP = P (J);
         P (J) = P (K);
         P (K) = TEMP;
         END G1;
         END L2;
PRINT:   DO J = 1 TO I − 1;
         P1 = P (J);
         PUT EDIT (P1 → NAME) (A(10), SKIP);
         END PRINT;
         END SORT_BS;
```

By using based variables with pointers, the program above requires less manipulation of stored data than a comparable sort program which does not use based storage. At the completion of the program, each generation of the based variable NAME remains at the storage address initially assigned to it by the compiler; only the values of the pointers in the array P are exchanged. In other words, sorting in the program consists of the possible exchange of the *values* of the pointer variables associated with each generation of NAME and *not* the exchange of the *generations of* NAME themselves. Figure 14.1 illustrates this method of sorting using based variables, where the value of each generation of NAME remains fixed and the values of the pointer variables change.

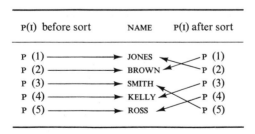

Figure 14-1. Sorting using based storage.

14.4   List Processing

An important use of based storage in PL/I is in list processing. A list is a sequence of variables linked together by pointers. An initial pointer contains the address of the first variable in the list, and associated with each variable is a pointer whose value is the address of the next variable in the list. The pointer associated with the last variable has the special NULL value, indicating that there are no more variables in the list. Figure 14.2 illustrates how a simple list is organized in based storage. In PL/I programming it is convenient to employ structure variables (Section 8.5) in forming lists, because a based structure variable can contain a pointer variable as a component in addition to other variables as components.

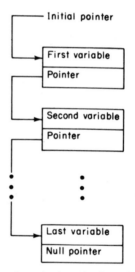

Figure 14.2.   Organization of a list in based storage.

Sample Program 26:   LIST

As an illustration of the basic scheme for constructing a list using based storage, let us consider a program which reads a maximum of 100 names, stores them as a list, and prints them in the order in which they appear in the list. In the program, NAME is declared as a based structure variable whose first component variable represents the value of the current generation of NAME and whose second component variable is a pointer containing the address of the next generation of NAME.

```
LIST:      PROC OPTIONS (MAIN);
           DCL 1 NAME BASED (R), 2 VALUE CHAR (80), 2 NEXT PTR,
             (P, INITIAL) PTR;
           ON ENDFILE (SYSIN) GO TO RELEASE;
     L1:   DO I = 1 TO 100;
           ALLOCATE NAME;
           GET LIST (VALUE);
           IF I = 1 THEN INITIAL = R;
           ELSE P → NEXT = R;
           P = R;
           END L1;
RELEASE:   FREE NAME;
           P → NEXT = NULL;
           R = INITIAL;
   PRINT:  DO WHILE (R ¬ = NULL);
           PUT EDIT (VALUE) (A (80), SKIP);
           R = NEXT;
           END PRINT;
           END LIST;
```

It should be observed that sorting or deleting names in the list formed by the foregoing program may be accomplished simply by changing the values of the pointers NEXT associated with each of the names, and does not require any physical movement in storage of the names themselves. This kind of programming facility and ease is what is so appealing about the use of based storage in the manipulation and processing of lists.

In case of record I/O a value is assigned to a pointer with the following type of READ statement:

READ FILE (name 1) SET (pointer);

where "name 1" is the file identifier and "pointer" a pointer variable. This statement causes a record to be read into a buffer and the pointer value to be the starting address of the buffer. A reference to a based variable qualified by this pointer is considered a reference to the record itself. The foregoing READ statement can be used only with buffered sequential files.

To allocate storage in an output buffer for a based variable the LOCATE statement must be used as follows.

LOCATE name 1 FILE (name 2) SET (pointer);

where "name 1" is the based variable identifier, "name 2" the file identifier, and "pointer" the pointer identifier.

If the SET option appears, the specified pointer refers to the address of the buffer; if the SET clause is not used in the LOCATE statement, then the pointer qualifying the based variable "name 1" points to the buffer.

If a variable is written on an output device following a LOCATE statement, then the storage allocated to the variable is automatically released. The storage allocated with a READ statement is released by the next READ statement.

EXERCISE

1. Using based storage, write a program which reads in four data elements A, B, C, and D, forms the list (A, (B, C), D) and prints out the sublist (B, C), where (A, (B, C), D) is represented as:

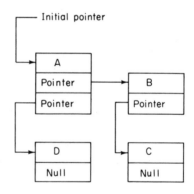

Solutions to Exercises

Chapter 2

1. Valid are (c), (e), and (h).

Chapter 3

1. Arithmetic variables are B, C, and D in the first expression, and A, B, C, and D in the second.
2. (1) GO TO L;
   (2) W = R;
   (3) W = Z;
   (4) GO TO L;

3. ASSESS6A: PROCEDURE OPTIONS (MAIN);
     DECLARE (USER, DUEDATE, RATE, DATE, FINE, BOOK,
       HOWMANYFINES, HOWMUCHMONEY) FIXED;
     HOWMANYFINES, HOWMUCHMONEY = 0;
     /*INITIALIZE TO VALUE 0*/
     GET LIST (RATE, DATE);
   L: GET LIST (BOOK, USER, DUEDATE);
     IF USER = 0 THEN GO TO FINISH;
     FINE = (DATE − DUEDATE) * RATE;
     IF FINE < = 0 THEN GO TO L;
     /*A NEGATIVE FINE INDICATES THAT BOOK IS NOT
      OVERDUE*/
     HOWMUCHMONEY = HOWMUCHMONEY + FINE;
     HOWMANYFINES = HOWMANYFINES + 1;
     PUT SKIP LIST (BOOK, USER, FINE);
     GO TO L;
  FINISH: PUT SKIP LIST (HOWMANYFINES, HOWMUCHMONEY);
     END ASSESS6A;

Sample Input Data
 10 31
 213645 987 23
 363666 999 17
 426583 333 26
 434656 555 13

Output
 10 31
 213645 987 80
 363666 999 140
 426583 333 50
 434656 555 180
 4   450

Chapter 4

1. ASSESS7A: PROCEDURE OPTIONS (MAIN);
     DECLARE USER CHARACTER (25) VARYING,
      DAYS FIXED (2), RATE FIXED (2), FINE FIXED (3);

```
L1:   GET LIST (USER, DAYS, RATE);
      IF USER = 'XXX' THEN GO TO STOP;
      /*A DUMMY NAME 'XXX' FOLLOWS LAST USER*/
      FINE = DAYS * RATE;
      PUT SKIP LIST (USER, 'OWES THE LIBRARY ',
            FINE, 'CENTS FOR OVERDUE MATERIALS.');
      GO TO L1;
STOP: END ASSESS7A;
```

```
2.  CATALOG1:  PROCEDURE OPTIONS (MAIN);
               DECLARE (NAME CHARACTER (20), TITLE
                     CHARACTER (30), CALLNO CHARACTER (10),
                     AUTHOR CHARACTER (20)) VARYING;
       GET:    GET LIST (AUTHOR);
               IF AUTHOR = 'XXX' THEN GO TO STOP;
               PUT LIST (AUTHOR);
    SEARCH:    GET LIST (NAME, TITLE, CALLNO);
               IF NAME = '000' THEN GO TO GET;
               IF NAME = AUTHOR THEN GO TO PRINT;
               GO TO SEARCH;
     PRINT:    PUT SKIP LIST (TITLE, CALLNO);
               GO TO SEARCH;
      STOP:    END CATALOG1;
```

As an alternative to reading in the NAME-TITLE-CALLNO file every time a search is made for books by more than one author, as required in CATALOG1, the names of all such authors could be read initially and stored in the computer. The use of multiple IF statements would then allow only one pass through the NAME-TITLE-CALLNO file to determine the titles and call numbers of books by the desired authors. The use of arrays, to be discussed in Chapter 8, is well suited to handle this type of multiple search process.

Chapter 5

```
1.  CONVERT:  PROC OPTIONS (MAIN);
              DCL STRING CHAR (3);
              I = 0;
              PUT EDIT ('XYZ', 'XYZ') (A(3), X (5), A (3));
```

```
GET:    GET LIST (STRING);
        PUT EDIT (STRING) (SKIP, A (3), X (5));
        STRING = TRANSLATE (STRING, 'TF', '10');
        PUT EDIT (STRING) (A (3));
        I = I + 1;
        IF I = 4 THEN GO TO STOP;
        GO TO GET;
STOP:   END CONVERT;
```

2. Replace the assignment statement labeled FINISH by

```
FINISH:   W = SUBSTR (TITLE, M, LENGTH (TITLE) − M);
```

As an alternate solution, insert the following after the assignment statement labeled FINISH.

```
W = SUBSTR (W, 1, LENGTH (W) − 1);
```

3.
```
PARSE1:     PROCEDURE OPTIONS (MAIN);
            DECLARE (TITLE CHARACTER (80), W CHARACTER (10))
                VARYING;
NEXTTITLE:  GET LIST (TITLE);
            IF TITLE = 'XXX' THEN GO TO STOP;
            PUT LIST (TITLE);
            M = −1;
            L = 1;
GETWORD:    M = M + L + 1;
            L = INDEX (SUBSTR (TITLE, M), ' ') − 1;
            IF L < = 0 THEN GO TO FINISH;
            W = SUBSTR (TITLE, M, L);
            PUT SKIP LIST (W);
            GO TO GETWORD;
FINISH:     W = SUBSTR (TITLE, M);
            PUT SKIP LIST (W);
            GO TO NEXTTITLE;
STOP:       END PARSE1;
```

4.
```
PARSE2:     PROCEDURE OPTIONS (MAIN);
            DECLARE (TITLE CHARACTER (80), W CHARACTER (10))
                VARYING;
NEXTTITLE:  GET LIST (TITLE);
            IF TITLE = 'XXX' THEN GO TO STOP;
            PUT LIST (TITLE);
```

```
                M = −1;
                L = 1;
GETWORD:        M = M + L + 1;
                L = INDEX (SUBSTR (TITLE, M), ' ') − 1;
                IF L < = 0 THEN GO TO FINISH;
                W = SUBSTR (TITLE, M, L);
                IF (W = 'THE') | (W = 'AN') | (W = 'OF') | (W = 'BY') |
                   (W = 'AND') THEN GO TO GETWORD;
                PUT SKIP LIST (W);
                GO TO GETWORD;
FINISH:         W = SUBSTR (TITLE, M);
                PUT SKIP LIST (W);
                GO TO NEXTTITLE;
STOP:           END PARSE2;
```

5.
```
    PARSE3:     PROCEDURE OPTIONS (MAIN);
                DECLARE (DOCNO, TITLE, W, FULL) CHARACTER (80)
                   VARYING;
NEXTTITLE:      GET LIST (DOCNO, TITLE);
                IF TITLE = 'XXX' THEN GO TO STOP;
                FULL = TITLE;
                /*SAVE ORIGINAL TITLE*/
GETWORD:        L = INDEX (TITLE, ' ');
                IF L = 0 THEN GO TO FINISH;
                W = SUBSTR (TITLE, 1, L − 1);
                /*LOCATE LEFTMOST WORD IN TITLE AND STORE IN
                   'W'*/
                IF (W ¬ = 'FOR') | (W ¬ = 'OF') | (W ¬ = 'ON') |
                   (W ¬ = 'BY') | (W ¬ = 'THE') | (W ¬ = 'AND')
                   THEN PUT SKIP LIST (W, FULL, DOCNO);
                TITLE = SUBSTR (TITLE, L + 1);
                /*REMOVE LEFTMOST WORD AND STORE SHORTEN
                   TITLE BACK IN 'TITLE'*/
                GO TO GETWORD;
FINISH:         W = SUBSTR (TITLE, 1, LENGTH (TITLE) − 1);
                /*STORE IN 'W' THE LAST WORD OF TITLE WITHOUT
                   SEMICOLON*/
                PUT SKIP LIST (W, FULL, DOCNO);
                GO TO NEXTTITLE;
STOP:           END PARSE3;
```

Sample Input Data
'EIX69X090009'   'DESIGN PROCEDURES FOR BAY AREA;'
'000000'   'XXX'

Output

DESIGN	DESIGN PROCEDURES FOR BAY AREA;	EIX69X09009
PROCEDURES	DESIGN PROCEDURES FOR BAY AREA;	EIX69X09009
BAY	DESIGN PROCEDURES FOR BAY AREA;	EIX69X09009
AREA	DESIGN PROCEDURES FOR BAY AREA;	EIX69X09009

Chapter 6

1. $L = L4, X = 40$
2. 701231
   F. SMITH   RPO 3729   MODERN MATH   C. SIMS

3.   INVERT1: PROC OPTIONS (MAIN);
                DCL (TITLE, ABBRTITLE) CHAR (80) VAR, (TYPE, MAIN)
                CHAR (30) VAR INITIAL (' '), WORD CHAR (12)
                VAR, NEXTSTEP LABEL;
                /*'TITLE' IS THE ORIGINAL TITLE, 'ABBRTITLE' IS
                THE TITLE AFTER REMOVAL OF PREPOSITIONS AND
                CONJUNCTIONS, 'TYPE' IS THE IDENTIFIER FOR
                JOURNAL TYPE, 'MAIN' IS THE IDENTIFIER FOR THE
                MAIN BODY OF THE TITLE*/
      START: GET LIST (TITLE);
                IF TITLE = 'XXX' THEN GO TO STOP;
                PUT SKIP LIST (TITLE);
      NEXTWORD: L = INDEX (TITLE, ' ');
                IF L = 0 THEN
                DO;
                L = INDEX (TITLE, ';');
                NEXTSTEP = LAST;
                END;
                ELSE NEXTSTEP = NEXTWORD;
      GETWORD: WORD = SUBSTR (TITLE, 1, L − 1);
                IF (WORD = 'AND')|(WORD = 'BY')|(WORD =
                'FOR')|(WORD = 'OF')|(WORD = 'THE') THEN GO
                TO SHORT;

```
              IF (WORD = 'JOURNAL') | (WORD = 'TRANSACTIONS') |
                  (WORD = 'REVIEW') | (WORD =
                  'COMMUNICATIONS') THEN
              DO;
              TYPE = TYPE ‖ WORD;
              GO TO SHORT;
              END;
              MAIN = MAIN ‖ WORD ‖ ' ';
    SHORT:    TITLE = SUBSTR (TITLE, L + 1);
              GO TO NEXTSTEP;
     LAST:    MAIN = SUBSTR (MAIN, 1, LENGTH (MAIN) − 1);
              IF TYPE = ' ' THEN
              DO;
              ABBRTITLE = MAIN ‖ ';' ;
              GO TO PRINT;
              END;
              IF TYPE = WORD THEN
              DO;
              ABBRTITLE = MAIN ‖ ' ' ‖ TYPE ‖ ';';
              GO TO PRINT;
              END;
              ABBRTITLE = MAIN ‖ ',' ‖ TYPE ‖ ';';
    PRINT:    PUT SKIP LIST (ABBRTITLE);
              GO TO START;
     STOP:    END INVERT1;
```

Chapter 7

1. None
2. THE TEXT IS: IT IS BETTER TO DO AS I SAY, SAID HE, THAN DO AS I DO.
   THE INDEX WORD IS: DO
   THE NUMBER OF OCCURRENCES OF THE INDEX WORD IN THE TEXT,
   AND THEIR LOCATIONS, ARE RESPECTIVELY

3	5	12	15	0
0	0	0	0	0
0	0	0	0	0
0	0	0	0	0
0				

3. The output is the same as in Exercise 2 except that the integers 5, 12, and 15 are replaced by 17, 44, and 52, respectively. This is because I serves as an index to count the number of words in the input text while M serves to identify the position within the text of the first character of each word.

4. SENTENCE COUNT $= 2.0$
    AVERAGE WORD COUNT $= 6.0$
    AVERAGE LETTER COUNT $= 2.61$

5.   COUNT1 :   PROCEDURE OPTIONS (MAIN);
                   DECLARE TEXT CHAR (500) VARYING,
                       SYMBOL CHAR (1),
                       (STATEMENTCOUNT, WORDCOUNT,
                       LETTERCOUNT) FIXED;
        PROCESS : GET LIST (TEXT);
                   STATEMENTCOUNT, WORDCOUNT, LETTERCOUNT $= 0$;
                   J $= 1$;
           L1 :   DO I $= 1$ BY 1 TO LENGTH (TEXT);
                   SYMBOL = SUBSTR (TEXT, I, 1);
                   IF (SYMBOL = '.') $|$ (SYMBOL = '?') THEN
           G1 :   DO;
                   STATEMENTCOUNT = STATEMENTCOUNT $+ 1$;
                   IF I $=$ J $+ 1$ THEN GO TO CONTINUE;
                   WORDCOUNT = WORDCOUNT $+ 1$;
                   END G1;
                   ELSE IF INDEX (', : ;' , SYMBOL) $\neg = 0$ THEN
                       WORDCOUNT = WORDCOUNT $+ 1$;
                   ELSE LETTERCOUNT = LETTERCOUNT $+ 1$;
        CONTINUE : J $= 1$;
                   END L1;
                   PUT SKIP LIST ('SENTENCE COUNT $= $ ',
                       STATEMENTCOUNT);
                   PUT SKIP LIST ('AVERAGE WORD COUNT $= $ ',
                       WORDCOUNT $/$ STATEMENTCOUNT);
                   PUT SKIP LIST ('AVERAGE LETTER COUNT $= $ ',
                       LETTERCOUNT $/$ WORDCOUNT);
                   GO TO PROCESS;
                   END COUNT1;

6. NO, NO, NO, SAID SHE. SAID HE, WHAT AM I TO DO?
    A $= 4$
    D $= 3$

E = 2
H = 3
I = 3
M = 1
N = 3
O = 5
S = 3
T = 2
W = 1

7. PROCESS: GET LIST (TEXT);
   Include the dummy text '#' at the end of the input stream, and insert in the program the following IF statement immediately following the GET LIST statement:

IF TEXT = '#' THEN GO TO STOP;

where STOP becomes the label of the END FREQ1 statement.

8.   FREQ1A: PROCEDURE OPTIONS (MAIN);
                        DECLARE ALPHA CHAR (26) INIT ('AB
                            CDEFGHIJKLMNOPQRSTUVWXYZ'),
                            TEXT CHAR (160) VARYING,
                            LETTER CHAR (1),
                            (COUNT, PREVIOUS_OCCUR, NEXT_OCCUR,
                            PUNCT_COUNT,
                            TOTAL_COUNT) FIXED;
            PROCESS: GET LIST (TEXT);
                        PUT LIST (TEXT);
                        /*IN ORDER TO FIND THE TOTAL COUNT OF LETTERS,
                        ALL PUNCTUATION CHARACTERS AND BLANKS
                        MUST BE COUNTED AND SUBTRACTED FROM
                        THE TOTAL LENGTH OF THE TEXT*/
                        PUNCT_COUNT = 0;
            COUNT_PUNCT: DO I = 1 TO LENGTH (TEXT);
                        IF VERIFY (SUBSTR (TEXT, I, 1), ', ; : ?') = 0 THEN
                            PUNCT_COUNT = PUNCT_COUNT + 1;
                        END COUNT_PUNCT;
                        TOTAL_COUNT = LENGTH (TEXT) − PUNCT_
                        COUNT;
            L1:   DO I = 1 TO 26;
                        LETTER = SUBSTR (ALPHA, I, 1);
                        COUNT = 0;

```
        PREVIOUS_OCCUR, NEXT_OCCUR = INDEX (TEXT,
            LETTER);
        IF PREVIOUS_OCCUR = 0 THEN GO TO
            NEXT_LETTER;
L2:     DO WHILE (NEXT_OCCUR ⌐ = 0);
        COUNT = COUNT + 1;
        NEXT_OCCUR = INDEX (SUBSTR (TEXT,
            PREVIOUS _OCCUR + 1), LETTER);
        PREVIOUS_OCCUR = PREVIOUS_OCCUR + NEXT_
            OCCUR;
        END L2;
        PERCENT = (COUNT * 100) / TOTAL_COUNT;
        PUT SKIP EDIT (LETTER, 'OCCURS WITH A
            FREQUENCY = ', PERCENT, '%') (A(1), X(2),
            A(26), F(2, 0), A(1));
NEXT_LETTER:  END L1;
        GO TO PROCESS;
        END FREQ1A;
```

Chapter 8

```
1.  SHELFLIST1A:  PROC OPTIONS (MAIN);
        DCL (OLDLIST (200), NEWLIST (100)) CHAR (80)
            VARYING INITIAL ('AA'), (OLDCOUNT, NEWCOUNT)
            FIXED;
        I = 1;
GETO:   GET LIST (OLDLIST (I));
        DO WHILE (OLDLIST (I) ⌐ = 'XX');
        I = I + 1;
        GO TO GETO;
        END;
        OLDCOUNT = I − 1;
        I = 1;
GETN:   GET LIST (NEWLIST (I));
        DO WHILE (NEWLIST (I) ⌐ = 'XX');
        I = I + 1;
        GO TO GETN;
        END;
        NEWCOUNT = I − 1;
        PUT LIST ('THIS IS THE OLD SHELFLIST: ');
```

```
                    PUT SKIP LIST ((OLDLIST (I) DO I = 1 TO OLDCOUNT));
                    PUT SKIP LIST ('THIS IS THE SHELFLIST OF NEW
                        BOOKS:    ');
                    PUT SKIP LIST ((NEWLIST (I) DO I = 1 TO NEWCOUNT));
         UPDATE:    DO J = 1 TO NEWCOUNT;
         COMPARE:   DO I = 1 TO OLDCOUNT
                        WHILE (SUBSTR (OLDLIST (I), 1, 6) < SUBSTR
                        (NEWLIST (J), 1, 6));
                    END COMPARE;
                    IF I = OLDCOUNT THEN OLDLIST (I + 1) = NEWLIST
                        (J);
                    ELSE
         INSERT:    DO;
         MOVE:      DO K = OLDCOUNT TO I BY − 1;
                    OLDLIST (K + 1) = OLDLIST (K);
                    END MOVE;
                    OLDLIST (I) = NEWLIST (J);
                    END INSERT;
                    OLDCOUNT = OLDCOUNT + 1;
                    END UPDATE;
                    PUT SKIP LIST ('THIS IS THE UPDATED SHELFLIST: ');
                    PUT SKIP LIST ((OLDLIST (I) DO I = 1 TO OLDCOUNT));
                    END SHELFLIST1A;

2.   SORT:     PROC OPTIONS (MAIN);
               DCL (WORD (30), TEMP) CHAR (20) VAR;
     L1:       DO I = 1 BY 1;
               GET LIST (WORD (I));
               IF WORD (I) = 'XXX' THEN GO TO SORT1;
               /*LAST WORD HAS DUMMY VALUE 'XXX'*/
               END L1;
     SORT1:    DO J = 1 TO I − 1 BY 1;
     L2:       DO K = J + 1 TO I;
               IF WORD (J) > WORD (K) THEN
     G1:       DO;
               TEMP = WORD (J);
               WORD (J) = WORD (K);
               WORD (K) = TEMP;
               END G1;
               END L2;
               END SORT1;
```

```
DO J = 1 TO I;
PUT SKIP EDIT (WORD (J)) (A (20));
END SORT;
```

This exercise makes use of the binary coded internal representations of alphanumeric characters, discussed in Chapter 4. The program compares the first element in the array WORD, which is defined by the value of J, with all succeeding elements of the array, defined by the value of K; then the second element is compared with all succeeding elements; and so on. When the internal representation of WORD (J) is larger than WORD (K), indicating that WORD (J) is alphabetically higher than WORD (K), their values are exchanged by using a temporary location named TEMP. Observe that use of a third location in memory is necessary when two values are to be exchanged. If the scheme

```
WORD (J) = WORD (K);
WORD (K) = WORD (J);
```

is used, the initial value of WORD (J) is lost.

3. The SORT program for Exercise 2 can serve as the solution to this exercise. This is because the internal representation for punctuation is smaller than that for alphanumeric characters.

```
4.   MATRIX1: PROC OPTIONS (MAIN);
              DCL WORD (20, 10) CHAR (20) VAR INITIAL
              ((200) ' '), TEXT CHAR (100) VAR, WORD1
              CHAR (20) VAR, SWITCH FIXED BIN INITIAL (0),
              CTR FIXED BIN INITIAL (0);
              GET LIST (TEXT);
              PUT LIST (TEXT);
              M = 1;
     GETWORD: DO I = M TO LENGTH (TEXT) WHILE (INDEX (', . ; ',
              SUBSTR (TEXT, I, 1)) = 0);
              END;
              IF I = LENGTH (TEXT) THEN SWITCH = 1;
              IF I = M THEN GO TO CHECK;
              /*TWO PUNCTUATION CHARACTERS APPEAR
                ADJACENT*/
              WORD1 = SUBSTR (TEXT, M, I - M);
     L1:      DO J = 1 TO CTR WHILE (CTR > 0);
              IF WORD1 = WORD (J, 1) THEN DO;
              /*CHECK WHETHER WORD OCCURRED BEFORE*/
              DO K = 2 TO 10;
```

```
                        IF WORD (J, K) = 'X' THEN
INCREMENT:     DO;
                        WORD (J, K) = ' ';
                        WORD (J, K + 1) = 'X';
                        GO TO CHECK;
                        END L1;
                        /*THE ABOVE "END" STATEMENT ENDS ALL THE DO
                            LOOPS INTERNAL TO L1 LOOP*/
                        CTR = CTR + 1;
                        WORD (CTR, 1) = WORD1;
                        WORD (CTR, 2) = 'X';
CHECK:         IF SWITCH = 1 THEN GO TO PRINT;
                        M = I + 1;
                        GO TO GETWORD;
PRINT:         PUT SKIP EDIT ('WORD', 'OCCURRENCES') (A(20),
                            X(5), A);
                        PUT SKIP EDIT ('1 2 3 4 5 6 7 8 9') (X(20), A);
                        DO J = 1 TO CTR;
                        PUT SKIP EDIT (WORD (J, 1)) (A(20));
                        PUT SKIP EDIT ((WORD (J, K) DO K = 2 TO 10))
                            (A(2));
                        END;
                        END MATRIX1;
```

Sample Input Data:

IT IS BETTER TO DO AS I SAY, SAID HE, THEN DO AS I DO.

Output:

WORD	OCCURRENCES
	1 2 3 4 5 6 7 8 9
IT	X
IS	X
BETTER	X
TO	X
DO	X
AS	X
I	X
SAY	X
SAID	X
HE	X
THAN	X

```
5.   MATRIX2:  PROC OPTIONS (MAIN);
               DCL WORD (20, 10) CHAR (20) VAR INITIAL
                  ((200) ' '), TEXT CHAR (100) VAR, WORD1
                  CHAR (20) VAR, SWITCH FIXED BIN INITIAL (0),
                  CTR FIXED BIN INITIAL (0), TEMP (10) CHAR (20)
                  VAR;
               GET LIST (TEXT);
               PUT LIST (TEXT);
               M = 1;
     GETWORD:  DO I = M TO LENGTH (TEXT) WHILE (INDEX (', . ;' ,
                  SUBSTR (TEXT, I, 1)) = 0);
               END;
               IF I = LENGTH (TEXT) THEN SWITCH = 1;
               IF I = M THEN GO TO CHECK;
               WORD1 = SUBSTR (TEXT, M, I − M);
          L1:  DO J = 1 TO CTR WHILE (CTR > 0);
               IF WORD1 = WORD (J, 1) THEN DO;
               DO K = 2 TO 10;
               IF WORD (J, K) = 'X ' THEN
   INCREMENT:  DO;
               WORD (J, K) = ' ';
               WORD (J, K + 1) = 'X ';
               GO TO CHECK;
               END L1;
               CTR = CTR + 1;
               WORD (CTR, 1) = WORD1;
               WORD (CTR, 2) = 'X ';
       CHECK:  IF SWITCH = 1 THEN GO TO PRINT;
               M = I + 1;
               GO TO GETWORD;
       PRINT:  PUT SKIP EDIT ('WORD', 'OCCURRENCES') (A(20),
                  X(5), A);
               PUT SKIP EDIT ('1 2 3 4 5 6 7 8') (X(20), A);
        SORT:  DO J = 1 TO CTR − 1;
               DO K = J TO CTR;
               IF WORD (J, 1) > WORD (K, 1) THEN
               DO;
      INVERT:  TEMP (*) = WORD (J, *);
               WORD (J, *) = WORD (K, *);
               WORD (K, *) = TEMP (*);
```

```
                /*A ROW OF THE ARRAY WORD IS STORED IN TEMP*/
                END SORT;
                DO J = 1 TO CTR;
                PUT SKIP EDIT (WORD (J, 1)) (A(20));
                PUT SKIP EDIT ((WORD (J, K) DO K = 2 TO 10))
                    (A(2));
                END;
                END MATRIX2;
```

6. The program for Exercise 4, MATRIX1, serves as the solution for this exercise if the following modifications are made. Beginning with the PUT SKIP EDIT statement labeled PRINT, replace the last seven statements of MATRIX1 by

```
PRINT:       PUT SKIP EDIT ('OCCURRENCES', 'WORD') (A, X(30), A);
             PUT SKIP EDIT (' ') (A);
             DCL NEW (10, 20) CHAR (8) VAR, FREQ (9) CHAR (1)
                 INIT ('1', '2', '3', '4', '5', '6', '7', '8', '9');
TRANSPOSE:   DO L = 1 TO CTR;
             NEW (*, L) = WORD (L, *);
             END TRANSPOSE;
             DO L = 1 TO 9;
             PUT EDIT ((NEW (L, K) DO K = 1 TO 14)) (A(8));
             /*THE ELEMENTS OF THE ARRAY 'NEW' HAVING THE VALUE
             'X ' ARE PRINTED AS 'X          '*/
             PUT SKIP EDIT (FREQ (L)) (A(2));
             END;
             END MATRIX1;
7.   MATRIX3:  PROC OPTIONS (MAIN);
               DCL 1 WORDS (30), 2 COUNT FIXED BIN INITIAL (1),
               2 WORD CHAR (20), TEXT CHAR (100) VAR,
               WORD1 CHAR (20) VAR, SWITCH FIXED BIN
               INITIAL (0), CTR FIXED BIN INITIAL (0);
               GET LIST (TEXT);
               PUT LIST (TEXT);
               M = 1;
GETWORD:     DO I = M TO LENGTH (TEXT) WHILE (INDEX (', . ;' ,
               SUBSTR (TEXT, I, 1)) = 0);
             END;
             IF I = LENGTH (TEXT) THEN SWITCH = 1;
             IF I = M THEN GO TO CHECK;
```

```
        /*THERE ARE 2 PUNCTUATION CHARACTERS
            ADJACENT TO ONE ANOTHER*/
        WORD1 = SUBSTR (TEXT, M, I − M);
L1:     DO J = 1 TO CTR WHILE (CTR > 0);
        IF WORD1 = WORD (J) THEN
        /*CHECK IF WORD1 IS ALREADY SAVED IN THE ARRAY
            'WORDS'*/
        DO;
        COUNT (J) = COUNT (J) + 1;
        GO TO CHECK;
        END L1;
        /*THE ABOVE 'END' STATEMENT ENDS ALL THE DO
            LOOPS INTERNAL TO LOOP L1*/
        CTR = CTR + 1;
        WORD (CTR) = WORD1;
CHECK:  IF SWITCH = 1 THEN GO TO PRINT;
        M = I + 1;
        GO TO GETWORD;
PRINT:  PUT SKIP EDIT ('WORD', 'OCCURRENCES') (A(20), X(5),
            A);
        PUT SKIP EDIT ('1 2 3 4 5 6 7 8 9') (X(20), A);
        DO J = 1 TO CTR;
        K = COUNT (J)*2 − 2;
        PUT SKIP EDIT (WORD (J), 'X') (A(20), X(K), A(1));
        END;
        END MATRIX3;
```

Chapter 9

1. The set of all prime numbers less than 12.
2. (a) {1, 4, 6, 8, 10}   (e) {2, 3, 5, 7, 8, 9, 10}
   (b) {2, 5, 8, 9, 10}   (f) {1, 4, 6}
   (c) {3, 7}   (g) {8, 10}
   (d) {1, 2, 3, 4, 5, 6, 7, 9}   (h) {1, 2, 3, 4, 5, 6, 7, 9}
3. (a) $x_1\bar{x}_2$
   (b) $\bar{x}_1 + x_2$
   (c) $(x_1 + \bar{x}_2 + \bar{x}_3)(\bar{x}_1 + x_3)$
   (d) $\bar{x}_1(x_2 + \bar{x}_3)$
   (e) $\bar{x}_2 + x_1x_3$

4. In each pair the right-hand identity is obtained from the left-hand identity by replacing each AND operator with an OR operator and vice versa. The validity of each left-hand identity is established by applying De Morgan's Laws to obtain negations of both sides of the identity and showing the latter expressions are equivalent. Hence each pair of identities shown represents a dual pair.

5. (a) $\bar{x}_1 x_2$
   (b) $x_1 + x_2$

6. $x_1 x_2 x_3 + x_1 x_2 \bar{x}_3 + \bar{x}_1 x_2 \bar{x}_3 + \bar{x}_1 \bar{x}_2 \bar{x}_3$

7.

$x_1 x_2 x_3$	$x_1 x_2 x_3 + x_1 \bar{x}_2 x_3 + x_1 x_2 \bar{x}_3$	$x_1(x_2 + x_3)$
0 0 0	0	0
0 0 1	0	0
0 1 0	0	0
0 1 1	0	0
1 0 0	0	0
1 0 1	1	1
1 1 0	1	1
1 1 1	1	1

8.

$x_1 x_2 x_3$	$x_1 + \bar{x}_1 x_2 x_3$	$(x_1 + x_2)(x_1 + x_3)$
0 0 0	0	0
0 0 1	0	0
0 1 0	0	0
0 1 1	1	1
1 0 0	1	1
1 0 1	1	1
1 1 0	1	1
1 1 1	1	1

Chapter 10

1. Substituting B for X and $A\bar{B} + C$ for Y everywhere in the set of equations yields a set of Boolean identities in the variables A, B, and C.

2. Substituting BC for X and C for Y everywhere in the set of equations yields a set of Boolean identities in the variables A, B, and C.

3. $B = \bar{A}$

4. $B = AC + \bar{A}\bar{C}$

5. D_3

6.

	CONG	C-G	C-R	ECON	ED	POL	P-P	S-L	T	W-P
D 1		X					X		X	
D 2	X					X			X	X
D 3		X					X	X		
D 4		X	X			X				
D 5		X		X		X				X
D 6	X				X				X	X
D 7				X				X		
D 8		X				X	X			
D 9	X			X						X
D10	X	X	X							
D11								X	X	
D12		X				X	X			
D13				X	X					X
D14	X			X	X				X	
D15	X		X	X						

$Q = $ C-R AND (C-G OR P-P)
$Q = $ D4 + D10

7. $Q = $ D2 + D6 + D9 + D13 + D14
8. None of the documents satisfy the request.

Chapter 11

1. '011110'B
2. Z = BOOL (X, Y, '0110'B);
3. Z = BOOL (X1, X2, '1101'B);
4. (a) '111111'B
   (b) '111111'B
   (c) '111111'B
   (d) '111110'B

D2 fails to logically imply R because of the presence of $\bar{I}_6$ in R. This is confirmed by the fact that a 0 occurs in the last bit position of the binary vector R2, with the result that the test in (d) fails to yield a unit vector of all 1's.

5.

	D_1	D_2	D_3	D_4
I_1	0	1	1	0
I_2	1	0	0	1
I_3	1	1	0	1
I_4	0	1	1	0
I_5	1	0	1	0
I_6	0	1	0	1

$Q = D_2 + D_3$

6. (a) I2ANDI3 = '1001'B
   (b) NOTI4 = '1001'B
   (c) I2ANDI3ANDNOTI4 = '1001'B

The BOOL function in (a) applies the AND operator to the binary vectors I_2 and I_3. The BOOL function in (b) applies the NOT operator to the binary vector I_4. The BOOL function in (c) applies the AND operator to the resulting binary vectors I_2I_3 and $\bar{I}_4$. The occurrence of 1's in the first and fourth positions of the final vector produced in (c) establishes that documents D_1 and D_4 satisfy the search request $Q = I_2I_3\bar{I}_4$.

7. RETRIEVE1A: PROCEDURE OPTIONS (MAIN);
          DECLARE 1 REQUEST (2), 2 CONTENT BIT (20),
              2 IDENT FIXED (6), 1 DOCUMENT (20),
              2 CONTENT BIT (350), 2 IDENT FIXED (6),
              NUMBER FIXED (6), NAME CHARACTER (20)
              VARYING, FORM CHARACTER (54) VARYING,
              ONEHIT BIT (350) INITIAL ((350) '0' B);
          /*ONEHIT CONTAINS THE LIST OF DOCUMENTS
              SATISFYING EACH PRODUCT TERM OF THE
              SEARCH REQUEST*/
          GET EDIT (DOCUMENT) (B(350), X(4), F(6));
     NAMELY: FORMAT (B (20), X(54), F(6));
          /*20 ITEMS REPRESENTING THE COORDINATE
              INDEX ARE READ IN AND STORED UNDER THE
              ARRAY NAMED 'DOCUMENT'*/
     NEWREQUEST: GET LIST (NUMBER, NAME, FORM);
          /*THE GENERAL DATA CARD FOR A SEARCH
              REQUEST IS READ*/
          IF NUMBER = 0 THEN GO TO STOP;
          /*TEST IS MADE FOR ADDITIONAL SEARCH
              REQUESTS*/

```
                        PUT PAGE LIST ('THE DOCUMENTS LISTED BELOW
                            SATISFY SEARCH REQUEST NO. ' , NUMBER,
                            'WHICH WAS INITIATED BY, ' NAME, 'AND
                            SPECIFIES A COMBINATION OF INDEX TERMS
                            AS FOLLOWS: ', FORM);
                        SATISFY = 0;
                        GET SKIP;
                        /*PREPARE TO READ NEXT DATA CARD*/
        CONTINUE:       GET EDIT (REQUEST) (R (NAMELY));
                        /*DATA FOR A PRODUCT TERM OF THE CURRENT
                            SEARCH REQUEST IS STORED*/
                        IF BOOL (REQUEST (1). CONTENT, REQUEST (2).
                            CONTENT, '0110'B) = (20) '1'B THEN GO TO
                            CHECK;
                        /*TEST IS MADE FOR END OF THE CURRENT
                            SEARCH REQUEST*/
    NEXTDOCUMENT:       IF REQUEST (1).CONTENT = (20) '0'B THEN GO TO
                            NOT;
            L1:         DO I = 1 TO 20;
                        IF (INDEX (SUBSTR (REQUEST
                            (1).CONTENT, I, 1), '1'B) = 0)
                            THEN GO TO A;
                        IF ONEHIT = (350) '0'B THEN ONEHIT = DOCU
                            MENT (I).CONTENT;
                        ELSE ONEHIT = BOOL (ONEHIT, DOCUMENT (I).
                            CONTENT, '0001'B);
                        SATISFY = SATISFY + 1;
            A:          END L1;
            NOT:        IF REQUEST (2).CONTENT = (20) '1'B THEN GO
                            TO PRINT;
            L2:         DO I = 1 TO 20;
                        IF (INDEX (SUBSTR (REQUEST
                            (2).CONTENT, I, 1), '0'B) = 0)
                            THEN GO TO B;
                        IF ONEHIT = (350) '0'B THEN ONEHIT = BOOL
                            (ONEHIT, DOCUMENT (I).CONTENT, '1000'B)
                        ELSE ONEHIT = BOOL (ONEHIT, DOCUMENT (I).
                            CONTENT, '0010'B);
                        SATISFY = SATISFY + 1;
```

```
      B:   END L2;
  PRINT:   DO I = 1 TO 350;
           IF INDEX (SUBSTR (ONEHIT, I, 1), '1'B) = 0 THEN
               GO TO END;
           PUT SKIP LIST ('DOCUMENT NUMBER = ', I);
    END:   END PRINT;
           ONEHIT = (350) '0'B;
           GO TO CONTINUE;
  CHECK:   IF SATISFY = 0 THEN PUT SKIP LIST ('NONE OF
               THE DOCUMENTS LISTED IN THE INDEX
               SATISFY THE ABOVE REQUEST');
           GO TO NEWREQUEST;
   STOP:   END RETRIEVE1A;
```

Chapter 12

1. TEXT = 'THE VOICE OF THE TURTLE IS HEARD IN THE LAND'
    PHRASE = 'THE TURTLE'S VOICE'
    II = 0
    JJ = 0
2. TEXT = 'THE PRESENT * * * IS ALIVE AND WELL'
    PHRASE = 'KING OF FRANCE'
    J = 26

3. The program RESERVE is divided into three procedures. The main
one, called RESERVE, reads in all the data for the program. The second one,
called FINES, calculates and prints a fine, if any, for a returned book. The
third procedure CHECK scans the reserve list and, if the returned book was
on request, prints the information needed to notify the user who requested
the book. Because FINES and CHECK are both internal procedures to RESERVE,
the values of all the variables read in the procedure RESERVE are known in
the procedures FINES and CHECK.

```
RESERVE:   PROC OPTIONS (MAIN);
           DCL BORROWER CHAR (40) VAR, 1 BOOK1, 2 TITLE1 CHAR (80),
               2 AUTHOR1 CHAR (80), (DUEDATE, DATE, RATE) FIXED BIN,
               FINE FIXED DEC (5, 2), 1 USERS (100), 2 NAME CHAR (10),
```

```
           2 PHONE CHAR (6), 2 BOOKR, 3 TITLE CHAR (80), 3 AUTHOR
           CHAR (80);
           GET LIST (RATE, DATE);
           PUT DATA (RATE, DATE);
           GET SKIP;
READ:      DO I = 1 TO 100;
           GET EDIT (USERS (I)) (A(10), A(6), X(64), 2 (A(8)));
           IF USERS (I).NAME = 'XXX' THEN
           DO;
           I = I − 1;
           GO TO NEXT;
           END;
           END READ;
NEXT:      GET LIST (BORROWER, TITLE1, AUTHOR1, DUEDATE);
           IF BORROWER = 'XX' THEN GO TO STOP;
           CALL FINES;
           CALL CHECK (BOOK1);
           GO TO NEXT;
FINES:     PROC;
           PUT SKIP LIST ('THE BOOK: ');
           PUT EDIT (BOOK1) (SKIP, A(80));
           PUT DATA (DUEDATE);
           IF DATE < = DUEDATE THEN RETURN;
           FINE = (DATE − DUEDATE) * RATE;
           FINE = FINE/100;
           PUT SKIP EDIT ('USER: ', BORROWER, 'MUST PAY $', FINE)
              (A, A(40), A, F(5,2));
           RETURN;
           END FINES;
CHECK:     PROC (BOOK);
           DCL 1 BOOK, 2 TITLE CHAR (200), 2 AUTHOR CHAR (100);
  L1:      DO J = 1 TO I;
           IF (BOOKR(J).TITLE = BOOK.TITLE) & (BOOKR(J).AUTHOR =
              BOOK.AUTHOR)THEN
           DO;
           PUT SKIP EDIT ('CALL ', PHONE (J), 'ASK FOR ', NAME (J),
              'BOOK RESERVED IS: ', BOOKR(J)) (A, A(6), A, A(40),
              SKIP, A, A(80), SKIP, A(80));
           RETURN;
```

```
         END;
         END L1;
         PUT SKIP LIST ('THE ABOVE BOOK IS NOT IN THE RESERVED LIST');
         RETURN;
         END CHECK;
STOP:    END RESERVE;
```

Chapter 13

```
1. COMBINE:  PROCEDURE OPTIONS (MAIN);
             DECLARE INDEX FILE RECORD INPUT DIRECT KEYED,
                 QUERY CHAR (40), 1 ENTRY, 2 TERM CHAR (40),
                 2 DOCUMENTS CHAR (1000);
             ON ENDFILE (SYSIN) GO TO STOP;
             ON KEY (INDEX)
             BEGIN;
             PUT SKIP LIST ('NONE OF THE DOCUMENTS IN THE FILE
                 SATISFY THE TERM ', QUERY);
             GO TO SEARCH;
             END;
   SEARCH:   GET LIST (QUERY);
             READ FILE (INDEX) INTO (ENTRY) KEY (QUERY);
             PUT SKIP LIST ('THE FOLLOWING DOCUMENTS SATISFY
                 THE TERM ', QUERY);
             PUT SKIP LIST (ENTRY.DOCUMENTS);
             DCL DOC FILE DIRECT KEYED RECORD, DOCREC CHAR
                 (1000) VAR, DOCKEY CHAR (4);
             /*DOC IS THE FILE CONTAINING THE FULL DESCRIPTION
                 OF THE DOCUMENTS*/
      L1:    DO J = 1 TO 1000 BY 4;
             DOCKEY = SUBSTR (DOCUMENTS, J, 4);
             IF DOCKEY = '    ' THEN GO TO SEARCH;
             READ FILE (DOC) INTO (DOCREC) KEY (DOCKEY);
             ON KEY (DOC) PUT SKIP LIST ('ERROR ON FILE DOC
                 KEY = ', DOCKEY);
             END L1;
             GO TO SEARCH;
   STOP:     END COMBINE;
```

2. FILEGEN1 : PROC OPTIONS (MAIN);
                DCL NEW FILE RECORD, KEY (10) CHAR (1) INIT
                    ('0', '1', '2', '3', '4', '5', '6', '7', '8', '9'), 1 DATA,
                    2 NAME CHAR (40), 2 ADDRESS CHAR (40);
                OPEN FILE (NEW) OUTPUT KEYED SEQUENTIAL;
          L1:   DO I = 1 TO 10;
                GET EDIT (DATA) (A(40), A(40));
                WRITE FILE (NEW) FROM (DATA) KEYFROM (KEY (I));
                PUT SKIP LIST (DATA);
                END L1;
                CLOSE FILE (NEW);
                OPEN FILE (NEW) INPUT DIRECT KEYED;
          L2:   DO I = 10 TO 2 BY − 2;
                READ FILE (NEW) INTO (DATA) KEY (KEY (I));
                PUT SKIP LIST (DATA);
                END L2;
                END FILEGEN1;

3. FILEGEN2 : PROC OPTIONS (MAIN);
                DCL NEW FILE OUTPUT RECORD SEQUENTIAL KEYED,
                    KEY (10) CHAR (1) INIT ('0', '1', '2', '3', '4', '5', '6',
                    '7', '8', '9'), 1 DATA, 2 NAME CHAR (40), 2 ADDRESS
                    CHAR (40);
          L1:   DO I = 1 TO 10;
                GET EDIT (DATA) (A(40), A(40));
                WRITE FILE (NEW) FROM (DATA) KEYFROM (KEY (I));
                PUT SKIP LIST (DATA);
                END L1;
          P: BEGIN;
                DCL NEW FILE INPUT DIRECT KEYED;
          L2:   DO I = 10 TO 2 BY − 2;
                READ FILE (NEW) INTO (DATA) KEY (KEY (I));
                PUT SKIP LIST (DATA);
                END P;
                END FILEGEN2;

Chapter 14

1. The data list represented in the exercise is a data list where one
element has more than one successor. In PL/I such a data list is called a

multidimensional list. The element A points to the sublist (B, C) as well as to the element D.

Because a data list must contain a uniform structure, in order to solve Exercise 1, it is convenient to use the structure

> DCL 1 ELEMENT,
> 2 VALUE CHAR (10),
> 2 LEFT PTR,
> 2 RIGHT PTR;

For the first element, A, its associated LEFT pointer contains the address of the element B and its associated RIGHT pointer the address of the element D. The element B has in its left pointer the address of C and in its RIGHT pointer the NULL address. The elements C and D are both last elements in the data lists (B, C) and (A, (B, C) D), respectively, and their pointers have the value NULL. Such lists are used to represent organizational charts, networks, flows, chemical formulas, economic and social structures, and so on.

```
SUBLIST:  PROC OPTIONS (MAIN);
          DCL 1 ELEMENT, 2 VALUE CHAR (10), 2 LEFT PTR, 2 RIGHT PTR,
              (P1, P2, TOP) PTR;
          ALLOCATE ELEMENT SET (P1);
          ALLOCATE ELEMENT SET (P2);
          GET LIST (P1 → VALUE);
          /*READ IN THE VALUE FOR 'A'*/
          TOP = P1;
          TOP → LEFT = P2;
          /*SET LEFT POINTER FOR 'A'*/
          GET LIST (P2 → VALUE);
          /*READ IN THE VALUE FOR 'B'*/
          ALLOCATE ELEMENT SET (P1);
          GET LIST (P1 → VALUE);
          /*READ IN THE VALUE FOR 'C'*/
          P2 → LEFT = P1;
          P2 → RIGHT = NULL;
          P1 → LEFT = NULL;
          P1 → RIGHT = NULL;
          ALLOCATE ELEMENT SET (P1);
          TOP → RIGHT = P1;
          GET LIST (P1 → VALUE);
```

```
                    /*READ IN VALUE FOR 'D'*/
                    P1 → LEFT = NULL;
                    P2 → RIGHT = NULL;
      PRINTBC:      P1 = TOP;
           L1:      DO WHILE (P1 → LEFT ⌐ = NULL) & (P1 → RIGHT
                        ⌐ = NULL);
                    P1 = P1 → LEFT;
                    END L1;
                    PUT SKIP LIST (P1 → VALUE);
                    IF P1 → LEFT = NULL THEN GO TO STOP;
                    P1 = P1 → LEFT;
                    GO TO L1;
        STOP:       END SUBLIST;
```

Selected Bibliography

1 Introduction to Boolean Algebra

Robert R. Korfhage, *Logic and Algorithms*, Chapter 3, "The Propositional Calculus," pp. 42–67; Chapter 4, "A View of Binary Vectors," pp. 82–85. Wiley, New York, 1966.

Donald L. Dimitry, and Thomas H. Mott, Jr. *Introduction to Fortran IV Programming*, Chapter 15, "Logical Operations," pp. 253–262. Holt, New York, 1966.

2 Document Handling and Retrieval

Charles T. Meadow, *The Analysis of Information Systems*, Chapter 4, "Retrieval of Index Records," pp. 106–145; Chapter 6, "The Organization of Files," pp. 174–202; Chapter 8, "The Organization of File Sets," pp. 226–252. Wiley, New York, 1967.

Susan Artandi, *An Introduction to Computers in Information Science,* "The Retrieval of Documents," pp. 45–59. Scarecrow Press, Metuchen, New Jersey, 1968.

3   Programming for Information Handling

A PL/I Primer, IBM Manual C28-6808, Chapters 1–13, pp. 4–66.

S. W. Pollack, and T. D. Sterling, *A Guide to PL/I.* Holt, New York, 1969.

Donald L. Dimitry and Thomas H. Mott, Jr., *Introduction to Fortran IV Programming,* Chapters 1–3, pp. 1–73. Holt, New York, 1966.

Susan Artandi, *An Introduction to Computers in Information Science,* Chapter 3, "Computer Hardware and Software," pp. 61–92. Scarecrow Press, Metuchen, New Jersey, 1968.

4   Advanced Readings in the Logic of Document Retrieval

J. Verhoeff, W. Goffman, and J. Belzer, "Inefficiency in the Use of Boolean Functions for Information Retrieval Systems," *Communications of the ACM* **4** (December 1961), 557–559.

R. Tritschler, "Effective Search Strategies without 'Perfect' Indexing," *American Documentation* **15** (July 1964), 179–184.

W. T. Brandhorst, "Simulation of Boolean Logic Constraints Through The Use of Term Weights," *American Documentation* **17** (July 1966), 145–146.

Howard P. Iker, "Solution of Boolean Equations through the Use of Term Weights to the Base Two," *American Documentation* **18** (January 1967), 47.

Wolfram Uhlman, "Document Specification and Search Strategy Using Basic Intersections and Probability Measure of Sets," *American Documentation* **19** (July 1968), 240–246.

Wolfram Uhlman, "General Method for Matching Arbitrary Logical Statements in Mechanized Retrieval Systems," *American Documentation* **20** (July 1969), 253–258.

David Hsiao, and Frank Harary, "A Formal System for Information Retrieval from Files," *Communications of the ACM* **13** (February 1970), 67–73.

Eugene Wong, and T. C. Chiang, "Canonical Structure in Attribute Based File Organization," *Communications of the ACM* **14** (September 1971), 593–597.

Index

A

A-format item, 31–32
ADDR built-in function, 191
ALLOCATE statement
  used with array variables, 87–88
  used with based variables, 190
Alphabetization
  through internal representation of
    characters, 48
American Standard Code for Information Interchange, *see* ASCII
AND operator, 10, 99, 100
Arithmetic operations, 19–20
  basic operators for, 19
  use of parentheses in, 20
Arithmetic operators, 20
Array(s), 79–88
  declaration of, 79

dimension attributes of, 73, 80
dimensions and bounds of, 79
operations on, 81–88
  without subscript, 82
programming examples of, 83–88
storage allocation for, during program
  execution, 87–88
in structures, 90
subscripting of, 70, 82
use of asterisks for bounds, 81–82
Array variables, *see* Array
ASCII character representation, 49
Assembler, 5
Assembly language programming, 5
Assignment statements, 18–22
  general form, 18
  in input/output stream of data-
    directed I/O, 25
  for several variables, 18